MIDDLE ENGLISH STUDIES

Norman Davis, who retired in 1980 after a long and distinguished tenure of the Merton Chair of English Language and Literature at Oxford, is one of the world's leading authorities on early and medieval English. His many publications include revised editions of Sweet's *Anglo-Saxon Primer* and Tolkien and Gordon's *Sir Gawain and the Green Knight*, editions of *Non-cycle Plays and Fragments* and of the massive *Paston Letters and Papers of the Fifteenth Century*, and *A Chaucer Glossary*. He has served as a Delegate of the Oxford University Press, an editor of *The Review of English Studies*, and the Director of the Early English Text Society. This volume of essays by some of his many friends and colleagues is a small expression of their gratitude and admiration. Fourteen leading scholars have contributed new work on a variety of topics within the period *c.* 1200–*c.* 1500. These essays include studies of the MSS of Middle English texts and their relationships of Chaucer (and of the fate of *Sir Thopas* in the sixteenth century), of Langland, and of other medieval writers and works. There are a number of important philological contributions, including discussions of the scansion of *Havelok* and the evolution of Middle English *-en* and *-e*, Chaucer's spelling, North-Midland present indicative plural forms, and Early Middle English *drihtin*. The volume also contains a list of Norman Davis's published writings and a biographical note by D. M. Davin, formerly Academic Publisher to the University Press.

NORMAN DAVIS, 1970

MIDDLE ENGLISH STUDIES

Presented to
NORMAN DAVIS
in Honour of his
Seventieth Birthday

Edited by
DOUGLAS GRAY
and
E. G. STANLEY

CLARENDON PRESS · OXFORD
1983

Oxford University Press, Walton Street, Oxford OX2 6DP
London Glasgow New York Toronto
Delhi Bombay Calcutta Madras Karachi
Kuala Lumpur Singapore Hong Kong Tokyo
Nairobi Dar es Salaam Cape Town
Melbourne Auckland

and associated companies in
Beirut Berlin Ibadan Mexico City Nicosia

Oxford is a trade mark of Oxford University Press

Published in the United States
by Oxford University Press, New York

British Library Cataloguing in Publication Data
Middle English studies
1. Davis, Norman, 1913- 2. English literature—Middle English, 1100-1500—Addresses, essays lectures 3. English literature—Middle English, 1100-1500—History and criticism
I. Gray, Douglas II. Stanley, E. G.
III. Davis, Norman, 1913-
820.9'001 PR281
ISBN 0-19-811183-5

Library of Congress Cataloging in Publication Data
Main entry under title:
Middle English studies.
"A list of the published writings of Norman Davis": p.
Includes bibliographical references and index.
1. English literature—Middle English, 1100-1500—History and criticism—Addresses, essays, lectures.
2. English language—Middle English, 1100-1500—Addresses, essays, lectures. 3. Davis, Norman, 1913-
I. Davis, Norman, 1913- . II. Gray, Douglas.
III. Stanley, Eric Gerald.
PR251.M5 1983 820'.9'001 83-4094
ISBN 0-19-811183-5

Printed in Great Britain by
Butler & Tanner Ltd, Frome and London

Contents

Abbreviations

AN	Anglo-Norman
ASS	*Acta Sanctorum* (Antwerp, 1643–)
BL	British Library
Bodl.	Bodleian Library
CSEL	Corpus Scriptorum Ecclesiasticorum Latinorum
CT	*The Canterbury Tales*
CUL	Cambridge University Library
EETS	Early English Text Society (ES: Extra Series)
EHR	*English Historical Review*
EME	Early Middle English
Index	C. Brown and R. H. Robbins, *The Index of Middle English Verse* (New York, 1943)
JEGP	*Journal of English and Germanic Philology*
JWCI	*Journal of the Warburg and Courtauld Institutes*
MÆ	*Medium Ævum*
ME	Middle English
MED	*Middle English Dictionary*
MGH	*Monumenta Germaniae Historica*
MLN	*Modern Language Notes*
MP	*Modern Philology*
NQ	*Notes and Queries*
OE	Old English
OF	Old French
OED	*Oxford English Dictionary*
ON	Old Norse
ONF	Old Northern French
PBA	*Proceedings of the British Academy*
PMLA	*Publications of the Modern Language Association of America*
Pres. E.	Present-day English
RES	*Review of English Studies*
SP	*Studies in Philology*

STC	A. W. Pollard and G. R. Redgrave, *A Short-Title Catalogue of Books printed in England, Scotland and Ireland ... 1475–1640* (London, 1926); 2nd edn., revised and enlarged, Vol. ii (I–Z) (London, 1976)
Supplement	R. H. Robbins and J. L. Cutler, *Supplement to the Index of Middle English Verse* (Lexington, 1965)
TCD	Trinity College, Dublin

Norman Davis: The Growth of a Scholar

DAN DAVIN

EARLY in 1942, because of wounds and consequent temporary secondment from 23 NZ Battalion to more cerebral and safer activities in the GHQ, Cairo, Military Intelligence Department, I was guiltily seated one day at the Balkan desk and sorting through enemy newspaper cuttings for clues about enemy troop movements and general intentions in Bulgaria. One cutting included a picture that had something of the dim familiarity one discerns in ancient passport photographs. But this particular travesty, an involuntary disguise in effect, was not of myself: if an uncharitably trained eye served correctly and a memory in those days still sharp, it was a picture of an old friend from Otago and Oxford years. The translated caption confirmed this: the subject was indeed denominated Norman Davis. Moreover, the cutting informed me, this vile and venturesome person had been condemned in Sofia—*in absentia* also, I was relieved to note—for sabotage and for the part he had played in engineering the escape from Bulgarian clutches of an even more sinister and villainous character. His name, though not his person, was also well known to me; for he was the Georgi Dimitroff whom we knew to be obnoxious to the regime because he was the unrepentant leader of the Bulgarian Peasant Party. What odd company Norman seemed to have been keeping lately.

Could this really be the Norman Davis I had known, as the faint resemblance of the photograph and the correspondence of names, if not of probabilities, seemed to affirm? I began to scratch about in the henhouse of my memory. Finding no explanation there, I proceeded to make discreet inquiries elsewhere. In the Cairo of the war years—as in Cambridge ever since the late Sir Maurice Bowra was Oxford Vice-Chancellor—there was not much that one could not discover, if not ascertain, when one put one's mind and the old-boy network into action. The details might not be wholly reliable but they could at least be relied upon to be at once secret and picturesque. As far as I know, we did not harbour any Philbys or McLeans, but we had men of knowledge, creative discretion, imagination, and narrative power. So I learnt before long that Norman had been transferred, when war broke out, or very likely had transferred himself, from being a British Council lecturer at the University to becoming an Assistant Press Attaché at the British Legation in Sofia. Moreover, he was now safe and sound, after some perilous adventures by flood and field, though my sources would not reveal where he was or what he was doing, save that he had married a former Sofia colleague with an equally courageous record, and had grown mustachios—presumably for reasons of disguise (a not altogether adequate cover, if there is anything in the legend that Ronald Syme, passing him in some Middle Eastern power-corridor, failed to recognize him, but did so later when he heard him talking).

The reticence of my sources (long matched in post-war years by the modesty and discretion of Norman himself and his wife Lena) was in itself a sufficient indication that, from an enemy point of view, he had not become a reformed character, was up to no good, and indeed probably training for some very horrid and un-Aryan exploit. His initial crimes, those perpetrated in Sofia, were given mythical dimensions for me, somewhat later, by one Colonel Ross, who had been British Military Attaché in Sofia and was an authority on which Bulgarian Cavalry General's wife wore the most dominant breeches and on various other matters of martial, marital, and marginal interest. Over bulging brandies and with bulging eyes—somewhat bloodshot—he told me, at the Turf Club, hazy, heroic, and piquantly improbable stories of how he and Norman had planned prowling nocturnal expeditions round Sofia with sacks of explosives and with the object, in fact unrealized, of blowing up fuel-storage tanks. It seemed that, for a civilian and a chap who wore spectacles, he was not at all a bad sort.

There was less leisure for speculation in those hectic days and BBC-loud glades and the evenings spent at Groppi's café among other members of Groppi's Light Horse or the Gaberdine Swine, as my irreverent old comrades visiting Cairo from the Western Desert used unkindly to term us. Yet I recall, sometimes through a haze of gin, ouzo, or home-made vodka, as I lay in bed at night, musing now and then over the metamorphosis that must have occurred in the young scholar I had first met in Dunedin in 1931. Looking back now, from a maturer and less cocky judgement of human nature, I find the change both surprising and unsurprising: for, in age, one accepts more easily the double-barrelled quality of human life and thinks more in terms of development than of metamorphosis.

Since recollection is an old man's substitute for thought and Norman's subsequent career has been such as to impart, one hopes, a little value to anecdotage, I now propose to cast back the remnant of my memory to the earlier and later days of our acquaintanceship, and indeed friendship: for, because of preoccupation with strangers or family, it is seldom possible in Oxford to see one's friends and therefore some recompense to write about them; and I egregiously imagine that a little of the gossip that Norman himself would spurn may not be altogether without interest for his many and more indulgent admirers. In the course of doing so, and in so personal a piece, I shall have to assume that comparisons can be commodious and ask to be forgiven if I appear more frequently as his foil, especially in the earlier period, than is altogether decent; but where I bring the two of us into conjunction or comparison I can do so at least in the confidence that the advantage will not be mine.

Norman and I were born in the same year, 1913, but by a happy accident of months he was a year my senior at the University of Otago. Thus I can count myself lucky to have been, as a student, both his contemporary and his junior. We had each come to the University, in our successive years of 1930 and 1931, on the basis of Scholarships, awards open to all and keenly fought for but particularly vital to people like ourselves, the children of relatively poor parents and therefore dependent for advancement—a university education in fact—on such beginnings; and, once established in the university of our choice, which would usually be determined by its proximity to our families, in order to survive and go forward we would still be locked in constant struggle with the ablest young men and women of our generation for further prizes and scholarships.

Because Otago University was a Scottish foundation and took only less pride in education than in frugality, these further awards were neither numerous nor bountiful and were allotted not on a basis of financial need but of proven ability. So, along the humble road of our *cursus honorum*, it would have been unfortunate for me to have had to vie—vainly, I am sure— with so formidable a competitor. I had some share of not altogether common sensibility and what I now see to have been a starling's audacious facility; but Norman had quite uncommon common sense, a first-rate mind, and an obdurate and unerratic power of sustained assiduity. He had a wonderfully accurate ear (he is a brilliant mimic to this day, especially of Dunedin Doric), a splendid memory, and a peristaltic power of ingesting and digesting facts which none of us could match. All the better for me, then, that by a quirk of timing I was to find in him instead of a rival a setter of standards, an exemplar, and a pathfinder.

Otago was the senior New Zealand university: the canny Scots settlers of scarcely a hundred years before had quickly sought and obtained a University Charter, whereas the northern pioneers had been at the time more materially preoccupied. Like Dunedin itself, the capital of Otago Province, the University looked back still to Scotland. Its Medical School was dominant—it is distinguished to this day—and it had drawn heavily on Edinburgh for its originating talent and its original tradition. In the Arts Faculty, mainly orientated towards the utilitarian rather than strict scholarship, the staff were largely Scots or of Scots origin. Election to Chairs was strongly influenced by the local Presbyterian Synod, and all departments were run on a porridge-bag budget. Thus, for most subjects, in the Arts Faculty at least, the teaching staff was limited to a single Professor and a single Lecturer.

To get a B.A. the student had to pass nine 'units'—each unit entailing one year's successful work in a particular subject. In the first year he—and as often she—took four subjects; with two of these it was necessary to persist for three years through three advancing stages. The remaining two units were open to a limited choice and had to be studied only for a year, like the two discarded after the first year. Those students who decided to go on for an M.A. normally concentrated on one or other of their final B.A. subjects. Terms were of longer duration than those of Oxford or Cambridge, lectures were compulsory up to a high percentage of checked attendance, there were annual examinations in each subject (and sometimes dummy term examinations), and, in the final year of the two higher degrees, there was always at least one external, United Kingdom, examiner.

Since Norman's principal interest—though he was able and successful in all the subjects he undertook—was English, and especially English Language, I must enlarge a little on the nature of the then English Department. The teaching staff consisted of Professor Herbert Ramsay and Mr G. MacGregor Cameron. Ramsay had read Classics at St. Andrews (he used to tell us, relishing the splendours of his vanished youth, of how bravely the scarlet gowns of the St. Andrews undergraduates had swirled in the windiness of that sea-girt place), emigrated for health reasons to Perth University in West Australia, and moved thence to the Chair of English in Otago: a change that characterized the grudging acceptance of English as a subject in the older English universities and, by the adapted application of classical techniques in the analysis and establishment of texts, greatly affected the general academic approach to the establishment of sound editions of the great English classics from that time onwards.

Ramsay's move, however, might not have taken place had the electors all realized that he was a firm and uncompromising atheist who, although not outwardly radiant with human felicity, was convinced that heaven, if it existed at all, was here and now and that, like it or not, we had better make the best of it. In his view there was no better way of doing so than by the pursuit of the highest standards of learning and humane scholarship. He had that sort of candour which, had we known of it at the time, would have made Bloomsbury's notorious frankness seem bogus and debased, the blunt honesty of the best kind of traditional and now very likely extinct Scots dominie. He was not averse to shocking his more timid and conformist colleagues by such sayings as 'There is no doubt whatever that the Christian Church is the work of the Devil.'

As if this Hume-like infidelity were not enough, he was also a man of unshakably liberal sympathies and entertained at the same time a deep suspicion that the only majority ever to be trusted was that great majority, the dead. Either David Nichol Smith or H. W. Garrod once said to me, after a visit to the United States, that there were not yet enough great men dead there for it to be wholly habitable. Ramsay would have agreed: for, although he liked New Zealand in many ways, he harboured a feeling that the underground human compost needed a great deal of enrichment before the country would be as cultured as it was by then cultivated. It was still a place where Sykes's Cattle Drench was more familiar than the Psyche of Apuleius.

Worse still, Ramsay had a genuine liking, though not always overt, for young people, especially if they were high-spirited and intelligent. He was a man of moderate height, dark-haired, lofty of forehead though not high of brow, and he had a lean and furrowed, almost ravaged, face. There was in him something of a self-controlled volcano.

He lectured in the Lower Oliver Room and the large attendance was at least as voluntary as it was compelled. He covered the whole range of English literature and language, judiciously laced with references to the Classics. I have never heard a better lecturer—his melodious (forgive the paradox) Scottish burr still reverberates in my memory's ear—or one more able to combine depth of philological scholarship with literary sensibility and at the same time communicate a sober but infectious appreciation of both to even the most unpromising of his listeners. Sober on his part, that is: in some respects he resembled those Polynesian chewers of the kava nut, in his case the facts and their kernels, to produce a potion that produces a mild intoxication in the consumer. But he was a stern judge also and he suspected mere facility. On occasion he would say, 'A man of good native intelligence, well taught, may write quite a good essay on Wordsworth; if exceptionally intelligent or better taught, he may even write something interesting about Shakespeare; but, if you want to know his real quality, wait till you have seen his Gothic.'

Gregor Cameron, by then probably in his middle twenties, was an Otago graduate, rather shy and much influenced by Ramsay, whom he wholeheartedly and rightly admired, while at the same time resolute to become his own man. No doubt to avert any reproach or infection of provincialism in his own training, he was at that time working by correspondence for a higher degree in the University of London. Like Ramsay he was well-disposed towards the right kind of mutinous young and would even accompany favoured pupils to one of the local pubs—*The Bowling Green*, *The Captain Cook*, *The Royal Albert*, or *The Bobby Burns*. In so puritan and authoritative a community as ours then, this was a bolder course than it will sound to present-day university men, accustomed both to alcohol and to relations of easy friendship with their teachers. But those of us whom he thought worth it and capable of the requisite standard of conversation and conviviality realized the potential and even minatory disapproval on the part of the guardians of the unalterable law that such indiscreet accessibility entailed, and I hope were duly appreciative. At the same time, we understood why Ramsay, an older man and a man of a different tradition, preferred to entertain favoured pupils at home, where his wife and children were always lively and welcoming. And there are some of us still living who will not easily forget how on more than one occasion, when the authorities showed themselves unjustly censorious, both Ramsay and Cameron stood forward as champions of free speech and open evidence, not always without risk to their own prospects.

At this distance of time, I doubt whether our syllabus in literature came much further forward than the Romantics or at the latest than the Pre-Raphaelites and Browning; and I suspect that Ramsay would have preferred to spend such leisure as he had in reading Lucretius rather than Aldous Huxley. Cameron was more a post-War man, which in our retarded modernity meant that he would read us a paper at the Literary Society on George Moore or Yeats. (The first person to discourse to us on the virtually unknown T. S. Eliot was the newly arrived Professor of Philosophy, J. N. Findlay.) Cameron had read D. H. Lawrence, though I doubt if he shared the naif enthusiasm which some of us felt towards Lawrence. He was familiar too with as much of Proust as was to be found in the library of the local French Club and he was capable of finding more than obscenity in such smuggled copies of *Ulysses* as got through to us.

English was a very popular subject (not always for the best reasons), its more strictly linguistic component less so, though quite properly compulsory and brilliantly taught by both Ramsay and Cameron. Most of the students were likely to end up as teachers or move into business occupations where the fading rudiments of a higher education might prove of adventitious advantage. There was the usual tendency to scribble copious notes from lectures and from the textbooks, which were fewer and better than they are now. The results would be regurgitated, more or less recognizably, in examinations—much as they no doubt still are.

Real potential scholars were rare. In fact, today, looking back over those fifty years now drowned, I can recall few names that would still be recognized as international. In Auckland there were men like Pip Ardern, MacDonald, who edited Livy, Paddy Costello, who edited the Oxford Book of Russian Verse, Jack

Bennett, Jim Bertram, Mike Joseph, and, from a slightly earlier generation, Firth the anthropologist and Ronald Syme, the Roman historian. In Wellington there were a similar select few, John Beaglehole, for example, and, somewhat later, Robert Burchfield, our own Douglas Gray, and others who for the moment escape my memory. Christchurch at that time seemed more prolific in poets than scholars, but this is only an impression based on the accident of acquaintanceship. Among us in Otago, the best-known exports tended to be medical men, of whom at least two, John Stallworthy and Bill Hawkesworth, were to graduate from the subjunctive and become men of might in Oxford. And in London, to name only three, there were Harold Gillies, Archie MacIndoe, and Geoffrey Flavell. There were others who were to make a wider mark in London also in such fiercer fields as Fleet Street, Geoffrey Cox notable among them. But in the arts we seemed at that time to produce fewer scholars in the true sense—in my time perhaps only Dale Trendall, the authority on Greek pottery, and Norman Davis himself.

Norman, indeed, was the only student of my close acquaintance who had a natural sense of what scholarship really is. The rest of us, however intelligent, looked at what we were doing as a means to an end and not an end in itself, as a more or less agreeable way of progressing towards some sort of career. We had little notion of the passionate dedication to learning which burnt in Ramsay's mind like one of those peat fires that never go out, and he recognized in Norman's mind at least a spark of that same fire.

In those days I had a conceit of myself which time and comparison have done something, I hope, to purge, or at least submerge. I thought of myself not as a future scholar but as an imaginative writer. It was axiomatic then that you had to prove yourself in Europe, if you were ever to be recognized at home. You had 'to put New Zealand on the map', as they used to say in times when our country seemed perched very precariously on the world's edge and was thought of elsewhere as an off-shore appendage of Australia. The only escape route that seemed conformable to my abilities and penury and ambitions was that of the Rhodes Scholarship. I therefore devoted such intellectual, administrative, and athletic drive as I had towards securing one.

Fortunately, as well as being a veteran and skilled examinee, I was fond of more physical activities like Rugby and also found scope for my exuberance in the rhetoric of debating and literary societies and the editing of ephemeral undergraduate journals. I set rather a foolish value, too, on parties, delighted in the congenial pleasures of female company, which were civilizing also, and was at ease in the pubs with medical students and rowdier sporting companions, themselves somewhat less civilizing than the girls, who were so often better read and wider-minded. Moreover, this was the time of the all-pervading Depression. We were lucky in that we were too young to be subdued by it but forced by the surrounding misery to feel sympathy for its victims and vociferate questions on whether it was necessary. It was also the time of the rise of Hitler and Mussolini and the invasion of Abyssinia, and these distant events awakened us politically, extended our horizons, and compelled us in futile but necessary protest to release whatever altruism might be in us and develop our skills in argument and oratory.

Norman, on the other hand, was a very different kind of man, a man whose Gothic could be trusted but in ways that I did not at first appreciate. I had heard of him, of course, before I met him, since ours was no huge campus. Myself of poor Irish immigrant descent from the Gaeltacht, I had been brought up on the alas still living legend of Black Queen Bess, Bloody Cromwell, the Black North, and Black Protestantism. Since I knew Norman to be of Scots extraction, I automatically assumed that he would be a 'swot' and a 'wowser'. Fortunately, I was still young enough to learn; and toleration and the diminution of self-esteem are among the best things universities have unofficially to teach. By contact with him at lectures and in various societies I soon found that he was a character very different from the stereotype of my childish assumptions.

He was by no means uncompanionable, indeed the contrary,

but he did not set up to be an athlete, partly no doubt because bad sight compelled him to wear glasses, partly because he did not like wasting time as the serious pursuit of most team games required, and largely because he got enough satisfaction and exercise from tramping and climbing in the rather arduous hills of the bush-covered Otago hinterland. I doubt if he either drank or smoked. He might occasionally attend the 'bob hops'—informal dances in Allen Hall, heavily chaperoned, where your shilling ticket gave you admittance and a supper of saveloy sausages, but where alcohol had to be drunk surreptitiously from beer kegs in the basement or gin bottles in the cars parked outside. But he would never have found himself involved in our frequent petty scandals, the great tiny affair of the Leviathan Hotel in 1932 for example; still less was he the kind of man to have been so indiscreet as to threaten the then Pro-Chancellor of the University of New Zealand with physical chastisement for dancing too ardently with someone else's fiancée, as the present writer on one occasion was indiscreet enough to do.

Without being in any way priggish he contrived to be a prodigiously hard and steady worker and yet to enjoy himself in ways unreprehensible to the very moral and sober citizens who abounded in both the city and the university. He was not indifferent to the political questions that so much agitated many of us, but had the good sense to see that much of our passionate protestation was little more, practically, than bombinating in a vacuum. In his literary taste he preferred the accepted classics to our latest discoveries; and, with retrospective embarrassment, I now remember feeling superior to him in literary discrimination when, on one occasion, he was critical of realism in fiction and deprecated the childbirth passage in the then intellectually fashionable, and as I at present think over-valued, novel *Kristin Lavransdatter*.

He was not ambitious beyond a very proper desire to develop and use his talents to their fullest extent. He seemed secure in himself, strong in that natural good sense that has never left him. He was happy with *Beowulf* and the *Anglo-Saxon Chronicles*, with Sweet's *Anglo-Saxon Reader* and Sisam's *Fourteenth Century Verse and Prose*, with Langland and with Chaucer, with Chambers and Klaeber, with Wright's *Gothic Grammar* and its Gospel of St. Mark, and with the mysterious, muddled, and to me esoteric sound and spelling changes expounded so learnedly and so bafflingly by Wyld.

Not that others altogether failed to get pleasure from these things, too. But mine at least was literary rather than philological. Because of that training I too can claim to have fought in the last ranks at the Battle of Maldon and to have slain ogres and dragons along with Beowulf. But it was Norman who, while no doubt not insensitive to these luxurious proxies for heroic living and dying, found a more exquisite, if grimmer, pleasure in the untangling of philological knots with Ramsay and arguing at length the obscure Indo-Germanic provenance of language and the intricate etymological stemmata of words that seemed to us commonplace.

He was fearless in argument and never beat about the bush—unless at the annual Latin picnic in the Leith Valley. He had even then the sardonic humour that any man who sees life as it is—both noble and null—must have if he is to survive and remain able to work, to enjoy and to retain self-respect. He also had, and still has, the faith in basic things—truth, honesty, loyalty, tolerance, among the rest—and an inability to be taken in by the fashions that tempt even intelligent vanities to swallow down cant without eructation. He was sceptical, though not cynical, about feelings, but reverent towards fact.

By tradition, the Rhodes Scholarship had largely gone in New Zealand to men more noted for their excellence in 'manly outdoor sport' than in scholarship, though intellectual ability was never entirely excluded as a consideration and was even, about this time, coming to be thought of as genuinely a possible ingredient in the power of leadership by which Cecil Rhodes himself was so deeply, and perhaps narcissistically, seduced. Norman's unconscious modesty (if that is not a tautology) had prevented him from ever thinking of himself as a possible candidate. It therefore came as a surprise to him when Mrs Ramsay suggested to him in his third year that he should put himself forward for nomination. It was still more a surprise to him, as well as to his more ambitious and calculating rivals, when his unsanguine application met with unhesitating approval by the selectors in 1933. They have seldom shown better judgement, though, to be fair and the present writer's bias apart, they have seldom chosen badly.

So, in 1934, Norman departed from amongst us, to take up residence in Merton and to be taught by men whose existence to us in faraway Otago—there were no swift air passages then—was legendary rather than real. In Oxford he was to find that, if there were no Camelot and no Round Table—he was not the man to expect them—there were quadrangles as good as, and more real than, courts; other tables, high and low; and there were still alive and lively heroes of scholarship like C. T. Onions, Sisam, Tolkien and Turville-Petre, and Charles Wrenn.

Some two years later—after a hiccup in the selection system not perhaps unconnected with an earlier event I have already glanced at—I was myself to follow Norman to Oxford, once our Camelot, though to Balliol rather than Merton, and to read Greats rather than English. The man I now found was so transformed that I ought to have been less surprised in 1941 than I was at yet another transformation. He was extraordinarily kind to me by inaugurating the gauche provincial into the arcana of Oxford and I can still recall my pleasure in his discourse, as we walked up the High Street, on the etymology of the word Carfax and its ramified associations, though I should be hard put to it now to give an accurate rendering of his explanation. But it was not merely a learned philologist that I now encountered. He had become an enthusiastic rowing man, he had an unexpected and unrivalled command of the bawdy verses familiar to sporting and sparkish undergraduates, and he had acquired an extensive and profound knowledge of the subtly varying qualities of vintage clarets and burgundies, of cigars and venerable brandies and of the diverse effects on post-prandial intellectual interchange produced by ports of the best years and provenance.

Although I fear I got more pleasure than profit from his generous and copious instruction, being in those days a man of more appetite than discrimination, neither were to be much prolonged. For in 1937, the year in which Oxford and I had become more or less reconciled or resigned to each other, Norman himself, who had loved Oxford from the first, went off to lecture at the University of Lithuania in Kaunas, then only less remote and exotic than they have so tragically since become. From Kaunas he later returned to London and then set forth again, by the old Simplon Orient, for Sofia, where I first took up his adventures in this tortuous chronicle.

Our next meeting was to be in Oxford after the war, when no less a scholar than Kenneth Sisam, a former New Zealand Rhodes Scholar himself and by now Secretary to the Delegates of the Oxford University Press, had become my boss and mentor. He sternly enjoined me to annex to our learned future Norman's promise of learned authorship and certainty of diligence. Over the next few years Norman worked variously in London, Oxford, and Glasgow before finally returning to take up the Merton Chair. In Glasgow he became, along with Peter Alexander, editor of the *Review of English Studies*. He worked steadily on his great edition of the *Paston Letters* as well as on much else. He became a valued adviser to the Delegates and eventually a Delegate himself. It was over these years that I was to learn at last what he had known intuitively from the beginning: that the past is the compost of the future and its scholars, humble but indispensable, are the earthworms, the scarabs, the moles, who re-cycle the past to make the present both interesting and possible. But the past is also an epitaph susceptible of infinite anagrams, a kaleidoscope that reveals a new pattern to every new historian. To survive, and its survival is vital, the past must be continually changed, created afresh for every generation. Like the disappearance of the *Marie Celeste*, it is also an eternal mystery, itself a disappearance forever demanding a new explanation. But it is only by pursuing the insoluble that solutions are found for what can be solved. Enigmas are eternal and necessary and none the less there must always be men in search of an Ultra.

So, at the Clarendon Press, I came at last to understand something of the real value and stature of men like Norman Davis. In the context a pendent explanation may be permitted for the presence of such New Zealanders in Oxford and not in their own country. There is always a tendency at the centre to decay, for Ancient Greece to become Alexandrian, for Rome to decline. But values, by some law of delayed entropy, persist longer at the periphery and, as the Romans found, it is possible to defer decline by recruiting at the circumference. In our time, and I speak of forty years ago, there was one place on the circumference where the soil was fertile in talent but not adequate to nourish that talent when fully matured. Americans, Canadians, Australians, South Africans, could return to an academic base in an ample and welcoming hinterland; but for most of the New Zealanders of academic distinction there was no place at home, no choice but expatriation, however nostalgic, ambivalent, or wistful.

What Norman Davis has done, not merely in Oxford but in the whole field of international scholarship, needs no rehearsal from me. The testimony lies with his published works, his judicious editing, the influence acknowledged in so many prefaces, his innumerable pupils, his concourse of colleagues and friends. No more illumination—if that is what it has been—is called for from me of a man who would himself believe, and if necessary proclaim, that the only final test of a man is what he has done in whatever form of Gothic fate has allotted to him.

Chaucer's Spelling*

M. L. SAMUELS

THE problem of how Chaucer spelt is a long-standing one, on which new opinions have been expressed in the past decade.[1] But there are now also new sources of evidence which have not yet been considered. Firstly, A. I. Doyle and M. B. Parkes have shown conclusively that the work of the two scribes who copied four of our earliest manuscripts of the *Canterbury Tales* was not limited to Chaucer, but that it also included manuscripts of Gower.[2] Secondly, the spelling of the Fairfax and Stafford MSS of the *Confessio Amantis* has been authenticated as that of Gower's in a quite unexpected way,[3] and that provides us with an essential control for examining the copying habits of the two scribes already referred to. Thirdly, more is now known about the history of the language of London in the fourteenth and fifteenth centuries than was available to earlier scholars like

* The above article could not have been written without the extensive and essential help that I have received from Mr J. J. Smith, at present working on the language of the manuscripts of Gower's *Confessio Amantis*.

[1] M. B. Parkes and R. Beadle, Introduction to *Poetical Works of Geoffrey Chaucer: A Facsimile of Cambridge University Library MS Gg.4.27* (Cam-bridge, 1979–80), 47, iii. n. 40, and reference there quoted.

[2] A. I. Doyle and M. B. Parkes, 'The production of copies of the *Canterbury Tales* and the *Confessio Amantis* in the early fifteenth century', M. B. Parkes and A. G. Watson (edd.), *Medieval Scribes, Manuscripts and Libraries: Essays presented to N. R. Ker* (London, 1978).

[3] M. L. Samuels and J. J. Smith, 'The Language of Gower', *Neuphilologische Mitteilungen*, lxxxii (1981), 295–304.

Koch[4] and Wild,[5] and there is thus a fuller frame of reference for the evaluation of the new evidence.

I

It will be convenient to explain the frame of reference first. In my article 'Some applications of Middle English Dialectology' (1963)[6] the main London type to *c.*1380 was designated Type II, while 'Chaucerian' English of *c.*1380–1420 was called Type III. It is not intended here to revise that typology, which was based on certain striking differences, especially *þat i(l)che* 'the same', *werld*, *warld* 'world', and *eld(e)* 'old' in Type II compared with *þat ilke*, *thilke*, *world*, and *old(e)* in Type III. Nevertheless, the texts belonging to these two types were admitted to show considerable variation on other criteria. If we now place those texts in an order that is roughly chronological, and trace the fluctuations and more gradual changes shown by the other criteria, it should then be possible, by a refinement of the typology, to show what combination of features might be expected at given points in the fourteenth and early fifteenth centuries. The texts to be considered, in their more detailed classification, are as follows.

A. *Early and mid-fourteenth century, Type* II

1. Auchinleck MS (Edinburgh, Advocates 19.2.1), main hand.
2. Auchinleck MS, hand 3.[7]
3. The Early English Prose Psalter in BL Add. MS 17376.[8]
4. St. John's College, Cambridge, MS 256.

B. *Late fourteenth century, Type* II

5. Magdalene College, Cambridge, MS Pepys 2498, Bodl.

[4] J. Koch, *A Detailed Comparison of the Eight Manuscripts of Chaucer's Canterbury Tales*, Chaucer Society, 2nd Series, 47 (1913).

[5] F. Wild, *Die sprachlichen Eigentümlichkeiten der wichtigeren Chaucer-Handschriften*, Wiener Beiträge zur englischen Philologie, 44 (1915).

[6] *English Studies*, xliv (1963), 81–94.

[7] The principal works in this hand are *The Seven Sages*, *Floris and Blauncheflur*, *Sir Degare*, and *The Assumption of the Virgin*.

[8] Ed. K. D. Bülbring, EETS 97.

Laud Misc. 622, and BL Harley 874, all in a single hand.[9]

C. *Late fourteenth century, Type* III

6. The documents of East London provenance in R. W. Chambers and M. Daunt, *London English 1385–1425*, pp. 47–57, viz. Gilds of St. Katherine's, Aldersgate, Sts. Fabian and Sebastian, Aldersgate, and St. Paul's (Pouchmakers). These are selected as especially relevant to Chaucer's place of upbringing in Upper Thames Street.
7. Petition of the Folk of Mercerye, ibid., pp. 33–7. This is included because, of the remaining fourteenth-century London documents, it is that which is closest to those given in 6 above, and can therefore usefully add to the range of forms available for comparison.
8. Peterhouse, Cambridge, MS 75.I of the *Equatorie of the Planetis* (hereinafter *Equatorie*).[10] On the claim that this is in Chaucer's own hand, F. N. Robinson (Preface to his second edition of Chaucer's works) commented: 'Later investigation, while by no means disproving, has not conclusively substantiated this claim.' The reasons for including it here will appear later.

D. *Early fifteenth century, Type* III

9. The Hengwrt and Ellesmere MSS of the *Canterbury Tales*, i.e. Nat. Libr. Wales Peniarth 392 and Huntington Libr. 26.C.9 respectively.
10. Corpus Christi College, Cambridge, MS 61 of *Troilus and Criseyde*.
11. Trinity College, Cambridge, MS B.15.17 of *Piers Plowman*.
12. Huntington Libr. HM 111 (*olim* Phillipps 8151) and 744 (*olim* Ashburnham 133), and other autograph MSS of Hoccleve.[11]

[9] For published portions see *The Pepysian Gospel Harmony*, ed. M. Goates, EETS 157; *Kyng Alisaunder*, ed. G. V. Smithers, EETS 227; *The Recluse*, ed. J. Påhlsson (Lund, 1918).

[10] Ed. D. J. Price (Cambridge, 1955).

[11] See Doyle and Parkes, op. cit., p. 182, and, for texts, EETS, ES 61 and 73.

E. c.*1430 onwards, Type* IV (*'Chancery Standard'*)[12]

13. Typical forms in documents written by Chancery-trained scribes, in PRO, Early Chancery Proceedings and Exchequer T.R. Council and Privy Seal.

The result of applying eleven variational criteria to the above thirteen texts (or groups of texts) is shown in the table on pp. 22–3, and this will be used as the frame of reference for the discussion that follows.

II

Of the new sources of evidence already mentioned, the most important is the scribe of the Hengwrt and Ellesmere MSS, who has now been shown to have been the second of the five scribes who copied from Book II, l. 2686 to the end of Gower's *Confessio Amantis* in Trinity Coll. Cambridge MS R.3.2 ('Scribe B' in the nomenclature of Doyle and Parkes).[13] As a copyist of Gower, this scribe is very unusual in that he translates his Gower exemplar thoroughly (with a few notable exceptions) into the normal Hengwrt–Ellesmere spelling. That he was copying from a conventional Gower exemplar can be shown, firstly, by the relict forms from Gower in the other hands of the manuscript, and secondly by this scribe's habit of using *-ee-* for Gower's typical *-ie-* even in words where, when copying Chaucer, he would not have used *-ee-* at all, e.g. *mortal* in Hengwrt–Ellesmere but *morteel* and even *mortiel* (3. 2027) in Gower. A similar pointer is his use of *thei* as well as *they* when copying Gower, but of *they* only when copying Chaucer. These features agree with the now authenticated text of Gower,[14] but for most other features the gap between the two spelling-systems is very wide,

[12] For the term 'Chancery Standard' see op. cit. (above, p. 18 n. 6).

[13] Op. cit., p. 170. Recently, in *Studies in Bibliography* 35 (1982), 133–54, R. V. Ramsey has attempted to show that the Hengwrt and Ellesmere MSS are by different scribes. I answer his case in 'The Scribe of the Hengwrt and Ellesmere Manuscripts of the *Canterbury Tales*' (forthcoming).

[14] Samuels and Smith, art. cit.

as may be seen from the following comparison of regular forms from the Fairfax MS of Gower and Scribe B's stint in the Trinity MS:

Fairfax	Trinity	Fairfax	Trinity
þese	thise	mochel	muchel
tuo	two	yit, yet	yet
sche	she	togedre	togidre
ȝoue	yeue	hyhe	highe
her(e) 'their'	hir(e)	ferst	first
eny	any	euel	yuel
-ende	-ynge	oghne	owene

This imposition of an entirely different spelling-system on the Gower text is in itself interesting because it suggests (though it could hardly be held to prove) that the spelling so familiar to us from the Hengwrt and Ellesmere MSS is really that of Scribe B, not that of Chaucer. There may, of course, have been a closer similarity between Scribe B's and Chaucer's spelling than between Scribe B's and Gower's, and one could even posit the extreme view that Scribe B had learnt, or developed, his spelling system from continually copying Chaucer. However, Middle English scribes fall into various categories according to the consistency with which they copy literally or translate into their own spelling, and Scribe B clearly belongs to the latter category. He transforms Gower's spellings with such obviously practised ease and consistency that it is difficult to believe that he was acting any differently when he copied Chaucer.

If Scribe B's spelling is primarily his own, what can he tell us about Chaucer's? The answer is that for just a few items he shows forms that are 'constrained' by those of his exemplar. This practice was common in scribes who in other respects were thorough translators, and must be distinguished from the mere copying of forms alien to the scribe's normal practice. To use

	1 Auchinleck, main hand	2 Auchinleck, hand 3	3 Early English Prose Psalter	4 St. John's College MS	5 Pepys, Laud, and Harley MSS	6 East London docume[nts]
SUCH	swiche	swich(e)	swich swyche	swich(e) suich	swich suich	swich(e)
MUCH	miche(l)	moche(l) ((muche))	michel mechel	moche(l) muche(l) miche(l)	mychel	moche
SHALL pl.	schul(len)	sschulle sscholle	shul(le) schul	schulle(n) (schul(n))	schullen	schul(le) (schole)
IF	ȝif ((if, ȝiue))	ȝif	ȝif, ȝyf ((if))	ȝif ((if))	ȝif	ȝif
AGAIN(ST)	oȝain(s) oȝe(i)n oȝaines	aȝen ((aȝein))	oȝain(s) oȝayn(s) (oȝaines aȝeins aȝayn)	aȝein(s) aȝain(s) aȝayn agein	aȝein(s)	aȝen(s)
YET	ȝete	ȝit (ȝet)	ȝete ȝit	ȝit, ȝete	ȝutt ((ȝut))	— —
BEFORE	bifor(e) biforn (tofor(n))	bifore biforn (tofore toforn)	tofor(n)e (aforn)	tofore(n)	tofor(n)e bifor(n)e	byfore byforn beforn before (afore)
NOT	nouȝt no	nowt	nouȝt (noȝt, nauȝt)	nouȝt (noȝt nauȝt)	nouȝth (no)	nat (nouȝt nauȝt)
WORK vb.	wirche (werche, wirke)	—	wirchen wyrchen	werke werchen	wirchen	werche
THROUGH	þurth	þourgh (þour(g) þourgȝ þourh)	þurȝ þourȝ (þurwe þurȝt þur(t)h)	þorw (þourw þoruȝ)	þorouȝ (þorou)	thorwȝ thurwȝ (thorw þurwȝ)
SAW pret.	seyȝe seiȝe (seye)	segh(ȝ) seȝ segȝ(e)	seiȝ(e) (saiȝ)	se(y)ȝ sei	seiȝ	—

7 ition, 'olk of Mercerye	8 Equatorie	9 Hengwrt–Ellesmere	10 CCCC 61	11 Trinity Coll. Cambridge B.15.17	12 Hoccleve	13 Chancery Standard
h(e)	swich(e)	swich(e) ((such(e)))	swich (such)	swich(e)	swich	such
ch(e)	moche(l)	muche(l) (moche, meche)	muche(l) (michel)	muche(l)	moche, -il	muche (moche)
lle lle	shollen	shulle(n)	shullen	shul	shul(n)	shul(l) shullen
'if)	yif	if	if	if	if	if
in(s)	agayn(s) (agains)	agayn(s) ageyn(s) ayeyn(s)	aȝein(s) aȝeyns agayn(s)	ayein(s)	ageyn(s) agayn	ageyns(t) ageyn(e) (ayein(st))
	yit	yet	ȝet	yet	yit	yit, yet
re(e) re)	byforn (byfore)	biforn bifore	biforn byfore	before tofore (afore)	toforn beforn before	before afore
ght	nat	nat noght	nought nouȝt nat, nauȝt	noght	nat (not)	not
	wirke wyrk workest	werken wirkyng	werken	werche	wirke	werk(e)
rgh	thorw	thurgh	thorugh ((thorwgh))	thorugh	thurgh	thorugh
	say	saugh (seigh say saw(e))	saugh (sey seigh say saigh sauȝ)	seigh saugh	sy	sawe

the terminology of the most recent discussion of the subject,[15] Scribe B was here activating certain forms from his 'passive repertoire' under the influence of his exemplars. By comparing his treatment of certain items when copying from different exemplars, we can deduce which forms he would normally write and which derive from his exemplar:

Fairfax MS of Gower	SCRIBE B Trinity MS (Gower)	SCRIBE B Hengwrt–Ellesmere MSS (Chaucer)
aȝein	ayein	*agayn(s), *ageyn(s), ayeyn(s)
tofore ((afore))	tofore ((afore))	biforn, bifore
worche, werche	werche	werke, *wirke
sih, syh, sawh	saugh, seigh, *sigh(e)	saugh, seigh, *say, *saw

Naturally, it is not always possible to be certain of the scribe's own preferences, but one can at least be sure that certain forms were *not* those that he normally wrote, and these are marked with an asterisk. The forms for 'before' are evenly balanced; his use tells us which were in his exemplars, but not whether he had a preference or used them all in free variation. On the other hand, his normal form for Gower's *sih*, *syh* is *saugh*; *sigh(e)* is obviously a constrained usage, while *seigh* is most probably his own rarer variant which he used under the influence of his exemplars' forms, whether *sih* (Gower) or *say* (Chaucer).

From the above it may be fairly deduced that the following were in B's Chaucer exemplar: *agayn(s)*, *ageyn (s)*; *biforn*, *bifore*; *wirke*; *say*, *saw*. Furthermore, since editors and textual critics are fairly generally agreed that the Hengwrt and Ellesmere MSS are close to the archetype of the *Canterbury Tales*,[16] it is reason-

[15] M. Benskin and M. Laing, 'Translations and *Mischsprachen* in Middle English Manuscripts', in M. Benskin and M. L. Samuels (edd.) *So Meny People, Longages and Tonges: Philological Essays presented to Angus McIntosh* (Edinburgh, 1981), 55–106.

[16] See, e. g., F. N. Robinson's edition of Chaucer's works, p. xxxvii.

able to postulate (if only provisionally at this stage of the argument) that these forms are archetypal.

Another scribe who contributed to the Trinity MS of Gower is relevant here: the fourth hand, accordingly called 'Scribe D' by Doyle and Parkes. Their discoveries here are even more dramatic, for they show that this scribe also copied MSS Harley 7334 and Corpus Christi Coll. Oxford 198 of the *Canterbury Tales*, and, in addition, no fewer than nine other manuscripts, including seven of the *Confessio Amantis*. For our present purposes, however, this scribe is less promising, for three reasons. Firstly, his exemplars for the *Canterbury Tales* were less close to the archetype than those of the Hengwrt and Ellesmere MSS; secondly, his own dialect was probably not that of London;[17] and thirdly, his copying habits are less straightforward and predictable than those of Scribe B. His active repertoire admits of more variants, including, apparently, some that he has adopted from his work of copying, and the result is that some obviously 'Gowerian' spellings appear even when he copies Chaucer.[18] Nevertheless, amidst all this mixture, it is still possible to detect some differentiation in his forms for 'not' and 'such':

copying Trevisa[19]	copying Gower	copying Chaucer
nought, nouȝt, not, noȝt, nouȝ	nought, nouȝt, not, noȝt, noght, nough	nought, nouȝt, not, *nat
such(e), soche, *swiche	such(e)	such(e), *swich(e)

[17] He has a greater tendency to use western forms than other London scribes. It follows that his use of *þ* and *ȝ* is not of chronological significance.

[18] A full examination of Scribe D's work as a copyist is being carried out by Mr J. J. Smith.

[19] In BL Add. 27944. To judge from the other two hands, this MS was copied in London from an exemplar in language containing dialect strata from both London and elsewhere.

Since Scribe D's exemplars for the *Canterbury Tales* had passed through one or more Northern and Midland stages of copying, it is all the more remarkable that the Southern form *nat* survived, and this provides strong evidence that *nat* is the archetypal Chaucerian form; and the same may reasonably be assumed (though again only provisionally at this stage of the argument) regarding *swich(e)*.

In addition to the above new evidence, an older source—that of rhymes—may be considered here. It is often regarded with suspicion, since one can always claim that a form was used purely to achieve the rhyme, and that it was not the poet's normal form. Indeed, that will hold true of the forms for 'not', for although, as we have seen, there is evidence to support *nat*, *noght* was obviously more convenient for rhyming purposes and is Chaucer's normal rhyme-word for the negative. However, that objection does not apply to the variants for 'yet'. The rhyming indices[20] show that Chaucer rhymed commonly with words ending in both *-et* and *-it*, and that he had available to him a wide range of words with both endings; but he invariably rhymed on *yit*, not *yet*. Since there is evidence for both variants in London in the fourteenth, fifteenth, and sixteenth centuries,[21] there seem no valid grounds for rejecting the rhyming evidence that Chaucer's form was *yit*.

To sum up so far: the evidence points, with varying degrees of cogency, to the following eight forms as authorial or, at least, archetypal: *swich(e)*, *agayn(s)/ageyn(s)*, *yit*, *biforn/bifore*, *nat*, *wirke* (vb.) 'work', *say* and *saw* (past tense) 'saw'.

[20] W. W. Skeat, *Rime-Index to Chaucer's Troilus and Criseyde*, Chaucer Society, First Series, 84 (London, 1892); Isabel Marshall and Lela Porter, *Rime-Index to Chaucer's Minor Poems*, Chaucer Society, First Series, 80 (London, 1889); Henry Cromie, *Ryme-Index to the Ellesmere Manuscript of Chaucer's Canterbury Tales*, Chaucer Society, First Series, 45 (London, 1875).

[21] For the sixteenth century see E. J. Dobson, *English Pronunciation 1500–1700* (Oxford, 1957), II, §77.

III

If we now return to the table on pp. 22–3, it is remarkable how closely the above list of forms tallies with those in column 8 (the *Equatorie*) in practically every detail,[22] and that it tallies with those of that column *and no other*. Even if we grant that some of the indications gathered from our new evidence are hypothetical rather than factual, the resulting correspondence of the two sets can hardly be due to pure coincidence, and our attention is immediately drawn to the four forms *moche(l)*, *shollen*, *yif*, and *thorw*, in which the *Equatorie* differs from the traditionally 'Chaucerian' *muche(l)*, *shulle(n)*, *if*, and *thurgh* of Hengwrt–Ellesmere. Here, the most striking and relevant fact is that all four (but especially *yif* and *thorw*) are such as might be expected for Chaucer both chronologically and dialectally:

(i) *moche(l)* was a well-established London variant, as may be seen from columns 2, 4, 6, 7, 12, and especially 6 (East London documents contemporary with Chaucer); furthermore, Scribe B wrote *muchel* for Gower's *mochel* (which suggests that *muchel* was B's own form), and his occasional *moche* when copying the *Canterbury Tales* is therefore quite probably influenced by his exemplar.

(ii) *shollen* is paralleled as a variant in columns 3 (*scholle*), 6 (*schole*), and 7 (*sholle*); the *o*-forms seem to have been ousted by *u*-forms *c.*1400, in the same way as *sholde* was to be ousted by *shulde* some two to three decades later.

(iii) *yif* is of especial interest since, although this text is predominantly Type III, it is distinguished chronologically by this form from the fifteenth-century Type III texts. For this feature, the *Equatorie* is classed with the older Type II and with the East London documents of Chaucer's time.

(iv) *thorw* 'through' is less in evidence in texts of Type II, which usually show *þourgh*, *þurȝ*, *þurth* or similar forms;

[22] The past tense 'saw' occurs only once, as *say*. The absence of *saw* is therefore not significant, especially since *say*, as the earlier form, is the more important.

but it does appear in column 4, with a variant *þurwe* in column 3. Since the main forms throughout the fourteenth century were variants of *þurȝ* (reappearing as *thurgh* in Scribe B), it is possible that *thorw* was a local East London variant: it is surely significant that *thorw* and the related forms *thorwȝ* and *thurwȝ* appear in column 6, in the very documents that come closest of all in localization to Chaucer's place of upbringing. In any event, further support for the form as one appropriate to Chaucer comes from *wherthorw* in the Appeal of Thomas Usk.[23]

Thus the combined evidence resulting from the application of all eleven criteria provides very strong support indeed for the view that the *Equatorie* is in Chaucer's own spelling. If the combination is viewed historically as a late fourteenth-century London system, only one feature of it arouses comment, and that is the use of *-g-*, not *-y-*, in *agayn(s)*. Such forms are not typical of Types II or III; *aȝen(s)*, *aȝein(s)*, *ayein(s)* are normal in the late fourteenth-century documents, including the Appeal of Thomas Usk and the Proclamations of Nicholas Brembre[24] (which are not represented in the table on pp. 22–3). *Ayeyn(s)*, *ayein* seem likewise to have been Scribe B's preferred forms (cf p. 24 above), and the same is quantitatively true of the scribe of CCC Cambridge 61: probably both these scribes used *agayn(s)* only when influenced by their exemplars. Lastly, *ayein(s)* is the form used in another early-fifteenth-century Type III text (column 11). It is thus difficult to escape the conclusion that *agayn(s)* was an exceptionally progressive form for Chaucer to use. Since it was to form part of the written Chancery Standard in the fifteenth century, it was doubtless well enough known as a spoken form in late fourteenth-century London. We may surmise that Chaucer's adoption of it was due to his having encountered it more than most Londoners as a man of travel and affairs, but, since so

[23] Chambers and Daunt, op. cit., pp. 22–31.
[24] Ibid., pp. 31–3.

pronounced a feature is more likely to have been adopted earlier in his life, it might equally well be due to his period of service as a page at Hatfield, Yorks., in the later 1350s. But whatever the reason for this form, the very fact that it is unexpected yet vouched for by both Scribe B and the *Equatorie* is in itself significant.

IV

If the view urged above is accepted (viz. that the *Equatorie* is our best evidence of Chaucer's spelling), a number of further questions immediately arise. How does it relate to Chaucerian textual criticism and editorial policy? Are these features, singly or in combination, to be found in any subsequent manuscripts of Chaucer's work? If not, what is the explanation? Why is a prominent feature like *thorw* not represented in those manuscripts usually regarded as nearest to their archetype (Hengwrt, Ellesmere, Corpus Christi Coll. Cambridge 61)?

These questions are by no means easy to answer, but three general points may be stated in advance:

(i) The number of forms replaced is not large. Many remained in fifteenth-century Type III texts, so that typical features that we have grown accustomed to call 'Chaucerian' are in fact common to both the *Equatorie* and Hengwrt–Ellesmere: *thise* 'these', *hir(e)* 'their' as well as 'her', *swich(e)*, *sholde*, *byforn/byfore*, *nat*.

(ii) In a period of increasing standardization (at least regionally and locally, if not yet universally), it was inevitable that a certain proportion of variants should disappear.

(iii) If the variants do reappear in fifteenth-century manuscripts, we have to assure ourselves, by examining the other linguistic features of those manuscripts, that they are not the result of translation into dialects in which such variants still naturally occurred.

Of the variants in question, *thorw* is the most outstanding and in need of explanation. Accordingly, in what follows, 'through' may conveniently be adopted as a test-word.

Perhaps the best example of the problems that are encountered is CUL MS Gg.4.27 (*Canterbury Tales*, *Troilus*). This manuscript is generally agreed to be high in the stemma of the *Canterbury Tales*, and some have even regarded it as equal in authority to Hengwrt–Ellesmere.[25] Its main forms for 'through' are *þorw*, *thorw*, *þour*, *thour*, with less common *þorow*, *thorugh*, *tho*(*u*)*rgh* and *thurgh*. Since the dialect is a very pronounced East Anglian one into which *thorw* and *thour* fit exactly, it is reasonable to assume that these are the scribe's own forms, and that *thorugh*, *tho*(*u*)*rgh*, and *thurgh* come from exemplars. However, since this manuscript has been suggested as a better representative of Chaucer's spelling than Hengwrt–Ellesmere,[26] we need better proof that this allocation of forms is correct. The proof comes from another manuscript written by the same scribe, Bodl. e Mus. 116 (Mandeville and *Astrolabe*), where the only forms are *thorw*, *thour*, *thourw*. Since both manuscripts are written fairly consistently in the same dialect, it is difficult to see why the scribe should add *thorugh*, *tho*(*u*)*rgh*, *thurgh* in Gg. unless those were the exemplar's forms; and the presence of *thurgh* suggests that this manuscript goes back to a copy in the same later Type III language as Hengwrt–Ellesmere (that there was at least one intermediate stage of copying is shown by western relict forms). Other features for which Gg. has been praised as authentic (like the endings in *-ys*, *-yth*) are, like *thorw*, mere concomitants of its East Anglian dialect.[27]

The great majority of the rest of the *Canterbury Tales* MSS show *thurgh*, *thorugh*, and *through* or variants of these forms (*þurgh*, *þurȝ*, *þorgh*(*t*), *thorgh*, *thurh*, *þourh*, *thoruh*, *thorowȝ*,

[25] See above, p. 17 n. 1.

[26] See above, p. 17 n. 1.

[27] It is true that there are some similarities between late fourteenth-century East London texts and those of East Anglia, and these may perhaps have been caused by immigration. But that is no reason for selecting an East Anglian MS of Chaucer's works and pronouncing its language to be authentic.

thoro(u)gh, *thorou*, *thorow*, *thorouȝe*, *throuȝ*, *throuh*, *throwe*, *thrugh*). It is relevant to note that even of these MSS the proportion of dialectal MSS is high, and can be explained only by assuming that many London MSS of the early fifteenth century were written by immigrant scribes. Only a very few contain *thorw* or related forms (*þorwhe*, *thorghw*), and, here again, it belongs to their uppermost layer of dialect, as in the Lansdowne MS (SW Midlands) and the Delamere MS (NW Kent).[28] Although it is always possible that a more exhaustive search might prove the contrary, the strong impression remains that there are no manuscripts of the *Canterbury Tales* that can be proved to go back to a stage of the language earlier than the late Type III of Hengwrt–Ellesmere. We can only assume that *thorw* was replaced by *thurgh* at some point high in the stemma, or that it was replaced more gradually by successive copyings. If the evidence of the earliest MSS of the *Canterbury Tales* is considered to be more relevant than that of the rest, then the former explanation seems more probable.

If such a simple explanation is available in the case of the *Canterbury Tales*, the problem of the *Troilus* MSS is more complex. A longer period of copying and lost manuscripts antedates our first surviving ones of the early fifteenth century. Even the possibility of an antecedent copy in a language closer to Type II is not to be entirely ruled out, for Corpus Christi Coll. Cambridge 61 contains a thin sprinkling of such forms: *ich* 'each',[29] *noither* 'neither',[30] *ar* 'ere', *therwhile* 'while',[31] *werld* 'world',[32] *sygge* 'say'.[33] But Corpus Christi Coll. Cambridge 61

[28] Admittedly a *dialectal* connection between the Delamere MS and the *Equatorie* can be traced, for its *thorghw* (*thorwe*) belongs to the same enclave as the *thorw* of the *Equatorie*. But its language is of such a late and idiosyncratic kind that it could not be considered as even a remotely connected descendant of a manuscript written in the same language as the *Equatorie*.

[29] III. 1690, V. 831.

[30] III. 938.

[31] III. 538.

[32] IV. 1580.

[33] IV. 194.

is predominantly 'late Type III', and its claim to represent Chaucer's language is poorer than that of Hengwrt–Ellesmere, for its normal form for 'through' is *thorugh*, and this is unlikely to be original as the metre always presupposes a monosyllable, not a disyllable. (At II. 616 there is the single, tantalizing instance of *thorwgh*.)

A *Troilus* MS which might at first sight seem more attractive as a link with the *Equatorie* is St John's Coll. Cambridge L.I, since it contains the form *thorw* together with *yit*, *yif*, *swich*, *shol* pl. 'shall', *sholde*, *biforn*, *nat*, *thise*, *hir*(*e*) 'their' and 'her', *any*, occasional *ageyn*, and *say* 'saw'. But this apparent agreement is illusory, for there are in fact three layers in this text—a 'Chaucerian' layer, a northern layer, and a third (uppermost) layer in the language of a scribe from the borders of SE Shropshire, NE Herefords and NW Worcs. This last is shown by striking features like *-nn-* in words like *gronne* 'groan', *cheynne* 'chain', *-uu-* as in *thouusand*, and the forms *thikke* 'the same' and *-lische*, *-lysche* for the adverbial ending '-ly'. The forms *thorw*(*e*), *thor*(*w*)*gh*, *thorght* exactly fit the localization of that West Midland layer,[34] and the same probably applies to *yit*, *yif*, *shol*, and *sholde*. Once again, therefore, the Chaucerian layer is reduced to no more than the usual sprinkling of late Type III forms.

In BL Harley 2280, the position is similar. There are again three layers: Type III, shown by *thise*, *swich*, *nat*; Northern, shown by *scho*, *walde*, *omange*, *ath* 'oath', *sla* 'slay', *twa*, *gud*; and SW Midland, shown by *swuche*, *mony*, *fram*, *worldeles* gen. sg. 'world's'. Here, just as in the previous case, it is far more likely that *þorwgh*, *þorwh*, *þorwȝ* belong to the SW Midland layer and not to the Chaucerian one. In other MSS of *Troilus* (e.g. the Campsall MS and Harley 1239), *thorugh*, *thorow* (whether Type IV or dialectal) is the commoner form, but *thurgh*

[34] As evidence for this layer, two West Midland MSS may be compared: Bodl. Add. B. 107 (Castle of Love), and Trinity Coll. Oxford 16A (Prick of Conscience).

also occurs occasionally, suggesting that such MSS may also have passed through the normal 'late Type III' stage of copying.[35]

Thus, in the case of the *Troilus* MSS, the evidence does not even suggest a simple solution; it does not, this time, indicate that there might have been a stage, high in the stemma, at which *thorw* was replaced by *thurgh* or *thorugh*. That may, of course, have happened, but the evidence suggests no more than that it was gradually replaced by repeated stages of copying. Occasionally it may have survived because it happened to coincide with the dialectal copyist's regular form, but this cannot be proved; and there is no MS of *Troilus* in *London* language that preserves *thorw*, unless we are to consider the stray *thorwgh* in Corpus Christi Coll. Cambridge 61.

As was pointed out earlier, if viewed historically, the disappearance of *thorw* from both of the main Chaucerian MS traditions is not surprising. Though it is well supported by the relevant documents as the form that Chaucer might have used, it was never more than a minority variant in London and, especially if it was subject to repeated copying, was bound to be ousted by the better established Type III form *thurgh* and by the increasingly common *thorugh*, a variant in Type III and the normal form in Type IV.

V

It might be objected at this point that if there are no manuscripts of authentic works of Chaucer that preserve genuine and specific traces of the type of spelling used in the *Equatorie*, then, in spite of the chronological and dialectal evidence in its favour, the case for it remains unproven. But that would be unjustified, for not only does the type recur, but it recurs in manuscripts of two independent prose works of Chaucer, *Boece* and the *Astrolabe*.

[35] Many of the *Troilus* MSS are specifically dialectal and need not be considered here. Examples are BL Harley 3943 and 4912, BL Add, 12044, Bodl. Selden B 24, Selden Supra 56, and Digby 181.

CUL MS Dd.3.53[36] of the *Astrolabe* is clearly in two layers of language, one of which tallies with that of the *Equatorie* and the other belonging to a copyist. The copyist's forms do not amount to much more than a veneer, for he leaves many unchanged: *she*, *hir*, *swich*, *shal*, *wole*, *fro/from*, *than(ne)*, *yif*, *yit*, *agayn(s)*, *byforn*, *nat*, *seyn/sein* (inf.). Others he occasionally alters, leaving two strata, as follows:

exemplar	copyist	exemplar	copyist
thise	the(e)s, theise	whan	wan
it	hit	after	aftur
which(e)	wiche, wych	wirke, wyrke	werken
euerich	euerech	thorw	thorow, thorgh
any	eny, ony	-ed, -id	-et
moche(l)	mechel, michel	first(e)	furst(e)

CUL MS Ii.3.21 of *Boece* is a more complex case since its uppermost layer is in the language of the NW Kent-London border; and because the dialect of the scribe was quite close to that of his exemplar, the layers cannot be differentiated for every item. Obvious Kenticisms of the scribe are the *-y* infinitive ending (*answery*, *gadery*, etc.), *brengeth* 'brings', *by* 'be', *on-* 'un-', *seuende* 'seventh'; but other forms tally with those of the *Equatorie*: *thise*, *swiche*, *any*, *yif*, *yit*, *byforn*, *nat*, *myhte*, *thorw*. Those that occur in doublets will fit the two layers, as shown in the table on page 35. In only one case did the copyist wholly reject his exemplar's form: he wrote *ayein(s)* and *ayen(is)*, not *agayn(s)*. But this is not at all surprising, for the same

[36] The resemblance of the language of this MS to that of the *Equatorie* was noted by R. M. Wilson in his section on the language in Price's edition (op. cit., above, p. 19), pp. 146 f.

exemplar	copyist	exemplar	copyist
it	hit, hyt	thilke	thikke, thykke
whiche	weche, wych	world	wordyl
moche(l)	meche	fro, from	fram
shol(len)	shellen	lasse	lesse
wolt	welt	whan	wan

tendency existed in many other copyists of Chaucer (cf. p. 28 above).

The fact that the type of language found in consistently written form in the *Equatorie*, without scribal variants, recurs with an extra scribal layer in MSS of two known works of Chaucer can hardly be accidental. It adds strong support to the view advanced above regarding Chaucer's spelling, and, although it is not the purpose of the present article to urge more than that, it increases the likelihood that the *Equatorie* is an authentic and autograph work of Chaucer.

VI

Of the questions posed above on p. 29, one still remains—that of editorial policy. The *Equatorie* is a short text which could not provide a model complete enough for the wide-ranging lexis of Chaucer's major works. The *Boece* and the *Astrolabe* are longer, but they contain layers of language, and since only the more obvious boundaries between their layers can be ascertained, they too are not suitable as models. It might be possible to establish some kind of consensus from all three texts, but that is a task that lies in the future. Failing that, probably the nearest an editor could get at present to Chaucer's spelling would be to take a consensus of Hengwrt–Ellesmere and Corpus Christi Coll. Cambridge 61 and then, wherever feasible, to alter spellings in the directions indicated by the *Equatorie*. But that is not a counsel that would appeal to all editors; for those who prefer a single text, Hengwrt–Ellesmere is probably somewhat nearer to the truth than Corpus Christi Coll. Cambridge 61; but which of those two, Hengwrt or Ellesmere, is to be preferred? The differences between these two MSS pose a problem, for although in general the forms used overall are the same, their distribution in the two MSS varies considerably, the earlier type of variant being more frequent in Hengwrt, the later type in Ellesmere. Examples are: *-o-* vs. *-ou-* in words like *ynogh*, *thogh*, *thoghte*; *-a-* vs. *-au-* in words like *draghte*, *faght*; *seigh*, *say* vs. *saugh*; *neigh*, *heighe* vs. *ny*, *hye*. Furthermore, Hengwrt shows more cases of the noun plural in *-is*, which also occurs in the *Equatorie* and is supported by rhymes. It is difficult to tell whether these differences are due to changes in preference over a fairly long period in the scribe's life, or merely to the constraints of differing exemplars. If the former were the case, the order of copying must necessarily be Hengwrt–Ellesmere; if the latter, then either order of copying is possible. This problem, too, requires further study, but for our present purpose a solution is perhaps unnecessary: Hengwrt preserves a higher proportion of early spellings, and, if that is one of the editor's criteria, he can choose accordingly.

The conclusions reached above may be summarized as follows. New evidence available from the study of scribal habits in the earliest surviving manuscripts of the *Canterbury Tales* suggests that the only manuscript to preserve Chaucer's spelling is that of the *Equatorie of the Planetis*, and this evidence is supported by rhymes and by chronological and dialectal evidence. The same spelling system survives in contaminated form in two later MSS, one of *Boece*, the other of the *Astrolabe*. Many of the identifying features of this spelling coincided with that of the local London standard of the early fifteenth century, and are therefore represented in the best MSS of the *Canterbury Tales* and *Troilus* (Hengwrt, Ellesmere, Corpus Christi Coll. Cambridge 61). But certain remaining features, notably *thorw* and *yit*, found no place in this local standard, and were therefore replaced in the normal process of copying. Since it is not practicable for editors to extrapolate on a large scale from the *Equatorie*, they have the choice of adopting the spellings of Hengwrt as they stand, or of modifying them in the direction of those of the *Equatorie*.[37]

[37] In an article to appear in *Studies in the Age of Chaucer* (cf. above, p. 20 n. 13), I have now shown that the Hengwrt MS must be regarded as having been written earlier in the career of the scribe than the Ellesmere MS, and that the first of the alternatives given on p. 36 above is the correct one.

The Text of *The Legend of Good Women* in *CUL MS Gg.4.27*

GEORGE KANE

SOME differences between the text of the Prologue to *The Legend of Good Women* in Cambridge University Library MS Gg. 4.27 (henceforth called G) and that preserved in the other manuscripts of the poem are of such character or extent or both as to be most easily explicable by a hypothesis of authorial revision. But acceptance of that hypothesis implies a need to examine all differences between the two texts in its terms. At the same time, from the axiom of the necessary corruptness of texts, not all differences can be authorial. The problem of distinguishing between revision, that is, authorial variation, and the scribal variation inevitable in manuscript transmission is probably the most delicate operation in all textual criticism.

It is here complicated by the question which version is antecedent. To my knowledge that question has never been resolved in terms of absolute proof. There seems just now a tacit consensus that the G version is the revision. But the consensus seems to rest more on dissatisfaction with the subjectivity of the arguments for the antecedence of G than on the quality of those for G being the revision. Ideally, then, identification of scribal damage in both versions of the *Prologue* would be effected without reference to the direction of revision.

This essay gives the results of such an attempt. The method of obtaining them has been to examine the unique unoriginal variants of G in that part of the poem where revision is not presumed, namely the *Legend*; from that examination to form a 'profile' of the immediate scribes or scribe of G; and to set that profile against differences of a comparable scale between the two versions of the *Prologue*. The exercise was conducted in full awareness of its limitations, which are those that qualify all applications of the theory of textual criticism. Here, specifically, the decisions about direction of variation in all interesting or significant cases are subjective; the arguments on which they are based—that is the explanations of individual variations—are speculative; the result is 'only another hypothesis'. What is in question is not absolute proof but a plausible explanation of a class of phenomena, the essential object of all literary study.

The position of G among the manuscripts of *The Legend of Good Women* is obscure. Since in the *Legend* all manuscripts are copies of the same poem they necessarily have an exclusive common ancestor, if nothing else the author's copy. Beyond that, classification of the manuscripts by variation from a text formed upon full collation[1] places all the manuscripts except G in two large families. One of these, {<[T(FB)]TH>A^{3}}, is solid for the whole poem. The second comprises the remaining manuscripts except G as and when these are represented: before line 800 as <[P(TrA^{1})]S>, and soon after that point, at its fullest, as <[S(TrA^{1})][PR]>, then later in the poem with fluctuating subgroups. It is not possible to relate G confidently to either main group on the basis of agreement in unoriginal readings. It figures in more than 100 random agreements with single manuscripts, unrelated manuscripts, or subgroups, but shares no considerable number of unoriginal readings with either main group. In other words, most of its unoriginal readings were accumulated in the more recent stages of its tradition.

Classification of the manuscripts also reveals that in those recent stages of transmission the text of *The Legend of Good Women* in G was much corrupted. For this poem at least G is in no sense a 'superior' manuscript.[2] By the most conservative

[1] The collation was carried out by Janet Cowen of King's College London; the text is one she and I have prepared for an edition of the poem.

[2] F. N. Robinson, *The Works of Geoffrey Chaucer*^{2}, (London, 1957), p. xxxix. The scholarship of the subject has been very conveniently summarized

estimate the text of G in the *Legend* has more than 200 individual unoriginal variant readings of a substantive nature. In another more than 200 it forms 92 random groups by coincident variation: 10 groups of 2 manuscripts based on a total of 54 variants; 19 groups of 3 (44 variants); 24 groups of 4 (42 variants); 7 groups of 5 (17 variants); 15 groups of 6 (27 variants); 7 groups of 7 (7 variants); 9 groups of 8 (13 variants); and one group of 9 manuscripts based on a single variant. It shares another 30 odd unoriginal variants in a pair or with two to four other manuscripts, so clustered as to suggest contamination rather than coincident variation.[3] There is an identifiable scribal variation for every seven lines of G's text of the *Legend*.

Among the individual unoriginal readings of G unmistakably mechanical variations are the more numerous. The most frequent source of such variation seems to be inducement of the preceding copy. Its effect is identifiable in the following instances:[4] 603 nothyng to hym] to hy*m* nothyng (*position of* Hym *at head of line*); 840 slow] slayn (slayn 837); 880 leef] lyf (sle *preceding*, 903 yfere] that (That *prec.*); 920 to] for (For *prec.*); 1082 She] And (And 1066–71, 1074, 1075, 1079, 1080); 1102 And] Of (Of ... of ... of 1101) (*so Robinson*); 1138 his yonge] this blysful (blysful 1137); 1189 hire] oure (am-orou-s *prec.*); 1240 this whan] whil (whil that 1239); 1259 they] ȝe (ye 1257, 1259); 1263 may²] may it (may ... it *prec.*); 1267 so pryuy] so trewe (so trewe 1266); 1387 ful] wol (wel 1386); 1486 hem] hy*m* (his *prec.*); 1489 For] Or (Or 1488); 1526 That half so] That so (That to 1525); 1568 his] hire (hire 1567); 1591 of al] I clepid (cleped

in *The Poetical Works of Geoffrey Chaucer: A Facsimile of Cambridge University Library MS Gg. 4.27 with Introductions by M. B. Parkes and Richard Beadle* (Cambridge, 1980), iii. 46–56.

[3] These are the groups: TrG, 8 agreements after line 2000; TrA³G, 6 after 2200; STrA²G, 7 after 2000; TrA³A²G, 6 after 2000; STrA³A²G, 9 after 2000. These readings are excluded from the present analysis because of the possibility that they are present in G by scribal 'correction'.

[4] The spelling of the lemmata from which G's reading varies is Robinson's, unless our text differs. Variants peculiar to G are as spelled in the manuscript. Variants of groups in which G figures have the spelling of the manuscript first in the cited order of sigils.

1590); 1608 with] *and* (And 1604, 1605, 1606 (2), 1607); 1734 she let hyre eyen] h. e. l. s. (of hire werk she tok: *object in first position* 1733); 1752 was] is (h-is w-i-t *prec.*); 1756 His] This (Th-e 1755); 1924 And] But (But 1918, 1921); 1964 Mynos] Thesi*us* (Theseus 1960); 2000 To] And (and ... and 1999); 2056 As] So (So-ne ... knyght 2055, As/So myghte 2056); 2088 yow] the (ye-ve *prec.*); 2182 for] with (with *prec.*); 2187 I] that I (*so Rob.*) (that *prec.*); 2314 Of] For (*so Rob.*) (Or 2313), agros] aros (reste 2313); 2358 can] coude (coude 2357); 2487 him] she (she *prec.*); 2500 as] that (That *prec.*); 2501 which] that (That 2500); 2521 so] to (*so Rob.*) (to *prec.*); 2598 deyen] turne (turne 2596, Sa-turne 2597); 2658 dremes it is] d. is it (drem-es it *prec.*); 2686 That] And (And 2685).

Anticipation of following copy is another frequent source of mechanical variation in G's text of the *Legend*. Its effect is identifiable in the following instances: 810 drery] dredy (dredful 811); 881 am] al (c-al-leth *following*); 897 departe] depare (t-re-wely *fol.*); 1000 she] he (he *fol.*); 1003 sholde] schule (la-, lo-, -le *fol.*); 1058 biknew] he knew (he *fol.*); 1115 the] to (to *fol.*); 1149 thanked] thankyth (*present tense fol.*); 1202 fair] bright (bryghte *fol.*); 1213 go bet] bobet; 1242 upros] a ros (a-nd ... a-non *fol.*); 1264 Tak] Thak (Tak hede ... th-is *fol.*); 1352 But] But ȝit (yit *fol.*); 1425 yle] ylde (called *fol.*); 1437 boles] bole (dragoun *sg. fol.*); 1643 hereupon] here vp (upward 1645); 1660 wedded] weddyth (th-e th-ridde *fol.*); 1685 to] to me (memorye *fol.*); 1717 yate] ȝote (p-o-rter ... n-o-n *fol.*); 1726 walles] wal (fallen] fal G *fol.*); 1729 it stingeth] me thy*n*kyth (I thynke 1730); 1766 That] ȝit (Yit 1767); 1826 he] this (this *fol.*); 1986 any] *om* (m-an fol.); 2007 whan] what (that *fol.*); 2044 no man] non (con-ne *fol.*); 2094 is] nys (no *fol.*); 2101 final] fenal (en-de *fol.*); 2215 come] cone (contre/cuntre 2216); 2267 preyde] preyeth (th-at *fol.*); he] ho (wo-lde *fol.*); 2275 but] myghte (s-yghte *fol.*); 2484 recorde] recordith (deth ... corde 2485); 2613 flour] flourys (lef is *fol.*); 2660 which] wit (noot *fol.*).

Occasionally substitution of an unoriginal reading appears to have been induced by features of the text both before and after the point of variation: 1251 at] of (oo-n . . . an-o-thers w-o); 1330 hath he] he hath (he let 1326, he gan 1328, he lafte 1332, he . . . stal 1333); 1496 oure] hire (hire 1493, pleye . . . hire 1497, 1498; 1543 on] in (th-i-s . . . n-y-ght); 1786 this] the (he 1785, she 1786, 1787); 1933 com aboute] fil a. (caste lot 1933 *and* On riche or pore 1934 *suggest the collocation* 'lot fell'); 2072 As] And (And 2070, 2073).

Grammatical attraction, that is, subconscious scribal interest in the completion of an anticipated grammatical relationship, in consequence of which a delaying element of text is omitted, was probably responsible for the following accordingly mechanical variations: 933 a] *om.* (*adj* ~ *noun*); 999 with him] *om.* (*verb* ~ *adv.*); 1032 for to] *om.* (*adv.* ~ *verb*); 1173 For] *om.* (so 1172 ~ that 1173); 1174 ek so] *om.* (*conjunction* ~ *complement*); 1341 allas] *om.* (*demonstrative adv.* ~ *referent*); 1398 which] *om.* (*noun* ~ *modif. clause*); 1566 grete] *om.* (*prep.* ~ *object*); 1567 him] *om.* (*verb* ~ *direct object*); 1599 which] *om.* (*noun* ~ *modif. clause*); 1741 of him] *om.* (*subj.* ~ *pred.*); 1809 swich] *om.* (*prep.* ~ *obj.*); 2038 that[1]] *om.* (*conjunction* ~ *referent clause*); 2356 eek] *om.* (*modal verb* ~ *infinitive*); 2554 is] *om.* (*comparative conj.* ~ *referent*). Grammatical attraction can induce variation of word order, as at 1640 *shulde hir neuer*] *s. n. h.* (so Rob.) where the attraction drew together the modal verb and its intensifying adverb, and at 2137 *Theseus of hire hath leve take*] *T. hath of hire . . .*, where subject and predicate were drawn together. And it can produce an overlay of two constructions, as at 2053 *Oon of the gretteste men*] *On of the gretteste man.*

Inducement of a common collocation is the probable explanation of a further number of mechanical variations. That common collocations existed in Middle English is unlikely to be debated, and an experienced ear will recognize a store of them. The difficulty is that a particular word could figure in several common collocations. Nevertheless the following individual variants of G in the *Legend* seem explicable in this way: 642 he[2]] sche (he and she); 647 be] to be (bidden to); 887 noyse or] ony (withouten any, *and note* o-n-y/n-o-y); 944 olde] owene (his owene); 1003 to] the (the longe while); 1018 than] thus (thus hath); 1133 thise noble] *om.* (alle thyng(es)); 1203 folk] men (sike men); 1457 rede] ryde (gon or ride); 1934 on] or (*so Rob.*) (riche or pore); 1948 lad] gon (gon forth); 1996 this] the (*so Rob.*) (the fend); 1999 roum eek and space] bothe r. and s. (both ... and); 2266 to] with (wende with); 2449 olde] owene (*cf.* 944); 2539 folk] men (men may).

The scribe of G was evidently also prone to error through distraction by a variety of less easily classifiable features of his exemplar. In 773 *whan*] *that* looks like the product of uncertainty about how the grammar of the sentence would develop. In 784 *sholde*] *wolde* he was probably thinking '*they wolde meten*'. In 1737 his difficulty with *Embelished*, for which he substituted *Emblemyschid*, to the contrary effect, is the probable cause of his omission of *eek* from 1736 and the dislocation of 1738 and 1739.[5] Omission of *But* from 1770 probably was induced by the difficulty of the distinction being made, which arises from a special use of *delit* with moral colour, as in *fol delit*, 'sexual misconduct'. In 1977 *Than*] *This* (so Rob.) is the byproduct of an unconscious confusion of numbers registered in *suster*] *systeryn* at the end of the line (see below, p. 45). In 2008 *on*] *as* the substitution probably anticipates unconsciously 2009 *or*] *as* where the scribe did not see the meaning of *or*. In 2216 *to*] *to to* the dittography probably occurred through hesitation about the sense of 2215: surely her worse fate would be for no ship at all to come. In 2267 *preyde*] *preyeth* the distraction need have been no more than the length of the line. In 2345 *hir*] *his* relates to the scribe's difficulty with *fond*, sc. 'upon his arrival'. In 2508 *strem*] *storm* the distraction will have been the proper name; no manuscript reads Robinson's *Sytho*: the variants are *Sitonie*, *Scython*, *Sitoy* (*e*), *Sitoio*, *Cyteys*.

A number of the G scribe's unoriginal variants are elementary scribal aberrations. Misreading of *kk* is all that there is to 756

[5] These he first inadvertently omitted, and then, when he noticed his error, copied out of place without signalling that fact.

wikkede] *welkede*. Mistaking *t* for *c*, followed by subconscious misdivision, produced 1160 *to the*] *comyth*. Initial *s* of following *smerte* caused 1597 *sorwes*] *sorwe*. Suspension trouble produced 1581 *devourer*] *deuoure* and 2125 *manere*] *mane*. There are omissions by homoeoarchy at 800 *woman wolde*] *wolde*, 904 *to this*] *to his*, 1246 *hadde hir*] *hadde*, 2210 *she speketh*] *speketh*; by homoeoteleuton at 951 *forth with*] *forth*, 1429 *nowher was þer*] *nower was* (so Rob.), 1733 *werk she tok*] *werk tok*, 2396 *that it*] *that*, and 2579 *sholde be*] *shal be*. Eyeskip caused 1177 *him telle his*] *his* and 1536 *Hym*[6] *had leuer hymself*] *Hymselue*. And the omission of lines 2506, 2507 is as pretty an instance of homoeoarchy (*But tymes foure* 2504, *And foure tymes* 2506) as any textual critic could wish for. At 913 *as swythe*] *a swythe*, 1313 *leste degre*] *leste gre*, 1813 *At thilke*] *At Ilke* and 2525 *trusted I*] *truste I* (a corrector erased the pronoun) there are unmistakable auditory errors. Another class of auditory error resulting from the phonetic situation where [v] and [ð] are heard identically is instanced in 1473 *blyue*] *blythe* (so Rob.) rhyming with *aryve*, and 2176 *blyve*] *swythe* rhyming with *dryve*. The same idiosyncrasy[7] explains 1977 *syster fre*] *systeryn fre*, the adjective having been heard as the numeral.

Variation arising from the scribe's response to and participation in the meaning of the text naturally occurs, but is limited in variety and amount. A number of substitutions make the text more explicit: 815 that] that þat; 941 he] *and* he; 1055 whan] wha*n* that; 1454 With] And with; 1482 to²] for to; 1571 preyede] preyede to; 1702 that] *and* that; 1813 the] here; 1950 in] into; 2027 Whan] And wha*n*; 2064 ther] than; 2293 it go] he do; 2324 a] that (*so Rob.*); 2372 tolde] hire tolde; 2480 dighte] let ... dighte; 2683 As] And.

A number of his sustitutions make the text easier in other ways, grammatical, lexicographical, or somehow contextual: 718 estward in the world was tho dwellinge] tho was in that lond

[6] Robinson reads *He*, but G's omission is evidence for original *Hym*.

[7] The subject of many Cockney jokes. Langland may have been exploiting it in his alliteration of [f] with [ð] and [θ].

Estward dwellynge (*so Rob.*) *making the reference of* estward *clearer*; 737 which that] that which *establishing the somewhat remote reference to the wall* (718); 870 now] tho *in resistance to the present aspect of preceding* hath; 916 ago] Igo (*so Rob.*); 928 In thyn Eneyde and Naso] In Naso *and* Eneydos (*so Rob.*); 1163 hir] his *in resistance to the literary gender*; 1171 drem] slep *no dream having been mentioned*; 1247 to²] as; 1283 land] landys *because the generic singular is difficult*; 1339 unbynd me] brynge it *dismissing the figure*; 1351 rof hyre to the herte] rof hyre hert; 1423 Now] Tho; 1439 bethoughte] bethoute hy*m*; 1541 swich] whiche; 1753 wel thoghte he] he woste wel; 1812 Romayns] Romeyn (*so Rob.*); 1826 is falle] be falle *eliminating a change of construction*; 2248 hire] that; 2345 fond] say; 2396 fynde] wete; 2469 doth] don (*cf.* 1826); 2570 called was] was callid *to prose order*.

A small number of substitutions makes the text more emphatic: 603, 741, 1749 was] nas (*so Rob.*); 1099 his] al hese; 1367 Rede] Rede he; 1684 telle] ne telle; 1728 to] sore; 1821 verray] worthi; 2176 blyve] swythe; 2188 torente] al ... torent; 2293 that] eu*ere*; 2294 kneled and so] he so fayre hire; 2590 raft] beraft; 2714 ferre] forth (fer *Rob.*)

Ideally it would be determinable whether these variations of G to a more explicit or otherwise easier or to a more emphatic reading were deliberate. But the question has no general or simple answer. Such variations can have occurred as a consequence of imperfect attention to detail, the scribe picking up a block of lines or even as little as a couplet and modifying it at the moment of registration or during its retention in his memory. In theory the stronger his interest and response, the greater the likelihood that a substitution to—say—a more emphatic reading would be deliberate. In practice one has only the variants from which to gauge the strength and nature of response. In this instance they have proved disappointing, but it may be that their very drabness is significant.

The same principle applies to his more elaborate variations, or sophistications. Here, however, there may be a greater possibility of assessing deliberate alteration, of identifying the point at which the explanation of unconscious variation is acceptable. The remaining individual variations of G in the *Legend* can be arranged in terms of that possibility.

Thus 1175 *therwithal*] *ek thereto* is probably not an expression of stylistic preference but a subconscious compensatory substitution following accidental omission of *ek so* from 1174. And 1352 *yit*] *right* is unconscious smoothing after *But*] *But ȝit* variation at the beginning of the line, the scribe's disconcertment registered by his omission of *seith*. In 1730 G's line *It styngith me whan I thynke on that place* may well be from its poor sense an unconscious adjustment after the unconscious anticipation of copy, *it stingeth*] *me thynkyth* in 1729. By contrast in 2525 the sophistication is visibly deliberate: after *trusted*] *truste* substitution I^2 is erased so as to turn *truste* into a substantive object of *may I pleyne*.

In another group of variants that look like sophistications it is not possible to rule out unconscious substitution. Thus at 1143 *noble*] *holy* it seems not impossible for the radical substitution to have been subconsciously induced by 1140 *god*, 1141 *moder hye above*, 1142 *liknesse of the child*, 1144 *scripture*. At 1932 the absence of *yeer* from G might register a momentary misconception that the choice of victim would fall on every third man, or might be part of the variation through distraction that shows itself in 1933 (above, p. 43). At 2009 *To slen hym or*] *And slen hym as* could be a subconscious misconception of how the fight would go or a deliberate 'correction'. At 2215 *come*] *ne cone* the negative, of which the *m n* error is a subconscious reflex, could be a thoughtless reaction to the text immediately preceding or a deliberate change based on the scribe's failure to identify the worst feature of Ariadne's predicament. At 2430 *And*] *That* (so Rob.) the scribe may equally well have unconsciously misread the line as a result clause or deliberately rejected its character as the resumptive assessment of Demophoon's whole situation.

A small group of sophistications have an unmistakable look of being deliberate. The relation of the variants at 785 *grave under*] *graue out of* and 788 *this grave*] *there graue* is too complex for an unconscious substitution. At 1131 *clothes broches and ek rynges*] *clothis and ek brochis ryngis* the variation looks very like a conscious move toward parallelism with 1132 *Some for to were and some for to presente.* At 1166 *waketh walweth*] *waileth and sche* is designed to reduce the undignified element in Dido's behaviour. In 1217 *wilde hertes*] *bestys wilde* (so Rob.) the substitution was designed to elevate the action, the scribe having missed the poet's intention of anticlimax. At 1370 *gentil*[1]] *tendere* he again mistook Chaucer's tone. In 1468 *whylom*] om. he misunderstood the modification of the adverb and excluded it as inappropriate. In 1737 *Embelished*] *Emblemyschid* he could not accept that tears might be an adornment. In 1815 *bothe at ones*] *bothe at onys bothe* he corrected his initial error to another order than that of his exemplar by cancelling *bothe*[1]. In 1994 *That*] om. is the result of his failure to see that the conjunction introduces the whole process specified in 1994–6.

Another group of variations comprises sophistications of the metre: 587 at] vnto (obeysaunce *being read as tetrasyllabic*); 725 Tisbe] And Tysbe (*so Rob.*) (*'correcting' a 'headless' line*); 759 but] but if (*after loss of final* e *from* herte); 1246 loved] I louyd (*after omission of* hire); 1337 ful] *and* ful (*loss of final* e: ofte); 1391 payed] hath payed (*loss of final* e: goode); 1433 moche] meche othir (*loss of final* e: moche *pl.*); 1482 to] for to (*loss of final* e: take); 1718 abyde] gan abyde (*loss of final* e: dore); 2027 Whan] And wha*n* (*originally a headless line*); 2134 oughte us herof] o. herof vs (*so Rob.*) (*smoothing the rhythm of a heavily modulated line*); 2184 hath] hath now (*so Rob.*) (*loss of final* e: herte); 2324 hath] hat he (*loss of final* e: force); 2328 loude] loude a (*loss of final* e: loude); 2419 brende] it brende (*loss of final* e: torche) (*so Rob.*); 2554 harder] hardyere (*after omission of* is); 2593 houses] howses that (*after omission of* his).

There is a pattern discernible in the independent variation of G in the *Legend*.[8] The amount of elementary mechanical error

[8] The analysis leaves a residue of differences between readings of G and the large family for which plausible explanations have not recommended them-

induced by misreading of letters, difficulty with suspensions, homoeoarchy or homoeoteleuton, and auditory confusion is small. At that level copying appears to have been pretty attentive.[9] There is a somewhat larger number of variations attributable to the subconscious effect of linguistic conditions, that is grammatical attraction and inducement of common collocations. The largest class of variation derives from preoccupation with meaning. While the scribe is copying he has in mind as well as in memory the context of the words immediate to his pen and thus is subject to a variety of unconscious error induced by preceding or following or surrounding copy. He also, unconsciously or deliberately, substitutes more explicit or otherwise easier readings; these make up about a fifth of G's independent variation in the *Legend*. The suggestion of indifferent intelligence in such variation is confirmed by the proportion of his sophistications, in themselves not numerous, based on misreading or misunderstanding. His metrical sophistication is elementary, mainly a register of objection to headless lines or syllabic surrogate for phonetically devalued historical or grammatical final *e*. The slightness or, just possibly, restraint of his emotional response to the stories appears from the relatively small number of more emphatic substitutions he makes. But of course he may have been puzzled or put off by the singular tone of the *Legend*. The impression is of a relatively careful, dull man, whose dullness actually increased his susceptibility to error.

That impression is strengthened by analysis of the several hundred unoriginal variant readings in which G agrees coincidentally with other manuscripts or groups of manuscripts. The most appropriate illustration of this will be from the instances where such variation has been admitted to Robinson's text of the *Legend*. From the excellence of his editorial flair they are not

selves. They are the following (G's reading is the second): 964, 2563 called/clepid; 1170 dere/leue; 1560 hir/it; 1911 caste/caughte; 1978 Phedra leve syster/leue systyr Phedra; 2119 assure/ensure; 2214 wrecched/wreche (*so Rob.*); 2367 by/with; 2618 And/zero; 2676 to/a.

[9] Compare Parkes and Beadle, op. cit., p. 54.

very numerous, and of course the more elementary errors are absent. The following are examples:

Variation induced by preceding copy: 794 likyng] hast PFfG (faste 790, laste 791); 815 forgladde] so glad TFBSTrThA^1G (so sore 814); 1139 tellith thus] telleth vs RG (th-th); 1263 I] ye TFBTrThG (ye 1257, 1259, 1260, 1263); 1269 dau*n*ce] daunces TrSPA^1RG (festes *prec.*); 1547 entent] assent TrA^1G (inn-ocent 1546); 1659 And . . . a . . . trayto*ur*] As . . . (a) . . . t. $A^3A^1A^2$G (as a traytour 1656); 1777 (than) he hath] (than) hath he FBSTrA^2G (tha ~ ath, *with further variation by omission of* than); 2239 this] his. SAG (his 2237); 2421 had] hath FBSThA^3G (possith *pres.* 2420); 2453 lyked] lyketh FBSTrThA^3A^2G (doth *pres.* 2452).

Variation induced by attraction to following copy: 1202 is fair as] as fair/bright as STrPA^1RG; 1357 I make] make I STrA^1G (I ~ my *fol.*); 2063 to] so SA^2G (swich *fol.*).

Variation induced by surrounding copy: 1285 thus] so SPRG (yn-o-gh, w-o-le, m-o-re 1284, ysw-o-re 1285; 1780 vnto] into A^2SG (in *prec.*, in 1781); 1967 ther] *om.* TFBSThA^3A^2G (happede ~ per cas); 1981 this] his TFBThG (he his 1980, he is *fol.*).

Substitution induced by a common collocation: 1241 yeden] came/comyn TFBSThPRG (comen out); 1639 ne] or ThG (lef or loth); 2102 on] vpon TFBTrThG (hereupon).

Variation to a more explicit reading: 968 the] his TFBThG; 1150 the] this TFBThA^1G; 1194 Vnto] Into STrA^1G; 1235 chaunge] c. her PRG; 1316 lat] and l. PRG; 1583 to] into TrSA^1G; 1784 Whe*þer*] Were it STr$A^3A^1A^2$G; 1795 swerd] poynt STr$A^3A^1A^2$G; 2168 seyde] s. that GSTrThA^2; 2676 Danaos sone] lyno TFBThA^3A^2G.

Variation to an otherwise easier reading. (i) *smoothing the tense:* 1114 nys] nas/ne was/was TFBTrThPA^1RG; 1163 hath] hadde SThPRG; 1273 wol] woldes FBSThPRG; 1409 hath] had TrA^1G; 1835 may] myght A^1SG. (ii) *to prose order:* 1626 am I] I am A^3G; 2477 agayn he wolde] he w. a. SA^3A^2G. (iii) *to fuller grammatical expression:* 2329 helpe] and h. SA^{3}A^{2}G; 2592 What] That what TrA^{2}G; 2637 Ne nolde] Ne I nolde GS. (iv) *to lexicographically easier readings:* 925 Bere] Be to TFBSTrThA^{1}G; 973 knytte] cutted TSTrThPA^{3}A^{1}G; 1472 lay the ship that Iasou*n*] that the ship of J. STrA^{1}G; 2332 Foreferde] For fere TrThA^{3}G.

Sophistication: 866 wax] was TFPA^{3}FfG *eliminating* box ... wax *echo*; 2092 you*r* gentilesse] giltles yow *misconceiving the argument* TrA^{2}G; 2255 full^2] eke SA^{2}G *eliminating repetition*; 2553 or] and TFBThG *objecting to Chaucer's alternative offerings for* intumulata (*Heroides* II. 136).

Variation to smooth metre: (i) *supplying a syllable after devaluation of final* e: 907 eue*r*] evyr yet A^{1}TrG; 1041 trouthe] and t. TFBSPA^{3}G (womanhede); 1063 hadde] she h./h. she STrPA^{1}RG (herte); 1649 name] a name TThA^{3}G, as] ryght as TrSA^{2}G (name); 1754 he] that he TrSA^{1}A^{2}G (more). (ii) *supplying a syllable after other loss:* 1015 to] vnto TFBSThG (comen] com); 1971 compleynt] compleynyng STrA^{1}A^{2}G (stoden] stode). (iii) *regularizing stress pattern:* 1776 he forth rit] forth h. r. SA^{3}A^{2}G; 2684 streyneth her] hire streyneth TrA^{2}G. (iv) *adjusting because the hiatus is not valued:* 1024 Had ben in this temple] Hadden in this temple ben TFBSTrThA^{3}G. (v) *adjusting because elision is not valued:* 2337 to his^2] to SG.

There is no difference of character or quality between these readings, where G agrees with other manuscripts, and those in which it varies alone. The likelihood is that they were admitted to the text of the *Legend* not for their quality but because its editor's ignorance of the frequency of coincident variation led him to be impressed by the mere fact of G being in agreement with other manuscripts. They reflect the distractions and preoccupations of the same dull and limited mentality exhibited in G's unoriginal solo variation.

The demonstrated character of G's scribal variation has an immediate bearing on the question of revision in the *Legend*. The whole pattern of that variation is such as to establish a primary unlikelihood that any differences between the *Legend* text of G and that of the large family are authorial. Those differences which have been discussed are the results of scribal variation in G or its immediate tradition. Where the text of G is superior the explanation is scribal variation in the tradition of the large family. There was no revision of the *Legend*.

There is further bearing on the two texts of the *Prologue*. Decision whether any given difference between those texts is authorial has hitherto had to be based on simple judgements of literary criticism. Is the difference of a kind one can imagine Chaucer wanting to make? That question now has a complement. Is the difference one within or beyond the demonstrated limits of the G scribe's capacity to effect? And if within those limits, is it, from conforming to his habits of variation, better interpreted as not the product of authorial revision? The position is thus altered. Axiomatically the G text of the *Prologue* contains scribal errors. Because we now know the characteristics of its immediate scribe's variation, we can identify them by editorial techniques rather than by arbitrary critical judgements. Knowledge of his *usus scribendi* has introduced an element of system into the procedure.

So, immediately, it is clear that the larger differences which distinguish the two texts would have been quite beyond his conception and execution. His incapacity to grasp the larger sense of his exemplar is indicated in the *Legend* when his copy shows no sign of disconcertment at the break of sense on ff. 417^{v}–419^{v} (449^{v}–450^{v}), where he copies lines 394–429 before 358–93[10] without registering that he noticed the inconsequence. We can be confident that any substantial difference between the two prologue texts is not by G and therefore presumably authorial.

As to the smaller differences, the indication is that any which relate intelligently to the meaning or feeling of their context, or show any command of expression, or answer to the better hypotheses of revision, are not to be attributed to him.

There is, however, a substantial residue of differences where

[10] I have not been able to find where Robinson gives this information.

G's readings do not answer to such description but can be related to the character of its scribe. The text of G in the *Prologue* contains more than 40 unique variant readings of the kinds identified as scribal in its text of the *Legend*, and in about the same density (one in about 12 lines as opposed to one in about 11). It also contains 40 variants of such kinds in which it agrees with one or more manuscripts of the larger family.[11] The similarity of the G readings in those situations to G's individual variations in the *Legend* suggests that they are scribal. If that suggestion is correct, Robinson's texts of the prologues can be improved at a number of points.

Where G's lines are unique Robinson did identify and correct 10 scribal errors.[12] G's tendency to metrical smoothing points to an eleventh in 225, where the 'and' in *Vp on the softe* and *sote grene gras* looks like an attempt to repair the rhythm after phonetic devaluation of the weak adjective inflexion, and incidentally suggests that the whole form of the line is scribal, the original being as in F 118. There is more interesting meaning to *smale gras* than to *grene*.

Where there are corresponding lines in the two prologues Robinson admitted to his text of G, in which they will inevitably be read as revisions, a number of readings which on the showing of the present analysis should be attributed to the G scribe. He did, to be sure, express awareness of the difficulty of decision, but then invoked the 'peculiar authority' of G[13] in support of their adoption.

It will be recalled that in the *Legend* many G variants were explicable as induced by the preceding context. That explanation

[11] Again, if these readings are scribal, the agreements are by coincident variation. They are mainly in one or two readings; the exceptions are STrA¹G, 9; SG, 5; PG 5; A¹G, 4; TrA¹G, 4. All agreements are in trivial variation.

[12] He actually ventured a silent conjectural emendation *metri causa* in G Prol. 189, where the manuscript reads *adam made*. The readings G 271 *me* (MS *ne*) and G 398 *this* (MS *his*) are apparently typesetter's errors: they are absent from the first edition. It is not clear whether G 374 *be* (MS *he*) is an emendation for 'sense' or someone's error. The original was certainly *he*: compare F 388.

[13] Robinson, p. 913.

will account for two differences between thetexts of the *Prologue*: 4 *yet*] *this* (*that* 3) and 48 *this flour*] *these flouris* (*floures* 38, 41, 42, *dayesyes* 43). Difficulty with local meaning of the kinds instanced in G's *Legend* variants appears also in its *Prologue* text. In 377/357 *tiraunt ne crewel*] *tyraunt* and *crewel* the scribe took *tiraunt* in its more general abusive sense (*OED*. s.v. 6 and 3, 4) or else did not know the sense 'despotic'. In 490/480 *the lyke*] *the lestyth* he mistook the finesse of Alcestis' 'even though it may not please you', and substituted a word implying the subsidence of desire in the Dreamer, and uncharacteristic of her general attitude to him. Two G *Prologue* readings are more explicit: 305/231 *estaat*] *degre*[14] *and* 413/398 *in*] *with*. Four readings in the G *Prologue* are easier: 78/66 *thogh*] *If* where *thogh* has the less immediate meaning 'supposing that' (*OED*, s.v. *Though* 2); 123/111 *surmounteth*] *surmountede* and 128/115 *hath*] *hadde* smoothing the tense; 217/149 *flourouns smale*] *manye flourys* (other manuscripts agree with G in this variation at 220/152 and 529/517). Three G readings look like metrical smoothing: 5 *dwellyng*] *that dwellyth* regularizes the rhythm; 127/115 *sore*] *sore hadde* compensates for devaluation of the adverbial inflexion on *sore*;[15] and 447/437 *If that*] *That If that* puts a head to a headless line. Here the scribe may seem to have been caught in the act: the capitalization *That If that* very possibly reflects an exemplar in which the line began *If that*. The resemblances between these readings of G and the individual G variants in the *Legend* makes them look very like scribal products. They are to be sure not very numerous, the few in fact that eluded Robinson's flair and good taste. But they have a serious bearing on the nature of Chaucer's revision here and in other works.

So does a passage with somewhat larger and more serious differences between the texts of the two prologues which, in the

[14] This is a very elegant instance, identifiable as such from a Gower quotation: *Thei thoghten wel sche hadde be In hire astat of hih degre. Confessio Amantis* II. 1224, quoted in *MED*, s.v. *Degre* n., 4 (a).

[15] There is the same variation at 502/490; see below, p. 57.

light of the demonstrated variational habits of the G scribe, are more likely to be his work than Chaucer's. This is 139/127–152/138. G's text here reads as follows.

Some songyn on the brau*n*chis clere
Of loue *and* that Ioye It was to here
In worschepe *and* in preysyng of hire make
And of the newe blysful somerys sake
That su*n*gyn blyssede be seynt volentyn
At his day I ches ȝow to be myn
with oute repenty*n*ge myn herte swete
And therwithal here bekys gu*n*ne mete
The honour *and* the humble obeysau*n*ce
And aft*er* dedyn othere obseruau*n*cys
Ryht on to loue *and* to natures
So eche of hem to cryaturys

Merely from its sense and metre this passage cannot be authorial in form, and editors have recognized its necessary corruption.[16] The question is whether the passage also owes some of its present form to revision, or whether it is simply a much debased form of the text represented in F 139–52. The answer is critical because of the adjacency of a major difference between the texts with an unmistakable look of revision. It can however, now be considered without concern for any 'peculiar authority' of G.

Straightaway, then, the form of G 127, 128 is seen to derive from unconscious omission of *And al his craft* through *And*-*And* eyeskip, possibly encouraged by the run-on grammar of the original (F 138, 139). Then, deliberately or unconsciously, the now too short line is filled out with *on the braunchis* from (original) F 143. Next, by inducement of the common collocation *song(en) of loue*, there is omission of *layes* from 127 with metrical padding by supply of *and that*. After G 130 there is omission of two lines like F 143, 144, probably unconscious, the inducements being homoeoarchy (compare F 141, 144 *In*, 142,

[16] Robinson (p. 913) records his unease and gives or even adopts conjectural emendations by earlier editors. But he presumably thought of the passage as revised, and so it looks as he prints it in his text. How many persevere at referring to his critical notes?

145 *And*) or a subconscious feeling of having already copied F 143 (*on the braunchis* G 127), or both in conjunction; even the difficulty of F 144, which calls for observation of the restlessness of small birds, might have contributed. G 131's evidently unoriginal *That* attempts to smooth the sense after the loss, and G 132 *For on his*] *At* actually echoes *That* and registers preoccupation with whether the smoothing will do.

It is not quite so easy to account for the just as manifestly corrupt form of G 135–8. *Yelding*] *The* in 135 resists explanation. But 136 *To love*] *And aft*er may again be the product of resistance to a run-on line; 137 *That longeth*] om.] *Ryht* can have occurred through attraction between *observauncys* and (*on*) *to* with subsequent padding; the desperate form of 138 might be prudish censorship of a naughty original like F 152.

The differences between the two texts of the *Prologue* in 139/127–149/135 were clearly not produced by revision. Whether revision has anything to do with the differences in the rest of the passage seems not finally determinable. But the whole passage can be seen as a sum of the sort of corruptions the G scribe was capable of, and if G's text here is seen as a scribally corrupted reflex of that of F, the level of quality in the sophistications is just about right for him. Why there should be so much corruption in such a short passage can only be guessed at. In any event it does not seem good editorial practice to attempt to restore a revised text here.

What has been shown about the quality of G's *Legend* text has also relevance to about 40 variant readings in G's *Prologue* at points where the two versions have corresponding lines, in which G agrees with one or more manuscripts of the larger family. Of those readings Robinson adopted 13 in his text of F, presumably as the originals of both versions. Another six he did not adopt for F but let stand in G, presumably as revisions. The quality of the readings in both groups fails to support his judgement. They conform to the types of G's characteristic individual variation in the *Legend* and might better be interpreted as the products of coincident variation by G and another manuscript or subgroup.[17]

Of the G readings Robinson adopted for F one is explicable as produced by attraction to preceding copy: 449/439 *as*] *what* PSA^{1}G (*with* prec.). Three register misreading of the original: 11 *men hath*] *men han* TFBThG taking the impersonal pronoun for the plural noun; 403/389 *And it so be*] *And if so be* STrA^{1}G missing *And* = 'If'; 404/390 *dredeful*] *sorouful* STrA^{1}G substituting an attitude of Christian penitence for the abject submission of a disarmed rebel after defeat, *in his bare sherte*. Two are substitutions of easier readings: 131/119 *of*] *from* STrA^{1}G, 261/215 *of*] *for* STrA^{1}G. The rest sophisticate the metre. Two smooth the stress pattern, that is eliminate modulation: 1 *I haue*] *haue I* STrA^{1}G, and 141/129 *In worshipynge*] *In worshyp and* TrA^{1}G. One, 480/470 *vnderstonde*] *and u.* SG 'normalizes' a headless line, at cost of the dramatic effect of the cæsura. And four supply compensatory syllables: 121/109 *gomme*] *gomme or* TFBG and 502/490 soore] sorer A^{1}STrG after devaluation of final *e*; 435/425 *blyve*] *as blyve* STrA^{1}G after loss of the infinitive inflexion of *sweren*; 508/496 *and*] *and that* STrG in failure to appreciate or from objection to the punctuational hiatus *Love and*.

The six cases where Robinson lets G's reading stand, presumably as authorial revisions, are of similar quality, conforming to G's characteristic variations. One is explicable as induced by preceding copy: 313/239 *it*] *hym* PG (*his* prec.). Another is a more explicit reading: 306/232 *the*] *that* TrA^{1}G. Another is easier: 529/517 *florouns*] *flouris* TBSTrPA^{3}A^{1}G. And three sophisticate the metre: 221/153 *fyn*] *fyne and* A^{1}G where *perle* has become a monosyllable; 238/170 *se*] *wel Ise* SG compensating for loss of the end syllable in *myghte*; and 317/243 *It*] *For it* SG putting a head to a headless line.

Robinson had flair, *Fingerspitzengefühl*, but why the readings

[17] The subgroups are TrA^1, which over the whole poem agree in about 300 unoriginal variants, and STrA^1, which agree in 36 unoriginal variants.

in the first group seemed to him like the originals of both versions and those in the second like revisions it is hard to conceive—unless he was merely influenced by sigils. Both groups belong to the same classes: readings within the capacity of the G scribe and therefore not necessarily either original or authorial revisions; of kinds explicable by the processes of scribal error; and of kinds to which, where G's individual variation is exposable to analysis, he showed himself prone.

Accordingly, even in the *Prologue* G has in a strict sense no 'peculiar authority'. More correctly the manuscript is remarkable in respect of *The Legend of Good Women* only because of the paradoxical situation where it uniquely preserves an authorial version of the *Prologue* copied by an immediate scribe notably subject to error.

Two considerations emerge. One is that G's text of any other work by Chaucer does not merit automatic respect; it is as good as G's particular exemplar of that work, subject to the damage done by its immediate scribe, can be shown to be.[18] A manuscript is as good as its readings. The other is that G's variation in *The Legend of Good Women* affords a remarkable demonstration of classes of changes which here, specifically, Chaucer did not make in his revisions, and which should not readily be imputed to him in other situations.

[18] Compare Parkes and Beadle, op. cit., p. 47.

Chauncer's Use of *gan*: Some Recent Studies

TAUNO F. MUSTANOJA

I HOPE Norman Davis will find this modest contribution to his anniversary volume acceptable and will not be too much disturbed by the unavoidable personal element in it. It is, to a certain extent, an attempt to review a number of reactions to certain interpretations proposed in my *Middle English Syntax*[1]—a book which owes much to his generous help at the time when it was taking shape.

One of my major problems while working on the book, particularly when dealing with a poet of the calibre of Chaucer, was to find out what precisely the author wished to convey by choosing the particular syntactical construction he did. And in this, as might be expected, a particularly difficult task was the tracing of any overtones, emotional or other.

I was particularly confronted with problems of this kind while I was working on the chapter on the verb *gin* (*gan*, *can*), and was digesting Elizabeth Homann's then fairly recent study entitled 'Chaucer's Use of *Gan*.'[2] The gist of her argument was that *gan*, the preterite of *gin*, was not merely a colourless auxiliary, a mere metrical aid. In line 532 of *The House of Fame*, for example, in

I gan beholde more and more
To se the beaute and the wonder

gan beholde appeared to her to mean 'looked straight at fully', 'absorbed the meaning of', 'gazed on and into significantly'. She

[1] *A Middle English Syntax*, Part I, Mémoires de la Société Néophilologique de Helsinki, 23 (Helsinki, 1960). Referred to as *MES*.

[2] Homann, Elizabeth R., 'Chaucer's Use of *Gan*,' *JEGP*, liii (1954), 389–98.

felt that it brought into the narration a sense of immediacy and, further, an accumulative interest dictated by desires and emotions. To prove her case, she adduced a passage from *Troilus and Criseyde*, II, 264–5,

> And with that word he gan right inwardly
> Byholden hire and loken on hire face . . .,

and quoted its verbal counterpart from *Il Filostrato*:

> e nel bel viso
> Cominciò forte riguardarla fiso . . .

Although I was by no means persuaded by many things she said in the course of her argumentation, something in her approach seemed to fall in with my own line of thinking about language as a means of expressing the many sorts of processes in the human mind, and I arrived at the following reserved formulation about it: 'Even while using the *gan*-periphrasis mainly for metrical purposes, consciously or unconsciously the poet often achieves a special stylistic effect by means of this construction . . . We have good reason to believe that in addition to metre and rhyme other stylistic considerations play a certain role in a good poet's choice between the simple preterite and the *gan*-periphrasis.'[3]

A few years later Professor Hamilton Smyser took up the matter in *Speculum*, in an article in which he subjected Miss Homann's views and my acceptance of them to a rather severe criticism, mainly in the light of earlier studies on the subject.[4] Admitting that my attitude in the matter was conservative compared to what Miss Homann said at length in her article, and that I had pointed out that the *gan*-form, favoured by Chaucer, served mainly the purpose of metrical convenience, Smyser went on to say that 'If the *gan*-form "implied both intellectual activity and aesthetic participation" in line 532 [of *The House of Fame*,

[3] *MES*, p. 612.

[4] H. M. Smyser, 'Chaucer's Use of *Gin* and *Do*', *Speculum*, xlii (1967), 68–83.

quoted above], then it must imply the same thing in line 531, which Miss Homann does not quote but which runs: "[This egle] Which that so hye gan to sore". If in line 531 it seems to bring something else than intellectual and aesthetic participation—such as, let us say, a sense of exhilarating motion tinged with acrophobia—then we are simply sampling the "feelings" of passages in Chaucer, not defining the meaning or meanings of *gan*. Miss Homann says that the word *behold* has "emotional significance". A more accurate statement might run something like this: "in our day *behold*, a word of Biblical and poetic associations, is obsolescent and is used only in emotional contexts... This is not to deny that the word *behold* can appear in an emotional context in Chaucer; it does so frequently. The point is that the "emotional significance" comes from the context, just as the variegated meanings which Miss Homann attributes to *gan* come from various selected contexts.'

J. Kerkhof, whose *Studies in the Language of Geoffrey Chaucer*[5] came out a year before Smyser's article, assumed (pp. 30–2) much the same restrained attitude to Miss Homann's 'bold attempt to explain the subtle uses to which *gan* is put by Chaucer'. He conceded that 'Chaucer no doubt knew better than any of his contemporaries how to avail himself of the latent possibilities of language and that it is, therefore, quite plausible to assume that to him and his listeners the *gan* constructions had overtones that escape us', but he could not help thinking that Miss Homann was making too large a claim for Chaucer when she said that he 'with his keen sensibility to time and space, setting and character behaviour utilized *gan* to add vitality to dramatic scenes, intensity to emotional situations, and an inner meaning and depth to his characters'. He pointed out that Chaucer used *gan* in numerous instances as a colourless auxiliary of the periphrastic preterite. But, just as it is difficult to decide whether *gan* has ingressive or descriptive force, he added, it is sometimes hard to distinguish between *gan* as a verb with descriptive force and *gan* as a stop-gap.

[5] (Leiden, 1966), 30–2.

The late Professor F. Th. Visser gave a considerable amount of space to the subject in his very comprehensive *Historical Syntax*.[6] His discussion was based on a large and detailed collection of quotations, the great advantage of which was that it took into account the whole history of the language.

Like Smyser, he took Miss Homann and me—and Otto Funke, too[7]—to task for reading into the Middle English periphrastic use of *gan* implications which could not be substantiated. The construction, he remarked, occurs exclusively in verse,[8] and must accordingly be regarded as a phenomenon of prosodic exigency. Visser did concede, however, that I had mentioned metrical reasons as the primary motive for the use of the periphrasis.[9]

There are two studies from the 1970s dealing with the Middle English uses of *gan*, both of them by Japanese scholars and both based on statistical illustrations of the occurrence of the construction in the poetry of the period. The earlier of the two, by Yoshio Terasawa,[10] confirms the prevailing view that the periphrastic use of *gan/can* is rare in the unrhymed alliterative poems of any genre. The frequency is clearly higher in the rhymed romances, ranging from the 1.3 per cent of *Ywain* to the 4.5 per cent of *King Horn*, and reaches its highest point (5 per cent) in *Pearl*.

According to Terasawa's statistics, *gan/can*, which is normally a feature of narrative poetry, occurs only in declarative statements. He disagrees in this respect with Visser, who in his *Historical Syntax*, §1480 (pp. 1577–9), lists a number of passages in which the verb is used in negative and interrogative contexts.

[6] *An Historical Syntax of the English Language*, Part III, First Half: *Syntactical Units with Two Verbs* (Leiden, 1969), 1571–81; also pp. 1379–80.

[7] Otto Funke, 'Die Fügung *Ginnen* mit dem Infinitiv im Mittelenglischen', *Englische Studien*, lvi (1922), 1–27.

[8] Visser, p. 1572.

[9] Ibid.

[10] Yoshio Terasawa, 'Some Notes on ME *Gan* Periphrasis', *Poetica* [Tokyo], i (1974), 89–105.

In most of these, Terasawa is convinced, *can* could be taken to mean 'be able to'.[11]

Professor Herbert Koziol's succinct but illuminating treatment of *gin*[12] has been elaborated and supplemented by Matsuji Tajima.[13] Like Terasawa, he has found that the periphrastic *con* (*gan*) is used commonly with the infinitive in the rhymed lines of *Sir Gawain and the Green Knight* and *Pearl* and is almost always used to place the infinitive in a rhyming position, but occurs only sporadically in the unrhymed alliterative lines of *Gawain*, *Purity*, and *Patience*.

Pearl stands out from the rest of the group by virtue of its striking predilection for *con*, which is used as an auxiliary not only of the preterite but of the present tense as well. Another peculiarity of this poem is the present tense form *coneȝ*, which occurs three times in it (e.g., *ȝyf hyt be soth þat þou coneȝ saye*, 482; also in lines 909 and 925) and was taken to be 'probably an auxiliary of the present tense' by E. V. Gordon in his edition of the poem.[14]

Tajima concludes his article by calling attention to the fact that the *Gawain* poet resorts almost exclusively to the periphrasis with *con* and only rarely makes use of the *do*-periphrasis.

This brief survey of the recent work done on Middle English *gin* (*gan*/*can*/*con*) is, perhaps, best concluded by a brief reference to Professor Michio Masui's authoritative work, *The Structure of Chaucer's Rime Words*.[15] Masui, referring to Franz Beschor-

[11] I take this opportunity to correct an erroneous interpretation in Visser's *Hist. Syntax*, iii, 1, p. 1576. In l. 3026 of the *Romance of Guy Warwick* (Auchinleck MS, EETS, ES 42), *Ac þe Sarrazins wers gan bitide*, *Sarrazins* is an indirect object, not the subject, of *bitide*.

[12] Herbert Koziol, *Grundzüge der Syntax der mittelenglischen Stabreimdichtungen*, Wiener Beiträge zur englischen Philologie, 58 (Vienna and Leipzig, 1932), 131–4.

[13] Matsuji Tajima, 'The Gawain-Poet's Use of *Con* as a Periphrastic Auxiliary', *Neuphilologische Mitteilungen*, lxxvi (1975), 429–38.

[14] *Pearl*, ed. E. V. Gordon (Oxford, 1953), p. 63, note on l. 482.

[15] Michio Masui, *The Structure of Chaucer's Rime Words: an Exploration into the Poetic Language of Chaucer* (Tokyo, 1964).

ner's statistical study,[16] mentions among Chaucer's favourite metrical techniques his fondness for ending his lines with verbs, particularly with infinitives with or without (*for*) *to*.[17]

As the final rounding off of the present survey I should like to add that the criticism directed against my interpretation of Chaucer's use of *gin* (*gan*) is in the main justified, though I hope to return to the subject on some later occasion. It is obvious at any rate that what has been said on the matter calls for a few rewordings in my chapter on *gin*. It seems apparent that the definition 'intensive-descriptive use' of *gan* (the term 'descriptive' comes from Funke) ought to be replaced by the more neutral one 'periphrastic' or 'metrical' use. There is also obviously reason to soften the tone of the statement beginning on p. 612, l. 21, so that it runs 'We have good reason to believe that in addition to metre and rhyme other stylistic considerations may have played a role in a good poet's choice between the simple preterite and the *gan*-periphrasis.'

[16] *Verbale Reime bei Chaucer*, Studien zur englischen Philologie, 60 (Halle, 1920).

[17] Masui, pp. 263–4.

Arcite's Injury

E. TALBOT DONALDSON

In Chaucer's *Knight's Tale*, Arcite, having won the tournament and been proclaimed the winner of Emily, is riding around the lists in triumph when a Fury frightens his horse, which reacts in such a way as to cause mortal injury to its rider. The passage describes the accident as follows:

> Out of the ground a furie infernal sterte,
> From Pluto sent at requeste of Saturne,
> For which his hors for fere gan to turne,
> And leep aside, and foundered as he leep;
> And er that Arcite may taken keep,
> He pighte hym on the pomel of his heed,
> That in the place he lay as he were deed,
> His brest tobrosten with his sadel-bowe.[1]

The traditional reading of these lines has Arcite's horse turning at the sight of the Fury, rearing to the side, and falling as he reared; and before Arcite knew what was happening, the horse pitched him on to the crown of his head, so that he lay on the ground as if he were dead, his chest having been shattered by the saddle-bow. Shortly afterwards, Arcite dies from the injury to his chest: there is no further mention of his having been pitched on his head, a circumstance that one would suppose would have caused, if not a broken neck, a fractured skull or a severe concussion. In Boccaccio, Arcite's horse rears and falls on its rider in such a way that the saddle-bow crushes his chest.[2]

[1] *The Works of Geoffrey Chaucer*², ed. F. N. Robinson (Boston, 1957), I. 2684–91.

[2] *Teseida*, IX. 7–9.

Chaucer's addition of Arcite's precipitous flight from his horse does nothing but lend a bit of indignity to his sad end.

Some years ago I suggested that the *pomel* of the sixth line in the passage above was not the top or crown of Arcite's head, as it is generally glossed, but an ornamental knob on the saddle-bow of his horse, against which Arcite was thrown when the horse reared.[3] I was wrong: the *pomel* is not an ornamental knob but the saddle-bow itself. Arcite's accident—which is roughly the same as when the driver of an automobile is thrown against the steering wheel—was by no means uncommon in the Middle Ages, its most notorious victim having been William the Conqueror. William, the story goes, was riding over the smoking embers of a town he had just razed when his horse was frightened by a blazing brand and reared, smashing William's body case with the pommel, or saddle-bow.[4] Modern historians use the word *pommel* in describing the accident,[5] and the *OED* records the meaning of *pommel*, 'The upward projecting front part of a saddle; the saddle-bow', from 1450,[6] a sense that perfectly fits Chaucer's line. In view of the fact that Arcite dies of an injury inflicted by his saddle-bow, it seems perverse to inflict a head injury on him by attaching to the word *pommel* a far-fetched nonce meaning of no large imaginative effectiveness: it is to be noted that *OED*, s.v *Pommel* (sb.), 4, 'A rounded or semi-globular projecting part. *Obs.* a. The rounded top of the head; the crown', cites as its authority this line, and this line only.

Nor does *pighte* in the same line mean 'pitched'. The original meaning of the verb is 'to thrust in', and all the uses in the *OED*

[3] *Chaucer's Poetry: An Anthology for the Modern Reader* (New York, 1958, 1975), p. 91, note to l. 1831.

[4] See Frank M. Stenton, *William the Conqueror* (rev. edn. (New York, 1966), 369; David C. Douglas, *William the Conqueror* (Los Angeles and Berkeley, 1964), 358.

[5] Discussing antique war-saddles, G. C. Stone says that the 'frame ... is called the tree, the front the pommel and the back the cantle', and notes that in the Middle Ages the pommel was often very high and prominent: see *A Glossary of the Construction, Decoration, and Use of Arms and Armor* (New York, 1934), 531.

[6] *OED*, s.v. *Pommel* (sb.), 5.

up until Chaucer's time suggest that the verb implies, if not penetration of an object, sufficient force to cause penetration if the object is penetrable.[7] *OED* lists this line as the earliest use of the verb meaning 'pitch', and the two other listed uses of the same sense before the sixteenth century are equally suggestive of penetration, as are the two early uses of the intransitive meaning 'fall'.[8] Arcite's horse did not throw him off, but stuck him on the saddle-bow, or, alternatively, Arcite stuck himself on the saddle-bow.[9] The wound may not have actually broken the skin, but it could have broken ribs and deflated a lung, and 'tis enough, 'twould serve.

I confess to some degree of puzzlement at the phrase 'of his heed'. It obviously does not refer to Arcite's head, and hence must refer to the horse's. It must mean something more than that the saddle-bow was located in the direction of the horse's head, which is idle information. I suspect it is a term from manage having to do with the position of the horse's head at the time of Arcite's encounter with the pommel: possibly 'off his head', the horse having thrown his head back at the same time that Arcite's forward momentum was hurtling him into the pommel. Now that the suggestion has been made that it is the horse's head and not Arcite's that the line mentions, I hope some expert in horsemanship will supply the missing link. Perhaps the splendid solver of philological problems to whom this volume is dedicated will solve this one too.

[7] *OED*, s. v. *Pitch* (v.[1]), 1–6. In Chaucer's only other use of the verb, it means 'pierced' : *ABC* 163, 'Longius his herte pighte'.

[8] *OED*, s.v. *Pitch* (v.[1]), 17. Under 'throw' are cited *Destruction of Troy*, '[Achilles with a spear] Pight on the prinse, persit his herte', where *persit* completes the action of *Pight*; and *Piers Plowman* C, 'Canstow . . . to þe cart picche?', where the action of pitching hay involves both penetrating the bottle and pitching it (cf. the tool-name 'pitchfork'). Under 18, 'fall headlong', *OED* cites Robert of Gloucester, 'to þen erþe he vel & pighte, þat al to peces he to rof', where it is likely that the faller made something of a dent in the earth; and *Gawain and the Green Knight*, of the arrows striking the boar: 'Bot þy poyntes payred at þe pyth þat pyȝt in his scheldes', the points being blunted by the toughness of the boar's shoulders that they were supposed to penetrate.

[9] *He* and *hym* might both refer to Arcite in a reflexive construction, though it seems more probable that *He* refers to the horse.

Sir Thopas in the Sixteenth Century

J. A. BURROW

TWENTIETH-CENTURY students of Chaucer have not paid much serious attention to their predecessors. A generous selection of earlier 'criticism and allusion' was long ago made available by Caroline Spurgeon; but the material is for the most part scrappy and miscellaneous, and much of it has no more than curiosity value. The writers, however, speak from a world nearer to Chaucer's own than ours is; and it would be strange if modern academic criticism did not have something to learn, directly and indirectly, from what they say—not least, perhaps, from those of their comments which seem least digestible to us. So there is a case for assaying at least some of this evidence more carefully and more sympathetically than has been done up to now. The present study offers the results of such an investigation, restricted to testimonies left by sixteenth-century readers of Chaucer's tale of Sir Thopas.

The first piece of evidence from the sixteenth century is William Dunbar's poem *Schir Thomas Norny*.[1] This contains no reference to Chaucer; but it is clear that the Scots poet had *Sir Thopas* in mind. He employs the tail-rhyme stanza with six lines, not otherwise common in narrative verse:

[1] Ed. J. Kinsley, *The Poems of William Dunbar* (Oxford, 1979). All quotations from Chaucer are taken from Robinson's second edition. On the relation of *Norny* to *Thopas*, see F. B. Snyder, *MLN* xxv (1910), 78–80, and E. R. Eddy, *RES*, NS xxii (1971), 401–9. Eddy points out archaic and Southern elements in the language of *Norny*, and notes a close parallel between *Norny*, 31–3 and *Ipomadon* A, 16–18. Dunbar's knowledge of tail-rhyme would not be confined to *Thopas*.

Now lythis off ane gentill knycht
Schir Thomas Norny, wys and wycht
And full off chevelry,
Quhais father was ane giand keyne—
His mother was ane farie queyne
Gottin be sossery. (1-6)—

Such introductions are commonplace, as Chaucer's imitation itself implies (*Thopas*, VII. 712-23); but the giant and the fairy queen certainly come from Chaucer's poem (807-16), as do the later references to Norny's success as a wrestler (22-4, *Thop.* 740-1) and as an 'anterous knycht ... at justing and at tornament' (31-3, *Thop.* 715-16, 909). Like Chaucer, Dunbar declares that his hero outdoes the famous knight Sir Bevis of Hampton (34-5, *Thop.* 899); and he also imitates the stanza in which Chaucer mentions Bevis along with Horn, Ypotys, Guy of Warwick, Lybeaus Desconus, and the mysterious Pleyndamour, as heroes outdone by Sir Thopas:

Was never wyld Robein under bewch
Nor ȝet Roger off Clekniskleuch
So bauld a berne as he;
Gy off Gysburne, na Allan Bell,
Na Simonis sonnes off Quhynfell
At schot war never so slie. (25-30)

Roger and the sons of Simon are unidentified; but Guy of Gisborne (not to be confused with Guy of Warwick) is the knight killed by Robin Hood in an early ballad preserved in the Percy Folio (Child no. 118), 'Robein under bewch' must be Robin Hood himself, and 'Allan Bell' is presumably the hero of another early outlaw ballad, *Adam Bell, Clim of the Clough, and William of Cloudesly* (Child no. 116). It seems, therefore, that Dunbar associated *Thopas* not only with metrical romances such as *Bevis of Hampton*, but also with the ballad poetry of the greenwood—just as Puttenham and Drayton were to do later in the century.[2]

[2] See below. One manuscript of *Thopas*, Royal College of Physicians MS 13 (dated 1460-80), anticipates Dunbar, Puttenham, and Drayton. It substitutes 'Robynhoode' for 'Beves' in Chaucer's list of heroes: see Manly-Rickert, *Text of The Canterbury Tales*, vii. 197, and A. B. Friedman, *NQ* cxcv (1950), 210.

Ballads figure hardly at all in modern discussions of *Sir Thopas*, although modern historians of balladry see close connections between the early ballads and the metrical romances of the later Middle Ages.[3] L. H. Loomis makes no use whatever of ballad material in her standard collection of *Thopas* parallels.[4] It is true that the earliest surviving copy of a greenwood ballad dates from the middle of the fifteenth century (*Robin Hood and the Monk*, Child no. 119); but some of the poems are certainly older than that. Langland knew of the 'rymes of Robyn Hood', and Chaucer in all probability knew them too.[5] No doubt the chief object of his imitation in *Thopas* was what we call metrical romance, especially the tail-rhyme variety; but Dunbar stands as a reminder that the distinction between romance and ballad should not be too sharply drawn. Chaucer's six-line stanza is closely akin to the standard four-line stanza of ballad, as the following balladized specimen will show:

> He dide next his white leere
> A breech and eek a sherte,
> And next his sherte an aketoun
> For percynge of his herte.
> (*Thop.* 857–62,
> lacking 858 and 861)

The language and style of early greenwood ballads in fact display many points of similarity to Chaucer's poem. This is particularly true of *A Gest of Robyn Hode* (Child no. 117), a poem first recorded in two early prints, but possibly, according

[3] See particularly David C. Fowler, *A Literary History of the Popular Ballad* (Durham, N.C., 1968), Chapters 3 and 4.

[4] W. F. Bryan and G. Dempster (edd.), *Sources and Analogues of Chaucer's Canterbury Tales* (Chicago, 1941), Chapter XX.

[5] *Piers Plowman*, B v. 395, edd. G. Kane and E. T. Donaldson (London, 1975). *Troilus*, II. 861, 'Thei speken, but thei benten nevere his bowe', evidently applies to Cupid the proverb 'Many men speak of Robin Hood that never shot in his bow': see the valuable collection of Robin Hood material, R. B. Dobson and J. Taylor, *Rymes of Robyn Hood* (London, 1976), 289–90. One scribe copying *Troilus* noted in the margin 'of Robyn hode' (MS Ph), another introduced 'robynhod' into the text (MS H4).

to Child, 'put together as early as 1400, or before'.[6] Like *Thopas*, the *Gest* is divided into fitts;[7] and it opens with a stanza whose structure resembles that of the opening stanza of Chaucer's poem as closely as anything cited by Loomis from the romances:

Lythe and listin, gentilmen,
    That be of frebore blode;
I shall you tel of a gode yeman,
    His name was Robyn Hode.[8]

We find in the *Gest* a knight who has distinguished himself, like Chaucer's hero, 'in ioustes and in tournement' (st. 116) and who carries a 'launsgay' (st. 134, *Thop.* 752 and 821). Sir Thopas also has something in common with the ballad's sub-chivalric world of 'good yeomen':

Therto he was a good archeer;
Of wrastlyng was ther noon his peer,
    Ther any ram shal stonde. (*Thop.* 739–41)

Loomis cites no parallels from the romances for Sir Thopas's love of archery—a pastime which is, of course, the chief love of the heroes of greenwood ballads. Wrestling is also an unknightly sport, practised by yeomen in the *Gest*:

But as he went at a brydge ther was a wrastelyng,
    And there taryed was he,
And there was all the best yemen
    Of all the west countree. (st. 135)

The hypothesis that the ballads themselves derived from earlier metrical romances similar to those imitated by Chaucer will account for some parallels; but it will not explain the wrestling and archery in Chaucer's poem, nor will it account for another

[6] F. J. Child, *The English and Scottish Popular Ballads* (Boston and New York, 1882–98), iii. 40. All ballad quotations are from Child.

[7] There are eight 'fyttes' in the *Gest*. *Adam Bell* (Child no. 116) concludes fitts at stanzas 51 and 97, using a form of words, 'Here is a fytte...', which resembles *Thop.* 888 more closely than either of the romance parallels cited by Loomis, pp. 499 and 500.

[8] The appeal to listeners is renewed at subsequent fitt-beginnings (stanzas 144, 282, 317), as in *Thopas* (833, 891–3).

very specific piece of evidence linking Sir Thopas with the world of 'Robein under bewch'. This is the occurrence, uniquely in Chaucer, of the greenwood expression 'merry men' in the description of the arming of Sir Thopas:

> His myrie men comanded he
> To make hym bothe game and glee. (839–40)

In the sense 'companions in arms' (*OED*, s.v. *Merry man*, 1), the phrase 'merry men' is familiar from many occurrences in the early Robin Hood ballads:

> Up than sterte gode Robyn,
> As man that had ben wode:
> 'Buske you, my mery men,
> For hym that dyed on rode'. (*Gest*, st. 340)[9]

Sir Thopas provides the first example of the phrase in *OED*, which also cites from *The Hunting of the Cheviot* (Child no. 162A) and *Gamelyn*:

> Tho was ȝonge Gamelyn
> Glad and bliþe ynough,
> Whan he fond his mery men
> Vnder woode-bough.[10]

Gamelyn is a forerunner of the Robin Hood ballads, and it is also associated with the *Canterbury Tales* in all the twenty-five medieval manuscripts which preserve it. Perhaps, therefore, it provides some kind of link between *Sir Thopas* and greenwood balladry. In any case, the reference to 'merry men' is the best evidence that Chaucer did know the 'yeddings' of yeoman outlawry in one form or another; and it helps to explain Dunbar's choice of heroes with whom to compare his own dubious protagonist.

Thomas and Thopas are, of course, both equally remote from

[9] Other examples may be found in *Gest*, stanzas 205, 281, 316, 382, *Robin Hood and the Monk*, stanza 9, *Robin Hood and Guy of Gisborne* (Child no. 118), stanza 5. The related expression 'merry meiny' occurs in *Gest*, stanza 262, and *Robin Hood and the Potter* (Child no. 121), stanza 4.

[10] Lines 773–4, edd. W. H. French and C. B. Hale, *Middle English Metrical Romances* (New York, 1930), printed here as a ballad stanza. *Gamelyn* also has a wrestling match (169–284).

any heroism, whether of good yeomen or of adventurous knights; but Dunbar's management of his burlesque is rather different from Chaucer's. In the eighteenth century, when the matter was best understood, critics distinguished two sorts of burlesque: the high sort 'in which mean and common subjects are ridiculously invested with the trappings of affected dignity', and the low sort 'in which lofty and sublime subjects are cloathed in the garb and stile of the vulgar'.[11] On this definition, Dunbar's poem is a straightforward case of high burlesque. The 'mean and common subject' is a court fool, Thomas Norny, whom Dunbar invests with the trappings of knightly and yeomanly heroism: he is *Sir* Thomas Norny, an 'anterous knycht' who has performed many a valiant deed in the Highlands and who always wins the prize at tournaments; and he is also an unrivalled dancer and wrestler, and a better archer than Adam Bell (who shot the Sheriff of Carlyle, and 'a better shotte in mery Carlyll, / Thys seven yere was not sene'). As in Dunbar's other tail-rhyme burlesque, *The Turnament* (Kinsley no. 52B), the comedy derives from a broad contrast between high heroic claim and low realistic disclosure. In Chaucer's poem, on the other hand, the contrast between mean subject and affected dignity is less clear-cut. Thopas, for one thing, is not a court fool or (as in Dunbar's *Turnament*) a tailor or a shoemaker. His birthplace, Poperinghe, sounds 'mean and common' enough, and Flanders lacks the right romantic associations for a 'fer contree'; but Chaucer's hero is, for all we discover, *Sir* Thopas by right, a real knight albeit a cowardly one. There is a difference, too, in the 'trappings of affected dignity'. It is hard to imagine that William Dunbar took seriously the heroic worlds of romance and balladry; but he does not seem concerned to ridicule such poetry in *Schir Thomas Norny*. Rather he accepts the minstrel manner, for the purposes of this poem, as establishing a norm against which the baseness of an absurd hero can be measured. But in Chaucer the minstrel manner is itself an object of ridicule—some would say, the chief

[11] 'K.W.', writing in 1773, cited by Richmond P. Bond, *English Burlesque Poetry 1700–1750* (Cambridge, Mass., 1932), 59.

object of ridicule. Here the trappings of affected dignity are themselves mean and common; and to that extent Chaucer's poem approaches *low* burlesque, where 'lofty and sublime subjects are cloathed in the garb and stile of the vulgar'.

Yet Sir Thopas himself is of course not 'lofty and sublime', even though he may be a knight rather than a jester. He is a ridiculous figure, portrayed in a broad and even farcical spirit of comedy which modern readers do not, I think, always catch. Two passing references by Dunbar's English contemporary, John Skelton, suggest a very robust response to the joke. There is, first, the curious question of Garnish's nose. In about 1514, Skelton engaged in a bout of comic 'flyting' with Christopher Garnish, gentleman-usher to Henry VIII. Skelton seems to have had *Thopas* in mind from the start, for in the opening passage of the first *Poem Against Garnesche* he refers to both 'Syr Tyrmagant' (4, cf. *Thop.* 810) and 'Syr Lybyus' (*Thop.* 900):

> Thow ye be lusty as Syr Lybyus launces to breke,
> Yet your contenons oncomly, your face ys nat fayer. (17–18)

And one of the worst parts of Garnish's face is his nose:

> Your tethe teintyd with tawny; your semely snowte doth passe,
> Howkyd as an hawkys beke, lyke Syr Topyas. (39–40)[12]

In his third poem, again, Skelton describes his adversary as 'nosyd lyke an olyfaunt' (71); and in the fourth he writes:

> thow hast a long snowte,
> A semly nose and a stowte,
> Prickyd lyke an unicorne. (130–2)

These passages indicate Skelton's response to Chaucer's memorable line, 'He hadde a semely nose' (*Thop.* 729). The

[12] Ed. A. Dyce, *Poetical Works of John Skelton* (London, 1843). Manly and Rickert record the variant *Topias* for *Thopas* in three manuscripts of the *Canterbury Tales* and *Thopias* in one. Skelton's association of Thopas with a hawk's beak has a curious parallel in a burlesque panegyric contributed by 'Αποδημουντόφιλος, 'the traveller's friend', to *Coryats Crudities* (1611), C 3–5. Describing the adventures of Coryate in 'dogrell' tail-rhyme, the author calls him 'this child Sir *Thopas* Squire' and credits him with an 'Eagles snowt' (l. 35).

Tudor poet evidently took it for granted that readers would understand this as a scornful irony, expressing 'per antifrasim, tanquam derisio', the very reverse of the truth.[13] Sir Thopas's nose was not seemly at all, but huge like a hawk's beak, an elephant's trunk, or a unicorn's horn, and so grotesquely in harmony with his bright red cheeks and lips and his enormous yellow beard. Most modern readers, I think, understand the joke differently, allowing Thopas a well-shaped nose, but seeing an anticlimactic incongruity in the detail—a knight's nose, like his complexion, being no business of the romance muse. But perhaps this is to read Chaucer's irony too delicately. Should we not assume that the hero's nose would be as grotesque as the rest of his face? Skelton may be right in inviting us to imagine a pure figure of fun, a carnival absurdity like Mr Punch, scarcely less outlandish than the three-headed giant whom he so inadequately confronts.

A later poem, *The Douty Duke of Albany* (*c.* 1523), shows how clearly Skelton understood the nature of this confrontation. Modern scholars have searched the romances for analogues to the basic plot of *Sir Thopas*; and they have found there adventurous knights, giant adversaries, and fairy mistresses.[14] But the event which forms the climax (such as it is) of Chaucer's story and gives it its distinctive shape could never figure in a regular romance: the maddening *conflictus interruptus* when Thopas, faced with the giant Olifaunt, 'drow abak ful faste' (827). Skelton, however, found in the events of his own day a comically exact parallel. In 1523, the Duke of Albany led an abortive Scots expedition against the English. Skelton claims that they ran away before they even encountered the enemy:

> Thou durst no felde derayne,
> Nor no batayle mayntayne
> Against our stronge captaine,
> But thou ran home agayne,
> For feare thou shoulde be slayne. (243–7)

[13] Geoffrey of Vinsauf, in the discussion from which I quote (*Poetria Nova*, 929–35), gives examples, such as calling an ugly man 'Paris'.

[14] See for instance F. P. Magoun, *PMLA* xlii (1927), 833–44.

His later allusion to Sir Thopas, whose promise after 'drawing back' to return on the following day is left unfulfilled, therefore has an exact point:

> But hyde the, sir Topias,
> Nowe into the castell of Bas,
> And lurke there, lyke an as. (287–9)

It does not require much critical acumen to see that *Thopas* is not a good poem—Harry Bailly could see that—and there is little to be learned from the fact that Sir Thomas Wyatt, imitating an Italian satire, chose Chaucer's 'drasty' piece to represent bad poetry in English. Wyatt declares his unwillingness to compromise with the corrupt and topsy-turvy world of the court, where men will say anything to please. *He* will not

> say that Pan
> Passithe Apollo in musike manyfolld;
> Praysse Syr Thopas for a noble tale,
> And skorne the story that the knyght tolld.[15]

This should not, I think, be taken to imply that *Sir Thopas was in fact preferred to the Knight's Tale* by courtiers of Henry VIII. On the contrary, most Tudor readers seem to have associated the poem with common and country occasions. Dunbar's references to Robin Hood and Adam Bell, popular heroes from Sherwood Forest, Barnsdale, and Inglewood, point in that direction, as perhaps does Wyatt's reference to Pan. But for a more explicit socio-regional characterization of Chaucer's poem we may turn to George Puttenham's *Arte of English Poesie*.[16]

In a part of this work probably written in the 1560s, Puttenham devotes a chapter (Book II, Chapter X) to an interesting question of poetic technique: the 'distances' separating a word

[15] 'Mine own John Poyntz', 48–51: *Collected Poems of Sir Thomas Wyatt*, edd. K. Muir and P. Thomson (Liverpool, 1969). The Alamanni original (ed. cit., pp. 347–9) speaks of preferring Maevius to Homer, Virgil, and Dante. Francis Thynne in his *Emblemes and Epigrames* (1600) also uses *Thopas* as the type of a bad poem: ed. F. J. Furnivall, EETS 64 (1876), pp. 3 and 77.

[16] Edd. G. D. Willcock and A. Walker (Cambridge, 1936). On dating see their Introduction, pp. xliv–liii.

in rhyme from its answering rhyme-word. 'Artificial' poets, he says, often employ long distances (three or more intervening lines), and so demand a more retentive ear than do 'common rhymers', who employ shorter distances. Very short distances reveal 'a certaine lightnesse either of the matter or of the makers head'. 'The over busie and too speedy returne of one maner of tune' gluts the ear—'unlesse it be in small and popular Musickes song by these *Cantabanqui* upon benches and barrels heads where they have none other audience then boys or countrey fellowes that passe by them in the streete, or else by blind harpers or such like taverne minstrels that give a fit of mirth for a groat, and their matters being for the most part stories of old time, as the tale of Sir *Topas*, the reportes of *Bevis* of *Southampton*, *Guy* of *Warwicke*, *Adam Bell*, and *Clymme* of the *Clough* and such other old Romances or historicall rimes, made purposely for recreation of the common people at Christmasse diners and brideales, and in tavernes and alehouses and such other places of base resort.'[17]

In his *Observations on the Fairy Queen of Spenser*, Thomas Warton cited this passage and drew from it the conclusion that 'Chaucer's pieces, or at least legends drawn from him, were, at that time, sung to the harp; for the tale, or rime, of Sir Topas is a poem of Chaucer now extant: so the Italians, at present, sing Tasso and Ariosto.'[18] It is hard to imagine how *Sir Thopas*, or even a legend drawn from it, could ever have formed part of a Tudor minstrel's repertory, given its fragmentary character; but Puttenham's testimony has value none the less. Like Dunbar, he associates Chaucer's poem with ballad and romance indifferently, citing *Adam Bell* alongside *Bevis* and *Guy*.[19] He also gives a lively sketch (which could be matched from medieval sources) of the social context to which such 'stories of old time' properly

[17] Ed. cit., pp. 83–4.

[18] Second Edition (London, 1762), I. 52–3.

[19] Thomas Warton neatly obliterates the distinction when he speaks of *Thopas* as 'a kind of burlesque on the old ballad romances', *Observations*, I. 139.

belong. They are recited by blind harpers and tavern minstrels, who give 'a fit of mirth for a groat'[20] at Christmas dinners, bridal feasts, and pub evenings.

Recent scholarship has tended to emphasize the bookish character of Middle English romances, giving the impression that most of them were composed by scribe-poets working in bookshops, and read by men such as Chaucer in books such as the Auchinleck Manuscript. Dieter Mehl makes the following observation, which may be taken as typical: 'That the romances were written to be recited in taverns and market-places, as is sometimes believed, is certainly a romantic fiction.'[21] But Puttenham's testimony at least proves that this so-called fiction antedates Sir Walter Scott; and it may prompt us to consider whether the modern reaction against 'romantic' notions of popular minstrelsy has not now gone too far. Those minstrels who looked so suspiciously like characters out of *Ivanhoe* have been succeeded by non-minstrels who look suspiciously like denizens of the bookish world inhabited by the modern scholars themselves. Perhaps this is a case of *counter*-romantic fiction. One cannot, of course, cite Puttenham as a trustworthy witness to conditions in Chaucer's day, almost two hundred years before; but he serves as a salutary reminder that Chaucer's sources for that 'rym I lerned longe agoon' may not all have issued from a London bookshop.

Puttenham's association of *Sir Thopas* with the 'recreation of the common people' certainly helps to explain why in the later Elizabethan period pastoral poets sometimes take Chaucer's poems as a model for their poetry of Pan. In Spenser's *Shepheardes Calender* (1579), the March Eclogue employs the six-line tail-rhyme stanza of *Thopas*, together with archaic and dialectal language, to suggest the rustic simplicity of the two

[20] 'Fit' here may be the same as Chaucer's 'fit' (888). In another chapter Puttenham speaks of having himself composed a (lost) romance in ballad metre 'by breaches or divisions to be more commodiously song to the harpe in places of assembly' (I. xix, ed. cit., p. 42).

[21] D. Mehl, *The Middle English Romances of the Thirteenth and Fourteenth Centuries* (London, 1968), 13.

shepherd boys, Willye and Thomalin. Although the diction has touches of Chaucer ('uprist', 'wroken'), there are no borrowings from *Thopas* itself; but E.K., in his note on *Spell*, cites the poem, managing to conflate three lines (712, 833, 893) into one: 'And so sayth Chaucer, Listeneth Lordings to my spell.'[22] In *Idea The Shepheards Garland*, a collection of pastoral eclogues published in 1593, Michael Drayton follows Spenser in drawing on *Thopas*. In the Fourth Eclogue, the old shepherd Gorbo proposes to Winken that they

> tell a tale of *Gawen* or Sir *Guy*,
> Of *Robin Hood*, or of good *Clem a Clough*.
>
> Or else some Romant unto us areed,
> Which good olde *Godfrey* taught thee in thy youth,
> Of noble Lords and Ladies gentle deede,
> Or of thy love, or of thy lasses truth.[23]

Drayton's editor is surely right to suggest that 'Godfrey is probably meant, like Spenser's *Tityrus*, for Chaucer.' Drayton follows Spenser in incorporating Chaucer into his pastoral world. Like Dunbar and Puttenham, too, he makes an association with romance and greenwood balladry. No particular work of Chaucer's is specified here; but in his Eighth Eclogue Drayton plainly imitates the metre and diction of *Thopas*, in the 'pretie Tale' which Motto learned from his toothless grandam when he was a boy. It begins as follows:

> Farre in the countrey of *Arden*,
> There wond a knight hight *Cassemen*,
> As bolde as *Isenbras*:
> Fell was he and eger bent,
> In battell and in Tournament,
> As was the good sir *Topas*. (123–8)

[24] Ed. cit., v. 11.

[25] Richard Hurd, in *Letters of Chivalry and Romance* (1788), described *Sir Thopas* as 'all DON QUIXOTE in little': ed. E. J. Morley (London, 1911), 172.

[26] *Pace* T. W. Nadal, 'Spenser's *Muiopotmos* in Relation to Chaucer's *Sir Thopas* and *The Nun's Priest's Tale*', *PMLA* xxv (1910), 640–56.

The allusions to Thopas and (with a pun on 'bold as brass') to Isumbras, hero of another tail-rhyme romance, may lead us to expect burlesque comedy; but the ensuing story of how Cassemen's daughter Dowsabell went a-maying and met a handsome shepherd is not ridiculous, and the Chaucerian phrasing and metre simply lend to the narrative 'a factitious and charming air of archaism'.[24]

In the pastoral poetry of Spenser and Drayton, *Sir Thopas* is assimilated into an old-fashioned rustic world; and in the process Chaucer's sharp and witty burlesque loses its edge. It may be noted that in his later and more famous poem *Nimphidia* Drayton draws upon *Thopas* for purposes which are clearly burlesque; but *Nimphidia*, published in 1627, looks forward to developments in mock-heroic which lie beyond the scope of this essay. Nevertheless, it is interesting to see Drayton couple Chaucer's name there with those of Rabelais and Cervantes. *Sir Thopas* eventually took its place alongside *Gargantua and Pantagruel* and *Don Quixote* in the ancestry of a new tradition of burlesque writing.[25]

Unlike Drayton, Spenser nowhere in his writings betrays his awareness—supposing that he was aware—of the burlesque character of *Sir Thopas*. It has been suggested that *Muiopotmos*, that grandiose narrative of a butterfly killed by a spider, owes something to Chaucer's burlesque; but the comedy of this poem, in so far as it derives from Chaucer at all, draws on the mock-tragedy of Chantecleer, not the mock-romance of Thopas.[26] If anything, it is the absence of verbal echoes from *Thopas* in such a poem which is significant. In *The Faerie Queene*, Spenser consistently treats *Thopas* as a serious romance—or at least as a source for details and episodes which are clearly not, in his

[24] Ed. cit., v. 11.

[25] Richard Hurd, in *Letters on Chivalry and Romance* (1788), described *Sir Thopas* as 'all DON QUIXOTE in little': ed. E. J. Morley (London, 1911), 172.

[26] *Pace* T. W. Nadal, 'Spenser's *Muiopotmos* in Relation to Chaucer's *Sir Thopas* and *The Nun's Priest's Tale*', *PMLA* xxv (1910), 640–56.

own poem, meant to be funny. *The Faerie Queene*, in fact, suggests a reading of *Thopas* quite different from that to be found in the other sixteenth-century sources (with one exception, to be mentioned shortly).

No importance can be attached to the fact that Spenser drew from *Thopas* two pieces of equipment for his archaic chivalric world: the boots of costly 'cordwaine' worn by Belphoebe and Tristram (II. iii. 27, VI. ii. 6; *Thop.* 732), and the jacket of 'checklaton' worn by the giant Disdain (VI. vii. 43; *Thop.* 734). Nor does Spenser's Blandamour (IV. i. 32) owe more than his name to Chaucer's mysterious 'Pleyndamour' (*Thop.* 900).[27] Other borrowings are more significant, however. In particular, Spenser seems to have vividly remembered and conflated in his imagination two separate stanzas in which Chaucer describes his hero resting in the open:

Sire Thopas eek so wery was
For prikyng on the softe gras,
So fiers was his corage,
That doun he leyde him in that plas
To make his steede som solas,
And yaf hym good forage. (778–83)

And for he was a knyght auntrous,
He nolde slepen in noon hous,
But liggen in his hoode;
His brighte helm was his wonger,
And by hym baiteth his dextrer
Of herbes fyne and goode. (909–14)

[27] The editions likely to have been used by Spenser, Thynne 1532 and Stow 1561, both read 'chekelatoun' for Robinson's 'syklatoun' and 'Blayndamoure' or 'Blaindamoure' for Robinson's 'Pleyndamour'. On the latter, see F. P. Magoun, *MP* xxv (1927), 129–31; on checklaton, compare Spenser's *View of the Present State of Ireland*: 'the quilted leather Iacke is olde Englishe for it was the proper wede of the horsemen as ye maye reade in *Chaucer* wheare he describeth: *Sr Thopas* apparrell and armour when he wente to fighte againste the Geaunte which Checklaton is that kinde of gilden leather', *Prose Works*, Variorum Edition, ed. R. Gottfried (Baltimore, 1949), ll. 2178–82. Spenser was not alone in deriving chivalric items from *Thopas*. John Bossewell, in *Workes of Armorie* (1572), f. 9^v^, cites Thopas's coat of arms: 'Bores heade. The fielde is *Sol* [gold], a Bores heade coped *Saturne* [black]. These were th'Armes of Sir

Lexicographical evidence supports J. M. Manly's observation that '*forage* usually is "dry fodder" and Sir Thopas was quite capable of the absurdity implied';[28] but the absurdity (if it is one) did not strike Spenser. Weary like Sir Thopas, Spenser's Redcross dismounts, 'And by his side his steed the grassy forage ate' (I. vii. 2). Similarly Prince Arthur, exhausted by his pursuit of Florimell:

> from his loftie steed dismounting low,
> Did let him forage. Downe himselfe he layd
> Upon the grassie ground, to sleepe a throw;
> The cold earth was his couch, the hard steele his pillow.
> (III. iv. 53)

In these lines there are two further recollections of the *Thopas* stanzas: 'Downe himselfe he layd' ('doun he leyde him') and 'the hard steele his pillow' ('His brighte helm was his wonger'). Spenser recalls the same two lines from Chaucer in an earlier and much more important context: Arthur's account to Una of his dream of the Fairy Queen:

> For-wearied with my sports, I did alight
> From loftie steed, and downe to sleepe me layd;
> The verdant gras my couch did goodly dight,
> And pillow was my helmet faire displayd. (I. ix. 13)

Nothing in the early modern career of Sir Thopas is so surprising as that Chaucer's burlesque should have contributed largely to Spenser's conception of Arthur's dream, the vision of glory which first draws the Prince into the world of faerie. Yet the contribution cannot be doubted. In the first part of his narrative (I. ix. 9–12) Arthur represents himself as having been a proud young scorner of 'that idle name of love, and lovers life'. Spenser clearly has Chaucer's *Troilus* in mind at this point,

Thopas, as in the metre made of hym maye appeare at large, in the workes of *Chaucer*. And for hys creste he bare a Tower / Wherein sticked a Lillye floure / Of coloures all most propre. Here note th'antiquitie of Creastes.'

[28] Note to ll. B 1968–73 in his edition of *Canterbury Tales* (London, 1928). Compare the words of the Reeve: 'Gras tyme is doon, my fodder is now forage' (I. 3868).

recalling how Troilus was first portrayed as a rebel against Cupid, and as an example of pride and folly:

> Forthy ensample taketh of this man,
> Ye wise, proude, and worthi folkes alle,
> To scornen Love, which that so soone kan
> The fredom of youre hertes to hym thralle. (I. 232–5)

Arthur represents himself to Una as a bad example of a similar sort:

> Ensample make of him your haplesse ioy,
> And of my selfe now mated, as ye see;
> Whose prouder vaunt that proud avenging boy
> Did soone pluck downe, and curbd my libertie. (I ix. 12)

This may seem a long way from *Sir Thopas*; but Spenser, as we shall see shortly, took good note of the stanza in which Chaucer described Thopas at the beginning of his adventure as a 'chaast' young hero for whom damsels pined in vain (742–7, cf. 791–3). He could, therefore, have associated Thopas with Troilus, as a type of proud youthful 'fredom' or 'libertie' soon to be thralled and curbed by Love. Hence it is not altogether surprising that Arthur's ensuing account of how he did fall in love (stanzas 12–15) should recall, as it clearly does, the *inamoramento* of Sir Thopas at several points. Like Thopas, Arthur rides out into a forest. Growing weary, he dismounts and falls asleep with his head pillowed on his helmet. He too dreams of a fairy queen, falls in love, and sets off in search of his beloved.

J. W. Bennett, who noted the parallels with *Thopas* and discussed them at length, suggested that stanzas 12–15 survive, though in a polished-up form, from Spenser's first version of *The Faerie Queene*, which she conjectures to have been a playful reworking and continuation of Chaucer's burlesque, done in the manner of Ariosto's continuation of Boiardo's *Orlando*.[29] But what comedy there is in Arthur's narrative seems to me to come from *Troilus*, not *Thopas*. Bennett is certainly right to say that

[29] J. W. Bennett, *The Evolution of 'The Faerie Queene'* (Chicago, 1942), 11–15.

sixteenth-century evidence for the reception of Chaucer's burlesque makes it unlikely that Spenser entirely failed to see the joke; yet we must surely affirm that the account of the vision itself betrays no hint of levity, either Chaucerian or Ariostan. It may be argued that Spenser, having adopted the established representation of Queen Elizabeth I as a 'Diana-like fairy queen'[30] and determined to introduce her in that guise into a romance of chivalry, simply took the most familiar of the not very numerous stories which offered him a link between a fairy queen and the world of errant knights, and used it without regard to its burlesque character. Yet, if we re-read Chaucer's account of Sir Thopas and the Fairy Queen with Spenser's poem in mind, we may find it a less incongruous model than such an account suggests. The ridiculous features in Chaucer's poem coexist with the true note of the faery. Unlike Spenser, Chaucer does not describe the dream itself—the narrative jumps, at line 784, from Thopas's preparations for sleep to his words on waking—yet this hiatus, so far from seeming incompetent, preserves the mystery of the affair, better in fact than Spenser's rather routine talk of 'goodly glee and lovely blandishment'. And there is something more than burlesque in the giant's later proclamation of the fairy queen:

> 'Heere is the queene of Fayerye,
> With harpe and pipe and symphonye,
> Dwellynge in this place.' (814–16)

Here, as in the inimitable opening of the *Wife of Bath's Tale*, the accompanying bathos and absurdities fail to dim the mysterious brightness of Chaucer's elf-queen.

Spenser saw other potentialities too in Chaucer's poem. Two passages in Book III of *The Faerie Queene* show him deriving from Sir Thopas's adventure, most unexpectedly again, an allegory of chastity. The first passage, III. vii. 37–61, introduces a giantess, Argante, armed with a 'huge great yron mace' (cf. *Thop.* 813), who first captures the Squire of Dames and

[30] Bennett, op. cit., p. 9.

Satyrane, and then is put to flight by the virgin warrior Palladine. After the giantess has gone, the Squire explains to Satyrane that she is the offspring of an incestuous union between the titan Typhoeus and his mother Earth, and that she has a twin brother called Ollyphant. The twins, sexually united at the moment of their birth, represent several varieties of erotic excess and perversion 'gainst natures law' (st. 49). Argante practises bestiality and heterosexual promiscuity, as well as incest; and Ollyphant, when he appears briefly in a later canto (xi. 3–6), is discovered in the act of pursuing a pretty boy. Just as Argante runs away from Palladine, so her brother cannot face Britomart:

> For he the powre of chast hands might not beare,
> But alwayes did their dread encounter fly. (III. xi. 6)

In his *Observations on the Fairy Queen*, Thomas Warton remarked that 'the giant Ollyphant here mentioned, is probably the same which Sir Thopas encounters in his expedition to the land of Fairy';[31] and J. W. Bennett has confirmed this suggestion by drawing attention to a remarkable variant in the first version of the text (1590).[32] In modern editions, which follow the second edition of 1596, the Squire of Dames speaks of

> the mighty Ollyphant, that wrought
> Great wreake to many errant knights of yore,
> And many hath to foule confusion brought. (III. vii. 48)

But the last line reads differently in the 1590 edition: 'Till him Chylde Thopas to confusion brought.' Bennett sees here another fragmentary relic of that continuation of *Thopas* which formed, in her reconstruction, Spenser's first attempt at *The Faerie Queene*. The conjecture is hazardous; but two things at least are clear. Spenser took over Chaucer's Olifaunt and incorporated

[31] *Observations*, I. 179. Spenser's adoption of Chaucer's giant into his allegory has a precedent, and possible inspiration, in *The Pastime of Pleasure*. Hawes's hero, in quest of his beloved, encounters resistance from a giant with three heads, like Olifaunt. The heads are interpreted allegorically as representing falsehood, imagination, and perjury: ed. W. E. Mead, EETS 173 (1928), ll. 4315–416.

[32] Bennett, op. cit., p. 19.

him, as a type of unnatural sexuality, in his book of Chastity; and he also at one stage imagined, though he probably never wrote, a continuation to Chaucer's unfinished story, in which Childe Thopas brought his giant adversary to confusion—presumably demonstrating, like Palladine and Britomart, 'the powre of chast hands'.

Bennett points out that Spenser's friend Gabriel Harvey, when annotating his copy of Speght's 1598 edition of Chaucer, characterized *Sir Thopas* as 'morall'—an epithet Harvey otherwise applies only to the *Clerk's Tale* and the *Parson's Tale*.[33] It is hard to imagine what he could have had in mind if not an interpretation similar to that implied by Spenser—from whom, indeed, he may have learned it. But how did either man arrive at such a moral reading of the poem, quite out of line with what we know of other sixteenth-century readings? Presumably the explanation lies in the stanza concerning the chastity of Thopas:

> Ful many a mayde, bright in bour,
> They moorne for hym paramour,
>   Whan hem were bet to slepe;
> But he was chaast and no lechour,
> And sweete as is the brembul flour
>   That bereth the rede hepe. (742–7)

If, following this lead, Spenser conceived of Thopas's ensuing love for the fairy queen as the kind of chaste love one should feel for Queen Elizabeth, then the giant Olifaunt could easily come to represent not a physical but a moral obstacle—the unchaste passions which might prevent the hero from achieving such a love. Giants were commonly associated with sexual practices 'gainst natures law', partly because their origins were held to lie in that episode before the Flood when the sons of God took wives from among the daughters of men (Genesis 6:1–5) and, in the words of *Cleanness* (l. 266), 'controeved agayn kynde contraré werkez'.

Before dismissing this interpretation out of hand, it is salutary

[33] Bennett, p. 19, referring to *Gabriel Harvey's Marginalia*, ed. G. C. Moore Smith (Stratford, 1913), 228.

to reflect that no modern critic has produced a fully satisfactory explanation of the crucial lines 742–7. Chaste heroes are not particularly characteristic of ballads and romances;[34] nor are they amusingly *un*characteristic of them—unless one takes chastity, in this context, as tantamount to effeminacy.[35] So the chastity of Thopas seems to make no clear contribution, either way, to the burlesque imitation. Even less convincing are the attempts to interpret the passage 'per antifrasim', as implying some kind of sexual impropriety. W. O. Ross, for instance, following Manly's suggestion (itself unconvincing) that *Thopas* is a satire on Flemings, suggests that Chaucer 'meant to call to the minds of his audience one more weakness of the people whom he was satirizing', since Flemings were notoriously unchaste.[36] Until we can do better than that, Spenser's interpretation must remain something more than a mere curiosity.

It is doubtful whether many Elizabethans would have agreed with Spenser and Harvey in reading *Thopas* as a 'morall' piece. More typical, no doubt, are the two dramatists, Lyly and Shakespeare, both of whom borrow the name of Chaucer's hero for comic purposes. In John Lyly's play *Endimion*, published in 1591, a year after the first three books of *The Faerie Queene*, 'Sir Tophas' is a pure figure of fun. Like Chaucer's hero, and like Skelton's Duke of Albany, Tophas is absurdly timorous. He exercises his martial arts on innocuous creatures such as wrens, trout, and sheep—recalling the hare, a 'wild beste' by anti-

[34] Loomis, *Sources and Analogues*, 493 n. 5, cites only two weak parallels from *Guy of Warwick*.

[35] So E. T. Donaldson, *Chaucer's Poetry: An Anthology for the Modern Reader* (New York, 1958), 935: 'The hero's notable chastity (perhaps symbolized in his name, Topaze, the stone of chastity) is unusual if not absolutely impossible in a knight of popular romance, and with a cruelty that has little to do with his being a bourgeois, Chaucer has exploited this chastity to make it seem downright effeminacy.'

[36] 'A Possible Significance of the Name *Thopas*', *MLN* xlv (1930), 174. Ross's contention that the hero's name itself suggests chastity has been questioned, notably by Conley, *SP* lxxiii (1976), 42–61; but Spenser may have understood it so.

phrasis, which threatens Thopas on his forest ride. Like Thopas, too, Lyly's Tophas is a braggart (compare *Thop*. 817–26, 872–4). Chaucer's coward knight can be seen, in Lyly's sub-plot, merging with the *miles gloriosus* of Latin comedy.[37] Evidently Lyly, like Skelton, read Chaucer's poem in the broadest spirit of farce.

In Shakespeare's *Twelfth Night*, it will be recalled, the clown Feste assumes the role of 'Sir Topas the curate' when he comes to torment the supposedly deranged Malvolio (Act IV, Scene ii). Unlike Lyly, Shakespeare takes nothing but the name from Chaucer; but his use of the name is interesting.[38] Shakespeare seems to have noticed that Chaucer harps on the honorific title 'Sir'. In his own short scene, the name 'Topas' occurs fifteen times, every time prefixed by 'Sir'. Malvolio repeats it with pathetic eagerness: 'Sir Topas, Sir Topas, good Sir Topas, go to my lady'; and again, 'Sir Topas, never was man thus wronged. Good Sir Topas, do not think I am mad.' In Chaucer's poem, too, the name is always preceded with a title—eight times with 'sir(e)', once with 'child'. The departure from Chaucer's normal usage here is greater than it may at first seem. 'Child Thopas' (830), echoed by Spenser in 1590, is an obvious abnormality. It involves an application of the word 'child' ('noble youth') paralleled in Chaucer's writing only in *Sir Thopas* itself (810, 817, 898). This is clearly meant to recall the usage of works such as 'Horn Childe and Maiden Rimnild' in the Auchinleck Manuscript. 'Sir(e) Thopas', on the other hand, may appear to be an unexceptionable form of reference in itself. Yet the evidence of the concordance suggests that this is not normal Chaucerian usage either.

'Sir(e)' is prefixed to the allegorical names Myrthe and Daunger in the *Romaunt of the Rose*; and the Canterbury pilgrims

[37] D. C. Boughner, 'The Background of Lyly's Tophas', *PMLA* liv (1939), 967–73. On the relationship with Chaucer, see also R. W. Bond (ed.), *The Complete Works of John Lyly* (Oxford, 1902), iii. 502–3.

[38] J. M. Lothian and T. W. Craik, in the New Arden edition (London, 1975), note to IV. ii. 2, ascribe the choice of name to 'Shakespeare's delight in incongruity', Chaucer and Lyly having used it of a knight. They also see a possible allusion to the idea that topazes heal lunatics.

commonly address each other as 'Sir Knight', 'Sir Clerk', 'Sir Man of Law', 'Sir Host' (*OED*, s.v. *Sir* (sb.), 6). But, prefixed to a true proper name, 'sir' occurs in Chaucer's works outside *Thopas* only five times; and of these five occurrences four evidently refer to priests—normal usage in Chaucer's time, as in Shakespeare's.[39] The Host and the narrator refer to the Nun's Priest as 'sir John' (VII. 2810, 2820); and the Friar speaks of wenches committing fornication with 'sir Robert or sir Huwe, or Jakke, or Rauf', in a context which suggests priests rather than knights (III. 1356–7). The only other occurrence is in the *Physician's Tale*, where Claudius addresses the corrupt judge as 'sire Apius' in his bill of complaint (VI. 178), no doubt out of respect for his learning in the law. It turns out, in fact, that Chaucer never outside *Thopas* prefixes 'sir' to the name of a knight—not in *Troilus* (never 'sir Troilus'), or the *Knight's Tale* (never 'sir Palamon'), or the *Franklin's Tale* (never 'sir Arveragus'). By contrast, in *Thopas* we find 'sir Thopas' eight times, and also 'sir Gy', 'sir Lybeux', 'sire Percyvell'—and even 'sire Olifaunt' (808), an absurdity comparable to Dunbar's 'Schir Thomas Norny' for a court fool. The distribution of this usage in Chaucer is unexpected, for the use of 'sir' with a knight's name is widespread in fourteenth-century texts. It occurs in courtly works such as *Sir Gawain and the Green Knight*, as well as more popular ones such as *Guy of Warwick*. Perhaps Chaucer regarded promiscuous use of the honorific in literature as a vulgarism, as insistence on titles often seems to be, when the occasion does not demand it. Such vulgarity would, of course, be entirely in place in *Sir Thopas*.[40]

[39] *OED*, s.v. *Sir*, 4: 'Placed before the Christian name of ordinary priests.' Viola says 'I am one that would rather go with sir priest than sir knight' (*Twelfth Night*, III. iv. 259–60).

[40] Dr Elspeth Kennedy refers me to L. Foulet, 'Sire, Messire', *Romania*, lxxii (1951), 330–3, 346–53, who notes that the fourteenth-century French chroniclers Jean le Bel and Jean Froissart do not prefix *sire* to knights' names. They confine the usage to wealthy bourgeois such as the Fleming 'sire Ghisebert Grute' (Foulet, p. 348). 'Dès le milieu du XIIIe siècle les chevaliers avaient adopté définitivement le "messire" comme signe distinctif, tournant le dos à *sire*, qu'ils

There is something to be learned, then, even from so slight an 'allusion' as Shakespeare's borrowing of a name. Let me end, however, with a substantial critical comment from the closing years of the century. In 1598, Thomas Speght produced a new edition of Chaucer's works, which was to remain standard for more than a century. Among his innovations was a set of Arguments to the individual works. His argument to *The Rime of Sir Topas* runs as follows: 'A Northren tale of an outlandish Knight purposely uttered by Chaucer, in a differing rime and stile from the other tales, as though he himselfe were not the authour, but only the reporter of the rest.'[41] 'As though he himselfe were not the authour, but only the reporter of the rest . . .' Has any modern critic expressed more concisely and forcefully the deeper purpose of Chaucer's remarkable burlesque?

abandonnaient, non sans dédain, aux bourgeois' (Foulet, p. 330). Perhaps Chaucer shared the disdain of his French contemporaries for the prefixed *sire*. His deposition in the Scrope–Grosvenor controversy, as recorded in the Chancery Roll, consistently employs the prefix *monsieur* ('Monsieur Robert Grovenour', etc): M. M. Crow and C. C. Olson (edd.), *Chaucer Life-Records* (Oxford, 1966), 370–71. The English usage would repay further investigation.

[41] *The Workes of our Antient and lerned English Poet, Geffrey Chaucer, newly printed* (1598), p. ciiiii. Speght's description of the tale as Northern, not borne out by modern scholarship, perhaps goes back to the association with 'countrey fellowes' found in Puttenham and in the pastorals of Spenser and Drayton.

Trajanus Redivivus: Another look at Trajan in *Piers Plowman*

PAMELA GRADON

THE figure of Trajan in *Piers Plowman* is one of the more puzzling personages in that puzzling poem. The purpose of this paper is to look again at this famous pagan as he appears in the B-text and to consider some of the ideas which he may embody.[1] Some preliminary indication of what seem to me the most important areas of discussion may be useful. Omitting for the moment the material in the speech which Skeat assigns to Loyalty, the relevant material in Passûs XI and XII of the B-text is as follows. The sequence opens with Scripture's claim that no sin can frustrate the healing power of mercy for those who are humble. Her speech is interrupted by Trajan 'broken out of helle'. Gregory, he says, bears witness that he was dead and damned as an infidel. Learned men know that 'al þe clergie vnder crist' could not snatch him from hell but only 'loue and leautee and my laweful domes'. Gregory perceived his good works and desired that he should be saved:

[1] For discussion of Langland see most notably R. W. Chambers, *Man's Unconquerable Mind* (London 1939), 136–48; T. P. Dunning, 'Langland and the Salvation of the Heathen', *MÆ* xii (1943), 45–54; George Russell, 'The Salvation of the Heathen: The Exploration of a Theme in *Piers Plowman*', *JWCI* xxix (1966), 101–16; for general discussion of the legend of Trajan see G. Paris, *La légende de Trajan*, Bibl. de l'école des hautes études, 35 (1878), 261–98; Arturo Graf, *Roma nella memoria e nelle immaginazioni del medio evo* (Turin, 1883), ii. 1–45; G. Boni, 'Leggende', *Nuova Antologia di Lettere, Scienze ed Arti*, cxxvi (1906), 1–39; J. R. Hulbert, 'The Sources of St. Erkenwald and the Trental of Gregory', *MP* xvi (1919), 485–93; L. A. Hibbard, 'Erkenbald the Belgian: A Study in Medieval Exempla of Justice', *MP* xvii (1920), 669–78.

Wiþouten bede biddyng his boone was vnderfongen
And I saued as ye may see, wiþouten syngynge of masses,
By loue and by lernyng of my lyuynge in truþe;
Brouȝte me fro bitter peyne þer no biddyng myȝte, (B XI. 150–3)[2]

The second passage referring directly to Trajan occurs in Passus XII. Imaginatif, in discussing the case of the penitent thief, compares his case to that of Trajan, who

tile noȝt depe in helle
That oure lord ne hadde hym lyȝtly out . . . (B XII. 210–11)

The third important passage relating to Trajan occurs at the end of this Passus. The Dreamer poses the question of the salvation of the infidel. Imaginatif claims that '*saluabitur vix iustus in die judicij—Ergo saluabitur.*' Trajan was a true knight but an infidel; nevertheless, he is saved and his soul in heaven; for there are three kinds of baptism, of font, of blood and of fire:

Ac truþe þat trespased neuere ne trauersed ayeins his lawe,
But lyueþ as his lawe techeþ and leueþ þer be no bettre,
And if þer were he wolde amende, and in swich wille deieþ—
Ne wolde neuere trewe god but trewe truþe were allowed.
(B XII. 287–90)

The significance of these details can perhaps be better understood if we look first briefly at the Trajan legend and the problems which it raised for theologians. For it is plain that the concept of suffrages for the damned which the legend implies was theologically problematic, and indeed the story of Gregory's punishment for praying for one of the damned testifies to the fundamental nature of the problem. Clearly it is impossible to review all the relevant material here. Three disparate examples will serve to illustrate a range of conventional (as distinct from academic or speculative) opinion. The first is from the Commentary of the Anonymous of Florence on Paradiso XX of Dante's *Divine Comedy*: 'Or potrebbe si dubitare qui, se la orazione fatta divota et umilemente da persona degna, potrebbe ajutare così gli dannati; . . . si considera da parte del dannato, dico che

[2] All references are to the edition of Kane–Donaldson.

no; imperciò che ... la volontà degli dannati è immutabile, come prova Tommaso nel iiij del suo Contra Gentiles q. 92; sì che mai non sono dispositi a bene nè a grazia neuna ...' He goes on, however, to admit that the absolute will of God could save the damned.[3] Our second witness is no less an authority than Augustine, in a passage from the *Enchiridion* which is quoted, for example, by William of Auxerre and is the basis of Wyclif's discussion of the problem in the *De Ecclesia*. 'Neque negandum est', he writes, 'defunctorum animas pietate suorum viventium relevari, cum pro illis sacrificium Mediatoris offertur, vel eleemosynae in Ecclesia fiunt. Sed eis haec prosunt, qui cum viverent, ut haec sibi postea possint prodesse, meruerunt.' Augustine then goes on to explain that such offerings for the dead may be valid or invalid according to the spiritual circumstances of those for whom it is offered. Thus, such suffrages are efficacious for the very good and the not very evil, 'pro valde malis etiamsi nulla sunt adjumenta mortuorum, qualescumque vivorum consolationes sunt. Quibus autem prosunt, aut ad hoc prosunt, ut sit plena remissio, aut certe ut tolerabilior fiat ipsa damnatio.'[4] I think it may be assumed that the damnation of which Augustine speaks would include the infidel such as Trajan. Our third witness is a gloss from Canon Law: 'Bonifacius Archiepiscopus quaesivit a Gregorio si liceat specialiter pro defunctis celebrare diuina, et oblationes offerre. Et respondet, quod pro catholicis licet; pro impiis autem specialiter hoc fieri non licet'; this is a gloss to the words: 'congruit ut sacerdos pro mortuis Catholicis memoriam faciat, et intercedat; non tamen pro impiis (quamvis Christiani fuerint) tale quid agere licebit.'[5] The views put forward by our three random witnesses are supported not only by the legend of Gregory's punishment to which we have already

[3] The Anonymous of Florence, *Commento alla Divina Commedia*, ed. P. Fanfani (Bologna, 1866), iii. 366–7.

[4] *Enchiridion*, cap. cx: *PL* 40. 283–4.

[5] *Decretum*, pt. II, c. XIII, q. ii, cap. xxi: *Corpus Iuris Canonici* (Lyons, 1624), i. 1039. Cf. Janet Coleman, *English Literature in History* (London, 1981), 249–52.

referred, but also by the various devices adopted to explain the salvation of Trajan. One view, suggested possibly by the passage from Augustine, was that, while Trajan remained in hell, his pains were mitigated. Such a view might also have been suggested by an ambiguous phrase used by John the Deacon which claimed that Trajan's soul was liberated by Gregory's prayer *ab inferni cruciatibus*;[6] a similar phrase is used by writers such as Landino,[7] the exemplum in BL MS Add. 33956,[8] and by Peraldus.[9] The author of the Annals of Magdeburg writes: 'non affirmamus ei plenam salvationem, sed accepisse per lacrimas Gregorii penam mitiorem.'[10] John of Salisbury also knows this version of the story.[11] The theologians too sometimes suggest that the effect of Gregory's prayer was merely the mitigation of the pains of hell. Thus, William of Auxerre, after discussing the problem of suffrages for the damned, in which he follows the Lombard,[12] reaches the following conclusion: 'Dicimus sine preiudicio melioris sententie quod illa que dicit quod suffragia non prosunt damnatis probabilior est ...'; and he refers to Trajan 'quem beatus Gregorius eripuit de faucibus inferni; ergo si ad preces unius sancti liberatus est totaliter aliquis a poenis inferni, multo fortius ad preces multorum sanctorum, immo ad preces totius ecclesie, liberatus erit quis de inferno a parte pene sue ...'[13] On the other hand, Aquinas seems to doubt whether a pagan (and a pagan was potentially damned) could be so relieved. Thus he writes: 'Dicendum quod in hoc omnes consentiunt quod damnatis post iudicij pena per suffragia ecclesiae nunc facta non minuetur, nec iterum infidelibus ante diem iudicij.' St.

[6] John the Deacon, *Vita S. Gregorii Pape*, *ASS*, xii Martii: Antwerp, 1668, p. 155[a].

[7] Christophoro Landino, *Comento sopra la Comedia di Dante* (Venice, 1497), p. clxiiii.

[8] BL MS Add. 33956, f. 35; cf. J.-Th. Welter, *L'exemplum dans la littérature religieuse et didactique du moyen âge* (Paris and Toulouse, 1927), 265–9.

[9] Peraldus, *Summae Virtutum ac Vitiorum* (Paris, 1668), p. 38[b].

[10] *Annales Magdeburgenses*, *MGH Script*. t. xvi. 112.

[11] *Policraticus*, v. viii: ed. C. C. I. Webb (Oxford, 1909), i. 317.

[12] *Lib. IV Sent.*, IV, d. XLV, c. 2.

[13] *Summa Aurea in IV Sent.* (Paris, 1500), ff. ccciv[va], ccciv[a].

Thomas then goes on to say that opinions differ as to the fate of the faithful damned before the day of judgement. Some say that prayers may diminish the pains of hell, some that the pains cannot be totally removed, and some that prayers merely give patience to endure. He then formulates for Trajan's case a different theory, well known from Dante, namely that he was brought back to life: 'Ad secundum dicendum quod de Trajano potest dici quod fit reuocatus ad uitam, et suscepta gratia ueniam consecutus cum et alii infideles resuscitati legantur. Non enim longitudo temporis preiudicat diuine potentie. Vel dicendum secundum quosdam quod poena fuit suspensa usque ad diem iudicij, nec tamen hoc est ad consequentiam pertrahendum, quia priuilegia paucorum non faciunt legem communem.'[14] A similar view is discussed by William of Auxerre[15] and by Durandus, who writes: 'Trajanus fuit vitae miraculosae restitutus, et tunc remissionem peccatorum consecutus est, nec prius erat sententia finali damnatus, sed conditionaliter; vel dicendum quod illud fuit singulare priuilegium diuinae gratiae.'[16] Wyclif also refers to this view but prefers to think that Trajan was rather illuminated by faith in Christ before his death and that he waited in hell for purgation and the prayer of Gregory.[17] On the other hand, some argued that Trajan was not in hell but in limbo. Such a view is referred to by Alexander of Hales: 'Sed quid de Trajano imperatore, pro quo oravit Gregorius ... Et si dicatur quod non des cendit nisi ad limbum, non ad inferius infernum, contrarium in Psalmo: *Eruisti animam meam ex inferno inferiori*'[18] And finally,

[14] *In IV Sent.*, IV, d. XLV, a. iii: Venice, 1593, xvii, pt. 3, f. 144[va]. Cf. *De Veritate*, q. VI, a. vi: *Opera Omnia* (Rome, 1975), xxii. 1 (2), p. 195; *In IV Sent.*, I, d. XLIII, q. ii, a. ii: ed. R. P. Mandonnet (Paris, 1929), i. 1012.

[15] *Summa Aurea*, f. ccciv[b].

[16] *In IV Sent.*, d. XLV, q. ii.

[17] Wyclif, *De Ecclesia*, cap. XXII: ed. J. Loserth (London, 1886), 517–48.

[18] *In IV Sent.*, III, d. XXII. 13: Bibliotheca franciscana scholastica medii aevi, 14 (Florence, 1954), 256. Cf. Bridget of Sweden, *Revelations*, IV. 13 (Nuremberg, 1521), sig. i5: 'Quicumque enim offert pro anima alterius unum Pater Noster acceptius est Deo pondere magno auri. Sicut patuit in illo bono Gregorio, qui oratione sua etiam infidelem Caesarem eleuauit ad altiorem gradum.'

some found a way round the difficulty by supposing, as St. Thomas implies, that the salvation of Trajan was a special privilege from which no general inferences should be drawn. Durandus refers to this view[19] and so does William of Auxerre; 'priuilegia paucorum non faciunt legem communem,'[20] he writes, and the same view can be found in Bonaventura: 'Verumtamen littera videtur loqui de tempore post mortem, in quo non solum difficile, sed etiam impossibile est, salvari decedentem in peccato; non quia hoc non possit divina potentia, sed iuste et rationabiliter oppositum decrevit divina iusticia; et si alicui unquam post mortem dedit gratiam, intelligendum est, quod ille non erat damnatus per sententiam, sicut legitur de Traiano. Aliqui etiam dicere voluerunt, quod hoc privilegium speciale fuit, ut Dominus ostenderet, quantum Sanctos suos diligeret.'[21]

It seems clear that Langland does not avail himself of any of these solutions to the problem of Trajan's salvation. His Trajan is not specifically in limbo but merely 'broken out of helle'; nor is there any evidence that his pain was mitigated; nor, though we are here on more difficult ground, does it seem that Langland thought that Trajan was brought back to life to receive baptism and infused faith. Dunning argued (and George Russell agrees with him) that Trajan was saved by the baptism of desire, *baptisma flaminis*. In the words of Imaginatif:

Troianus was a trewe knyght and took neuere cristendom
And he is saaf, seiþ þe book, and his soule in heuene.
Ac þer is fullynge of Font and fullynge in blood shedyng
And þoruȝ fir is fullyng, and þat is ferme bileue;
Aduenit ignis diuinus non comburens set illuminans. (B XII 283–7)

At first sight it does indeed appear that Trajan is in heaven as the result of one of these three baptisms, presumably, as Dunning suggests, the baptism of desire. But this is not without difficulty in regard to Trajan; for the baptism of desire appears often to require a desire for baptism. Thus Augustine writes: 'Invenio

[19] Loc. cit. [20] *Summa Aurea*, f. ccciv[a].
[21] *In IV Sent.*, IV, d. xx, Du. III: *Opera* (Florence, 1889), iv. 528.

non tantum passionem pro nomine Christi id quod ex Baptismo deerat posse supplere, sed etiam fidem conversionemque cordis, si forte ad celebrandum mysterium baptismi in angustiis temporum succurri non potest.'[22] Bernard (in a passage quoted by Dunning in pursuit of another argument) testifies to the same opinion: 'Sic sola fides et mentis ad Deum conversio, sine effusione sanguinis et sine perfusione aquae, salutem sine dubio operatur volenti, sed non valenti, prohibente articulo, baptizari.'[23] There is no evidence that Langland's Trajan desired baptism, nor that he could not have had it, had he so desired.[24] He did, after all, live in a Christian era; nor have I found any version of the Trajan legend which links him with the baptism of desire. It may be argued, however, that the reference is to a rather different definition of the baptism of desire, as put forward by Aquinas; namely, the baptism of repentance depending on belief in, and love of, God and repentance for sins.[25] This, however, does not seem to help. Far from repenting for his sins, Trajan proclaims in no uncertain terms his own merits; whether he believes in and loves God is less clear and depends to some extent upon our interpretation of the speech assigned by Skeat to Loyalty; to this we shall return, but it must be conceded that Trajan, as presented by Langland, seems singularly ill fitted for the Baptism of Repentance. I would, therefore, suggest that the conclusion that Trajan was saved by the baptism of fire is not without difficulty.

But if the final discourse of Imaginatif is less conclusive than might at first sight appear, is there any clue in the association of Trajan with the penitent thief which also appears in this section

[22] *De Baptismo*, IV. 22: *PL* 43. 173; cf. J. Corblet, *Histoire du sacrement de baptême* (Paris, 1881–2), i. 24–5, 151–6.

[23] Epistola LXXVII: *Opera*, edd. J. Leclercq and H. Rochais (Rome, 1974), vii. 191.

[24] On the contrary, Trajan was known by some authorities as a persecutor of the Christians; cf. Pliny, *Epistulae*, ed. R. A. B. Mynors (Oxford, 1963), X. xcvi, xcvii, pp. 338–40; Orosius, *Adversum Paganos*, ed. C. Zangemeister (Leipzig, 1889), pp. 252–3.

[25] Quoted by Dunning, op. cit., p. 52.

of the poem? Is there more to the association than their positions in hell and heaven? According to Augustine, in a passage we have already cited, the penitent thief was saved without baptism because, in the words of St. Paul, 'corde creditur ad justiciam, ore autem confessio fit ad salutem.'[26] Similar views are expressed by the *Catena Aurea*, which quotes Gregory's *Moralia* as claiming that the penitent thief had faith, hope, and charity;[27] while Bonaventura, in his Commentary on Luke, writes: 'in latrone hoc fuit *veritas fidei* et *confessio veritatis*, reprobando malum, approbando bonum et asserendo verum; fuit *etiam supplicatio orationis* ... Christus miram ostendit misericordiam ... quia poenitentiam latronis, quantumque seram, non refutavit.' In support of this view Bonaventura quotes the *Glossa Ordinaria*: 'Unde Glossa *Magna gratia in hoc latrone eminet; nullum membrum a supplicio habet praeter cor et linguam; totum, quod liberum habet, offert, credit corde, confitetur ore.*[28] Now it would be tempting to think that Langland saw Trajan saved by such an act of faith. George Russell has suggested that in Passus xv of *Piers Plowman* we have a reference to the theory of *clara visio* as propounded by Uthred of Boldon:[29] 'Saracenus, Judaeus et Paganus ... habebit claram visionem Dei ante mortem suam; qua visione manente habebit electionem liberam convertendi se ad Deum .... et si tunc eligerit converti ad Deum salvabitur ...'[30] Yet while Langland does twice present the penitent thief as making confession to Christ he does not seem to avail himself of the formula *credit corde*. This would seem to be in keeping with George Russell's observation that Langland's treatment of the theme of faith in the Trojan episode is sporadic and unclear and that only when we come to the discourse of Anima is the importance of faith in relation to salvation spelled out. We shall

[26] *De Baptismo*, loc. cit.; but, as Corblet point out, he later suggested that the penitent thief might have been baptized in prison.

[27] *Catena Aurea*, ed. P. A. Guarienti (Turin, 1953), ii. 305.

[28] Bonaventura, ed. cit., vii. 580.

[29] Russell, op. cit., pp. 112–15.

[30] M. D. Knowles, 'The Censured Opinions of Uthred of Boldon', *PBA* xxxvii (1951), 334. I here give Wilkins's longer version. See Knowles, p. 334.

return later to this passage, but I would suggest in the meantime that, while one should not perhaps press Langland's somewhat diffuse wording too far, there would seem to be little indication that he is claiming an act of faith as instrumental in the salvation of Trajan or the penitent thief.

I think, however, it must be conceded that there is one point which, as several critics have noticed, Langland emphasizes in regard to Trajan's snatching from hell. He seems to claim that he attained salvation, in the jargon of the theologians, *ex puris naturalibus*, a clearly Pelagian position. Since this is the one point that is clearly and unambiguously made, it might be useful to follow up this clue and see where it leads us. There are, in a sense, two aspects of this problem in regard to the pagan Trajan. On the one hand the question of whether the good works of a pagan have merit and, on the other, the more general question of whether even the Christian can attain merit without the grace of God. In regard to the first question we may note that, in the opinion of Augustine, the good works of infidels are of no value for salvation. For to proclaim an act good one must have regard not only to its object but to its purpose, and the actions of pagan heroes are spoilt by evil purpose; namely, the desire for glory.[31] Works which are good must be works which lead to salvation, and thus the ethical works of virtue, springing from the natural virtues, such as the infidel might be supposed to attain to, are defective. Such works can be attributed merely to free will and not to the grace of God. This gulf established by Augustine between natural and theological virtue (not without its relevance to Chaucer's *Troilus and Criseyde*) continued to exercise the minds of theologians, as can be demonstrated, for example, by Ockham's discussion of the problem in the thirteenth century.[32]

[31] *De Spiritu et Littera*, caps XXVI–VIII: *PL*, 44. 226–31; *Contra Julianum*, Bk. IV: *PL* 44. esp. 715–52. Cf. H. A. Oberman, '*Facientibus quod in se est Deus non denegat gratiam*: Robert Holcot, U.P. and the beginnings of Luther's theology', *Harvard Theological Review*, lv (1962), 317–42.

[32] Gordon Leff, *William of Ockham* (Manchester, 1975), 492; for a similar discussion in Thomas Buckingham see J. A. Robson, *Wyclif and the Oxford Schools* (Cambridge, 1961), p. 67 and n. 2.

On the other hand, Pelagians claimed that man *was* capable of deserving grace. Thus an act of the will, *initium fidei*, depending on natural virtue, preceded the reception of grace. Thus the Pelagian view emphasized the justice of God and argued that men received the reward of their merits. It is significant that Jerome's *Dialogus adversus Pelagianos* opens with the question *Num possit homo sine peccato, si velit, esse.*[33] The Sentences of Peter Lombard summarize the matter neatly: 'Sine (gratia) credant [the Pelagians] hominem posse facere omnia divina mandata ... caritatem autem negant divinitus dari, qua pie vivitur: ut scilicet sit donum Dei *scientia* quae sine caritate *inflat*; et non sit donum Dei ipsa *caritas*, quae ut scientia non inflet *aedificat*.'[34] Even if the attention of the Lombard were not sufficient testimony to an interest in these views in the later Middle Ages, other evidence would not be lacking. Not only was Bradwardine's *De Causa Dei* well known in the fourteenth century but, as is clear from Bradwardine's discussion, earlier Pelagian or semi-Pelagian works were known to the later Middle Ages. Thus, for example, Pelagius' Commentary on the Pauline Epistles appears in manuscripts of this period[35] and the *De Vita Christiana* of Fastidius,[36] attributed for a while to Augustine, was for this reason available, as well as pseudo-Jerome's *Letter to Demetriades*,[37] the authenticity of which is discussed by Bradwardine.[38] Whether the *Tractatus de Diuitiis* was available is

[33] *Dialogus adversus Pelagianos*: *PL* 23. 497.

[34] *Lib. IV Sent.*, II, d. XXVIII, c. 1.

[35] *Pelagius's Expositions of Thirteen Epistles of St. Paul*, ed. A. Souter, Texts and Studies, 9 (Cambridge, 1922–6). Ascribed manuscripts appear, for example, in St. John's College, Cambridge, MS G 15 (xii–xiii s.) from St. Albans; Corpus Christi Coll. Cambridge, MS 48 (l. xii s.); TCD MS A 2.2 (xii–xiii s.) which in the fifteenth century belonged to West Dereham in Norfolk; Eton College MS 26 (xii–xiii s.). Cf. Souter, i. 344; N. R. Ker, *Medieval Manuscripts in British Libraries*, (Oxford, 1977), 653–6. For the works of Pelagius, see G. de Plinval, *Pelage: ses écrits, sa vie et sa réforme*, (Lausanne, 1943).

[36] *De Vita Christiana*: *PL* 40. 1031–46.

[37] Epistola 1: *PL* 30. 15–45.

[38] Bradwardine, *De Causa Dei*, I. 35 (London, 1618, p. 312).

unclear.[39] Moreover, in addition to the inevitable discussion by theologians such as Ockham of the central problems raised by Pelagianism, such as free will and grace, we know also that the followers of Ockham, such as Adam Wodeham, Thomas Buckingham, Holcot, and others, were also interested by the issues associated with Pelagian thought.[40] These issues were known too from Pelagius' adversaries, Augustine and Prosper of Aquitaine, *Liber contra Collatorem*,[41] a rebuttal of Cassian, and Jerome's *Dialogus adversus Pelagianos*.[42] If further testimony were needed on might quote Uthred of Boldon's seventeenth proposition (which he later retracted): 'Quod quis potest mereri ex puris naturalibus, ita quod nichil requiritur a parte merentis preter naturalia ad eliciendum actum meritorium.'[43] If in what follows I seem largely to have ignored the works of the *moderni* in favour of earlier sources it is because I see no evidence in the material we are discussing of the intellectual subtleties and the elaborate escape routes, such as the *potentia absoluta* and *potentia ordinata* of God, provided by these writers. This is not, of course, to deny that they are important witnesses to the vitality of these issues at this period. Assuming then that Trajan's claim that he is saved for his merits (his clemency and his justice, those kingly virtues for which he was famed throughout the Middle Ages) suggests that he stands as proponent of the Pelagian argument, albeit in a fairly simplistic form, would such an assumption throw any light on other obscure elements in the Trajan sequence in *Piers Plowman*? I would suggest that in a number of cases it might. In the first place we may ask whether Trajan's explicit rejection of prayers and masses (the latter presumably a

[39] Ed. C. P. Caspari, *Briefe, Abhandlungen u. Predigten* (Christiana, 1890), 25–67.

[40] See William J. Courtenay, *Adam Wodeham: An Introduction to his Life and Writings* (Leiden, 1978), 116–33; cf. G. Leff, *Bradwardine and the Pelagians* (Cambridge, 1957); H. A. Oberman, *Archbishop Thomas Bradwardine: A fourteenth-century Augustinian* (Utrecht, 1958); Robson, op. cit.

[41] *PL* 51. 214–76.

[42] *PL* 23. 495–590.

[43] M. D. Knowles, op. cit., p. 338.

reference to the Trental of St. Gregory) can be so explained.[44] The emphasis is curious in that it seems gratuitous in the context and indeed necessitates an evasive treatment of the received legend. It is true that some versions of the legend may have been thought to suggest that Gregory merely wept at the thought of Trajan's merits and of his damnation,[45] but this seems an insufficient reason for emphatically rejecting the role of prayer and masses in Trajan's salvation. If, however, Langland was concerned to point out that Trajan was saved by his own merits, such a point is relevant. And indeed it is possible that a clue may be found in the Lombard: the Pelagians, he claims, 'destruunt etiam orationes quas facit Ecclesia, sive pro infidelibus et doctrinae Dei resistentibus, ut convertantur ad Deum; sive pro fidelibus, ut augeatur eis fides, et perseverent in ea.'[46] Here the Lombard is clearly talking, not about prayers for the dead, but about prayers which, on an orthodox view, were a necessary means of grace for the living. On the Pelagian view these were unnecessary, since man himself was capable of willing the first step towards faith, the *initium fidei* which depended on an act of the will, depending in turn on natural virtue.[47] This is not, of course, to claim that for the orthodox, *Dowel*, good works, are not necessary; rather the problem is one of the human will.

[44] This calls to mind the 'false signes' of one of the Wycliffite sermons Cf. *Select English Works of John Wyclif*, ed. T. Arnold (Oxford, 1869–71), i. 212/31; cf. also ii. 213/9–15; iii. 208/3–4, 336/35–337/5; *The English Works of Wyclif*, ed. F. D. Matthew, EETS 74 (1880), 177/1–12; Anne Hudson, *English Wycliffite Writings* (Cambridge, 1978), 3/73–92. But *The Twelve Conclusions* date from 1395 and dating of the other texts is uncertain, although they were probably written in the eighties or nineties. Their relevance to Langland is thus uncertain. As for Wyclif himself, his reference to the Trajan story in the *De Ecclesia* is as conventional as his condemnation of the modern Pelagians is astringent. Cf. Robson, op. cit., p. 211.

[45] Cf. Vincent of Beauvais, *Speculum Historiale*, x. lxviii: Venice, 1591, 132[va]. For some discussion cf. J. S. Wittig, '*Piers Plowman* B. Passus IX–XII: Elements in the Design of the Inward Journey', *Traditio*, xxviii (1972), 249–55.

[46] *Lib. IV Sent.*, II, d. XXVIII, c 1. Cf. D. M. Murtaugh, *Piers Plowman and the Image of God* (Gainesville, 1978), 103.

[47] See A. Vacant and E. Mangenot, *Dictionnaire de théologie catholique* (Paris, 1921), s.v. *Infidèles*.

While Augustine believed that the postlapsarian human will was incapable of merit without the grace of God,[48] Pelagius and his followers, he says, claimed 'secundum aliqua merita humana dari gratiam Dei',[49] or, in the words of Isidore of Seville, 'sufficere voluntatem ad implenda jussa divina'.[50] On this assumption not only do prayers of the kind referred to by Peter Lombard become unnecessary for salvation, but it might also be inferred that the prayers by which Gregory gained salvation for Trajan detracted in some measure from the pure justice of God's dealings with him. Trajan's rejection of prayers and masses may thus have been intended as an indication of the Pelagian standpoint which he represents in the poem.

In the matter of the penitent thief two points should be noted about the presentation of the story in B XII. 192–213. In the first place, unless we assume that the introduction of the penitent thief is due to random association with the thief who saved his life by knowledge of the neck-verse, we must assume that he is a further exemplar of *clergy*. He recognized Christ as redeemer, repented, and asked for grace. Whether this grace is to be understood as theological grace or merely as 'mercy' is not clear. His salvation is thus in a sense presented as initiated by himself. In the second place, he is presented somewhat unsympathetically as only occupying a lowly place in paradise.

For he þat is ones a þef is eueremoore in daunger,
And as lawe likeþ to lyue or to deye:
De peccato propiciato noli esse sine metu.
And for to seruen a Seint and swich a þef togideres,
It were neiþer reson ne riȝt to rewarde boþe yliche.
And riȝt as Troianus þe trewe knyȝt tilde noȝt depe in helle
That oure lord ne hadde hym liȝtly out, so leue I by þe þef in
heuene.
For he is in þe loweste of heuene, if oure bileue be trewe,
And wel losely he lolleþ þere by þe lawe of holy chirche:
Quia reddit vnicuique iuxta opera sua. (B XII. 206–13)

[48] *Contra Julianum*, Bk. IV. Cf. E. Portalié, *A Guide to the Thought of Saint Augustine* (London, 1960), 192–204.

[49] Epistola CCXV: *PL* 33. 971.

[50] *VIII Etymol.*, V. 63: *PL* 82. 304.

Now, while it is true that the words *Hodie mecum eris in paradiso* of the gospel account are a common *locus* for comment, I have found no exact parallel to Langland's exposition of this theme. The passage is indeed unclear but the basis of the comparison in ll. 210–11 appears to be that, as Trajan was in the depths of hell, whence God rescued him, so the penitent thief, also rescued from damnation, is in a lowly position in heaven. It would seem that the emphasis in the passage, however, is on the idea that the penitent thief is rewarded according to his deserts. While it is, of course, true that the concept of diversity of heavenly rewards is by no means peculiar to Langland, the grudging tone of Langland's remarks about the penitent thief in this passage suggests that he feels the story to be out of tune with his presentation of *Dowel* or reward for merit. Particularly odd is his use of the text from Ecclesiasticus (5:5), 'De peccato propiciato noli esse sine metu.' That the living should be concerned as to the sufficiency of their penitence is understandable; that the penitent thief should be so is strange. The point that Langland emphasizes is that the thief's demerit remains with him even in heaven. Moreover, Langland's treatment of the story here seem out of line with the usual treatment of the story. There is, however, another way of looking at this tale. In Prosper of Aquitaine we find the story discussed within the context of a rebuttal of the heterodox views of Cassian, a rebuttal which Bradwardine cites as anti-Pelagian.[51] In pursuit of his argument Prosper quotes a passage from the *Collations* of Cassian: 'Si enim dixerimus nostrum esse bonae principium voluntatis, quid fuit in persecutore Paulo? quid in publicano Matthaeo? quorum unus cruori ac suppliciis innocentium, alius violentiis ac rapinis publicis incubans, attrahitur ad salutem. Sin vero gratia Dei semper inspirari bonae voluntatis principia dixerimus: quid de Zacchaei fide? quid de illius in cruce latronis pietate dicimus qui desiderio suo vim quamdam regnis coelestibus inferentes, specialia vocationis monita praevenerunt?'[52] In this passage Cas-

[51] *De Causa Dei*, I. 35: p. 313.

[52] *Liber contra Collatorem*, VII: *PL* 51. 230.

sian is citing examples in some of which men might seem to have initiated their own salvation and in some of which, on the other hand, salvation seems to have come, not from human merits, but from the grace of God. And it will be noted that the penitent thief, with Zachaeus, belongs to the former category. In other words, the story of the penitent thief is being used as a proof text in the argument as to whether man can initiate his own salvation. Prosper is, of course, a proponent of the orthodox view, concerned to show that man could not initiate his own salvation, and he argues that the penitent thief manifested the work of the Holy Spirit in his repentance. But the important point for our argument is that the penitent thief is seen as relevant to the Pelagian argument. Like Trajan, he could be thought to argue man's ability to take the first step towards salvation.

More importantly, the Pelagian argument seem to throw some light on the parting words of Imaginatif to the Dreamer: '... *saluabitur vix iustus ...—Ergo saluabitur.*' A common interpretation of this text from 1 Peter 4:18 is that only by great tribulation shall a good man be saved. Thus Hugh of St. Cher declares in his comment on the passage that the just shall be saved 'per multos labores et cum magno certamine'.[53] Lyra quotes Acts 24 in elucidating this passage, 'quia per multas tribulationes oportet eum ingredi regnum caelorum,'[54] and Wyclif in his *Postilla* repeats the same view.[55] Even the just man cannot be justified in God's sight except by great tribulation and suffering. The same tenor can be observed in comment on the similar passage in Proverbs 11:31, 'Si iustus in terra recipit, quanto magis impius et peccator.' Hugh of St. Cher comments that the implications of the passage are that if even the martyrs suffer how much more the wicked;[56] or, as Lyra says, 'Si iustus in terra recipit *a Deo flagella sicut patet de sancto Iob*, quanto magis impius et pecca-

[53] *Postilla* (Paris, 1530–45), VI, f. cccvi^{b}.
[54] *Glossa Ordinaria* (Antwerp, 1617), vi. 1340.
[55] *Postilla super totam Bibliam*, MS Bodley 716, f. 152^{v}.
[56] *Postilla*, III, f. xxii^{va}.

tor *flagellabuntur a Deo in futuro*?'[57] The thought is again the same. The good man will suffer in this world. Far from proving that the good man will be saved, the text from 1 Peter emphasizes the great difficulty of salvation and the inadequacy of mere virtue. The point is clearly made in a passage from Augustine cited in the *Glossa Ordinaria*: 'Quaeritis causam quare iustus vix in Dei iudicio saluus esse possit, et quare, nisi quia Dei iustitiam tantam esse certum est, ut interdum quae videntur in hominibus nostro iudicio esse iusta, iudicio Dei inueniuntur iniusta, secundum illud *Homo videt in facie, Deus autem intuetur cor*?'[58] Jerome also interprets *vix* as implying the limitations of human virtue for salvation: 'Certe justus est, qui in die judicii vix salvatur. Salvaretur autem facile, si nihil in se haberet maculae. Ergo justus est in eo, quod floret multis virtutibus, et vix salvatur in eo, quod in quibusdam Dei indiget misericordia.'[59] On the other hand, Imaginatif, by his use of the emphatic *ergo*, seems to be using the text to prove that the just man *will* be saved—and presumably he will be saved because he is righteous. Now it is not merely assumption that the text could be so used. For if we look at the *De Vita Christiana*, a text of Pelagian origin, it is used in just this way. Fastidius is developing the argument that faith alone is insufficient for salvation: 'Sine causa dedit Deus mandata justiciae, si sola sine justiciae opere fides prodest.' The Gospel, he points out, says: '*Si vis vitam habere, serva mandata*: Non dixit, serva tantum fidem ... Nam si Deus peccatorem non punit, ubi est illud propheticum: *Si justus vix salvus erit, peccator et impius ubi parebunt*?'[60] Again it would seem that the words *vix iustus salvus erit* are being used in an argument about the importance of good works, of *Dowel*. The argument seems to run that salvation comes from keeping the

[57] *Glossa Ordinaria*, iii. 1652.

[58] *Glossa Ordinaria*, vi. 1340.

[59] *Dialogus adversus Pelagianos*: *PL* 23. 541.

[60] *De Vita Christiana*: *PL* 40. 1042, 1044. Cf. J. F. McNamara, 'Responses to Ockham's Theology in the Poetry of the "Pearl" poet, Langland and Chaucer' (Diss. Louisiona, 1968), 110.

commandments, which the Pelagians asserted it was within man's power to do. The sinner will be punished without doubt, for he will certainly not keep the commandments when it is difficult even for the just man to do so. The fulfilling of God's law is difficult but it is just this fulfilment which brings salvation. So when Imaginatif claims '*Ergo saluabitur*' he must surely be saying that it is righteousness that saves a man. It is true that within the context of what Imaginatif actually says he *could* have discussed faith and grace. The fact that he does not choose to do so must surely be taken seriously by any sober critic. All too often in Langland critical attention has been focussed on what Langland might have said rather than on what he did say. But, the reader may ask, what of the baptism of fire? I suspect that here Langland may be following a tradition to be found in the *Opus imperfectum* of Pseudo-Chrysostom, a work used elsewhere in *Piers Plowman*, according to which the baptism of fire is the baptism of temptation as suffered by Christ in the wilderness.[61] He is pointing to the hardships which the righteous man must suffer, hardships which indeed Trajan did suffer, according to the legend, when he condemned his own son to death for the murder of the widow's son. The parting words of Imaginatif seem to support this reading of the text:

Troianus was a trewe knyght and took neuere cristendom
And he is saaf, seiþ þe book, and his soule in heuene . . .
Ac truþe þat trespased neuere ne trauersed ayeins his lawe,
But lyueþ as his lawe techeþ and leueþ þer be no bettre, . . .
Ne wolde neuere trewe God but [trewe] truþe were allowed.
And wheiþer it worþ [of truþe] or noȝt, [þe] worþ [of] bileue is
gret,[62]
And an hope hangynge þerinne to have a mede for his truþe.
(B XII. 283–92)

[61] Pseudo-Chrysostom, *Opus Imperfectum in Matthaeum*, Homily v: *PG* 56. 661.

[62] The emendation seems to depend on the assumption that Imaginatif is praising faith; but rather he is praising faith in the value of righteousness, quite a different thing. I would keep Skeat's reading *the bileue is grete of treuth*, and translate: 'faith in righteousness is noble'.

And Imaginatif goes on to quote texts demonstrating his belief in divine mercy and proclaims his faith that:

> 'The glose grauntеþ vpon þat vers a greet mede to truþe.
> And wit and wisdom', quod þat wye, 'was som tyme tresor
> To kepe wiþ a commune: no catel was holde bettre,
> And muche murþe and manhod;' and riȝt wiþ þat he vanysshed.
> (B XII. 294–7)

Here again I would argue that the discussion that is being pursued in the Trajan sequence is an argument as to the importance of *Dowel* and man's capacity to *Dowel* within the scheme of salvation. The question posed is whether man can be saved *ex puris naturalibis* and the answer, with certain reservations to which I shall return, is that he can. Even the virtues of pagans avail for this purpose. It might perhaps be added that there are other areas of the poem which seem to be concerned with the same problem. Most notably the Pardon is a Pelagian document in its implications, proclaiming that man is capable of right action. This view the priest, as a representative of the church, rightly condemns. The Dreamer raises the same question at the beginning of Passus VIII with the text *Sepcies in die cadit iustus*. The friars give a perfectly orthodox reply which involves the concept of mortal and venial sin, a concept which we may note the Pelagians denied, since, on their view, for a single lie or idle word one ceased to be just.[63]

This brings us finally to the speech (B XI. 154–319) which Skeat attributed to Loyalty. I believe the view to be correct that while lines 154–170 are not spoken by Trajan (and to these I shall return), the rest of the speech may be. Yet its themes, love, poverty, and humility, seem at first sight to have little relevance to Trajan; nor is it clear why in the C-text the material should have been largely taken over by Recklessness. It is true, of course, that Trajan stands as an exemplar of Humility in Dante's *Purgatorio* but there seems not much evidence that such a tradition

[63] See Portalié, op. cit., pp. 188–9.

was known to Langland. But there is perhaps another reason why Trajan might have uttered the sentiments here attributed to him. We find in Bradwardine's *De Causa Dei* the following passage: 'Objiciunt autem Pelagiani contra praemissa de Predestinatione et Reprobatione [a topic, the reader will remember, introduced at B XI. 112] conantes ipsas vel omnino destruere, vel saltem ostendere ipsas esse secundum merita personarum ... Quare et Ioachim Abbas de Flore ... assignat duplicem rationem et causam Electionis, Praedestinationis, et misericordiae Dei, quarum prima est aptitudo ad misericordiam, salutem et bonum; secunda, actio ipsa bona.'[64] Thus, as Bradwardine explains, Joachim posits a double predestination for man, due, on the one hand, to man's aptitude for mercy and, on the other, to the good act itself. Basing his argument on the text in Romans 9:15–16, Joachim writes in regard to the first point: 'Ecce habes manifeste cur non volentis neque currentis, sed miserentis sit dei, cum liqueat luce clarius, quod non pro iusticia sua assumatur aliquis a deo, sed pro misericordia, non pro operibus, sed pro humilitate, non pro fortitudine sed pro infirmitate, non pro sapientia sed pro stultitia, non pro nobilitate sed pro ignobilitate ... Igitur electionis causa non iusticia est, sed abjectio, non consolatio mundi, sed afflictio, non quia ista simpliciter placent deo, sed quia pariunt humilitatem, quam solam requirit virtutem deus in angelis et hominibus.'[65] Thus Trajan would seem to be proclaiming a point of view which Bradwardine (though not the modern editor of Joachim) regarded as Pelagian. Trajan's merits were acceptable to God because of his humility and praise of poverty and we may note that according to Pelagius the rich who do not renounce their wealth on baptism are damned.[66] This is a view which Bradwardine urgently combats saying that the rich too can merit salvation while the poor and the beggar may be repro-

[64] *De Causa Dei*, I. 47: p. 436.

[65] *Dialogus de Praescientia Dei et Praedestinatione Electorum*, ed. J. Huck in *Joachim von Floris* (Freiburg im Breisgau, 1938), pp. 282–3. I am grateful to Dr Marjorie Reeves for help in tracking down this text.

[66] See Portalié, op. cit., p. 189; J. D. Mansi, *Sacrorum Conciliorum nova et amplissima Collectio* (Florence, 1960), iv. 311.

bate.[67] Trajan's argument, on the other hand, seems to be that of Joachim; while righteousness (*justicia*, *truthe*)[68] pleases God, it is poverty and humility which make these virtues acceptable, while wealth and the pride which accompanies it make him apt for reprobation. I am not, of course, arguing that the praise of poverty and humility makes the passage Pelagian. Such a claim would be absurd. What I am claiming is that Trajan, having proclaimed his salvation to be due to his merits and not to the prayers or masses of the church, goes on to expound also, as Joachim does, the place of humility and poverty in the scheme of presdestination and reprobation. It may also be noted that the whole Trajan sequence is introduced by the words of Scripture that no sin can frustrate God's mercy if humility follow. The nature and function of mercy is thus the opening chord, as it were, the rich complexities of which are explored in what follows. And it should perhaps be assumed that some of the resonances of the sequence are to be found in the *Adversus Pelagianos* of Jerome, who argues against his Pelagian adversary that 'Tunc ergo justi sumus, quando nos peccatores fatemur, et justicia nostra non est ex proprio merito, sed ex Dei consistit misericordia.'[69] This argument is taken further in Joachim by his insistence, not merely on humility as the channel of God's mercy, but upon actual poverty. Trajan, in fact, if indeed the speech be by him, neatly picks up and redirects the opening words of Scripture just as Imaginatif at the end of Passus XII proclaims his belief in the mercy of God, thus completing the complex interweaving of the themes of merit and mercy initiated by Scripture's citation of the text: '*Misericordia eius super omnia opera eius*.'

There are other passages in the poem which might reflect the late medieval debate on Pelagianism. It may be that the vision of Nature in Passus XII is part of this debate. Augustine tells us

[67] *De Causa Dei*, I. 47: p. 437.

[68] For *leaute* and *treuthe* in the sense of 'righteousness' (*justicia*) cf. *MED*, svv. and J. A. Burrow, *A Reading of Sir Gawain and the Green Knight* (London, 1965), 43.

[69] *Dialogus adversus Pelagianos*: *PL* 23. 505.

that the Pelagians teach that grace is the kind of nature wherein we have been created so that we possess a rational soul; and it is man's rational soul which enables him to obey the commandments and so to merit salvation.[70] There may be a significance too in the introduction of the whole debate with Scripture in Passus x by the Dreamer's question on baptism:

> '*Contra!*' quod I, 'by crist! þat kan I wiþseye,
> And preuen it by þe pistel þat Peter is nempned:
> That is baptized beþ saaf, be he riche or pouere. (B x. 349–51)

Such a provocative view forms a natural introduction to a debate which will involves the question of sacramental grace and works in the scheme of salvation. Clearly these are matters which might merit further investigation. But in conclusion I would draw attention to another aspect of the Trajan sequence in *Piers Plowman*. I have argued that Trajan is a proponent of the view that even pagan man can have merit in the sight of God. But I believe that he is also the proponent of another argument, not a theological but a social one. When the author addresses his audience in lines 154–70 he is not adducing the example of Trajan as a proponent of theological views but as a good ruler:

> Wel ouȝte ye lordes þat lawes kepe þis lesson haue in mynde
> And on Troianus truþe to þenke, and do truþe to þe peple.
> (B xi. 158–9)

In this the poet is in line with writers such as John of Salisbury, who depicts Trajan as the ideal ruler: 'Laudes uero Augusti totus orbis concelebrat, et Titum amorem humani generis suas scilicet delicias iocunda memoria ueneratur. Ego his omnibus Traianum praeferre non dubito, qui in solius virtutis cultu regni constituit maiestatem.'[71] Thus, as so often in Langland, the theological and the social fuse. Trajan is indeed an exemplar of *Dowel*; he is also a model for the rulers of Langland's day. As paintings depicting Trajan often combine the imagery of the good ruler

[70] *De Gratia et Libero Arbitrio*, especially caps. xii, xiii: *PL* 44. 895–7.
[71] *Policraticus*, v. viii: ed. cit., i. 316.

with the figure of Gregory, so Langland has presented us with a figure who translates *Dowel* into practical terms. Trajan is ideally suited to portray the interlocking moral and political concerns which are the theme of Langland's poem.[72]

[72] Janet Coleman's study, *Piers Plowman and the Moderni* (Rome, 1981) came to hand after this article was written.

The Middle English *Mirror* and its Manuscripts

THOMAS G. DUNCAN

SIX manuscripts survive of the Middle English translation of Robert de Gretham's Anglo-Norman *Miroir*.[1]

(1) B. Bodleian Library, MS Holkham misc. 40.[2] Written by five hands,[3] this MS dates from the late fourteenth or early fifteenth century and includes a complete text of the *Mirror*.

(2) C. Corpus Christi College, Cambridge, MS 282.[4] The text here is slightly defective at the beginning owing to the lack of the first and last leaves of the first gathering. The writing, in the same hand throughout, is later fourteenth century.

(3) H. Glasgow University Library, Hunterian MS 250. The hand of this MS belongs to the last quarter of the fourteenth century.[5] The last leaf of the final gathering is lacking and the text breaks off leaving the final sermon incomplete.

(4) Har. British Library, MS Harley 5085.[6] This is a

[1] Dr Anne Hudson kindly informs me that the Introduction to the *Mirror* is also found in CUL MS Ii.6.26.

[2] This MS is fully described in A. C. Paues, *A Fourteenth Century English Biblical Version* (Cambridge, 1904), pp. xiv–xv.

[3] There is a change of hands on f. 15^v not noticed by Miss Paues.

[4] See M. R. James, *Catalogue of the MSS. in Corpus Christi College, Cambridge* (Cambridge, 1912), ii. p. 48.

[5] See T. G. Duncan, 'Notes on the Language of the Hunterian MS of the *Mirror*', *Neuphilologische Mitteilungen*, lxix (1968), 204–8. A brief, rather inaccurate account of this MS appears in John Young and P. Henderson Aitken, *A Catalogue of the Manuscripts in the Library of the Hunterian Museum in the University of Glasgow* (Glasgow, 1908), p. 201.

[6] This MS is only listed, and dated to the fourteenth century, in *A Catalogue of the Harleian MSS. in the British Museum*, iii (London, 1808), p. 244. No detailed description has been published.

fourteenth-century MS in a fairly formal book hand. Although the text breaks off in mid sentence with several lines left blank on the final leaf, this occurs only in the course of material additional to the *Mirror* proper.

(5) P. Magdalene College, Cambridge, MS Pepys 2498.[7] This is another fourteenth-century MS in a single hand throughout. It lacks, at the end, a sermon found in all the other MSS, although the text ends without mechanical defect and, indeed, the final sermon here is followed on p. 212b by the comment:

> Of þe holy omelies now j wil blynne God
> bringe vs to þ*at* blisse þ*er*e ioye is eu*er*e jnne.

Owing to the loss of one leaf (pp. 170–1), the beginning of Tale XVI is missing in P.

(6) R. Rylands Library, Manchester, MS English 109.[8] This MS, in various fifteenth-century hands, has lost many leaves and been extensively damaged. The part containing the *Mirror* is the work of two hands, first one which could be late fourteenth-century[9] and then a smaller, very cursive hand which records the date of writing as 1432 on f. 126. This MS omits the fifth sermon of the *Mirror* but otherwise, though much is now missing, from a list of contents in a fifteenth-century hand on two medieval fly-leaves it appears that it originally contained not only the rest of the *Mirror* in full but also a considerable amount of extra material to some extent paralleled in B and in Har.

[7] See M. R. James, *Bibliotheca Pepysiana, A Descriptive Catalogue of the Library of Samuel Pepys*, part III (1923), 106–10. See also Margery Goates, *The Pepysian Gospel Harmony*, EETS 157 (1922), p. ii (facsimile) and pp. xi–xiv, and A. Zettersten, *The English Text of the Ancrene Riwle*, EETS 274 (1976), pp. ix–xxi, with facsimiles as frontispiece and facing p. 112.

[8] See M. R. James, *Catalogue of the Latin Manuscripts in the John Rylands Library at Manchester*, (Manchester, 1921), i. pp. 305–6; the English number of the MS is wrongly given on p. 305 as 229. A briefer description is found in M. Tyson, *Hand-list of ... English Manuscripts in the John Rylands Library, 1928* (Manchester, 1929), p. 24; Tyson did not notice that his parts (c) and (d) belong to one item, the *Mirror*.

[9] M. R. James mentions this as 'a hand of rather earlier aspect'.

The *Mirror* is a lengthy work; the shortest version, that of P, comprises an introduction and fifty-nine sermons. Its contents and purpose are thus described in the introduction:

> þe godspelles of sonnendays & a parti of þe
> seyntes þat ben in heuen, ich haue drawen hem
> out into englische, first after þe letter, &
> þen þe vnderstondi*ng*' & vndoinge schortliche,
> þat men may wel vnderstonden hem.

The account of the relationships of the six MSS which follows is a pilot study based on the evidence of variant readings in the exemplary tales found in the sermons. These tales—seventeen in all—give a reasonable sample of the *Mirror* in so far as they are spread throughout the work; the first occurs in the sermon for the second Sunday in Advent, and the last in the sermon for the twenty-third Sunday after Trinity. Though only brief extracts from the *Miroir* have appeared in print,[10] the Anglo-Norman texts of all the tales are conveniently found in Miss Marion Y. H. Aitken's study of the *Miroir*,[11] from which the Anglo-Norman quotations given here are taken. For each Middle English quotation a reference is given to the tale in which it occurs as numbered by Miss Aitken. Since only substantial variants germane to the determination of the MS relationships are relevant to the following discussion, other variations among the MSS in spelling, form, and wording are usually left unrecorded in the quotations.

The following stemma (see p. 118) can be demonstrated, with the exception of γ, at which point the evidence collected so far is contradictory.

Whereas numerous variants represent merely changes and errors which have arisen independently within the separate tradition of each MS, a pattern of readings which splits the MSS

[10] The most extensive of which is the highly inadequate edition of eight of the sermons in *Robert de Gretham: Miroir ou les Évangiles des Domnées* ed. Saverio Panunzio (Bari, 1967). See the review article by Linda Marshall and W. Rothwell in *MÆ* xxxix (1970), 313–21.

[11] M. Y. H. Aitken, *Étude sur le Miroir ou les Évangiles des Domnées de Robert de Gretham suivie d'extraits inédits* (Paris, 1922).

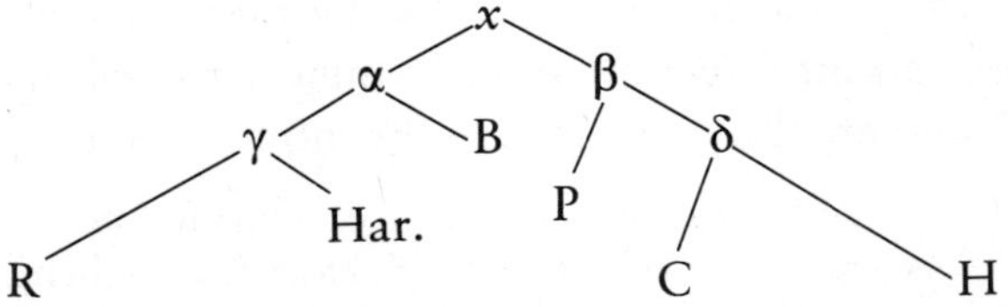

x
α β
γ B P δ
Har.
R C H

three against three—B, R, and Har. against P, C, and H—is fairly frequent. It is often impossible in these cases to be sure which reading is in error since both usually make good enough sense. However, where the English follows the French closely, comparison with the Anglo-Norman text reveals which must in all probability have been the original reading of the English translation.

The following shared errors establish α:

(i) Aitken, I

P, C, H and it nas nouȝth longe after þat god
ne took vengeaunce opon hy*m*

B, R, Har. & it was noȝt long aftur þat god
toke uengawnce oppon hym

Miroir Ne demura pas longement
Que Deus n'en prist le vengement

(Aitken, p. 137, 1015–16)

The negative in the second clause in P, C, and H has been taken over from the idiom of the French. The omission of 'ne' in B, R, and Har. appears to be a shared error, though such a change in favour of normal English syntax might have been arrived at independently.

(ii) Aitken, V

The king of England had a servant good, wise, and strong. In England there could not be found his equal. But one vice he had

P þat non ne miȝth do hym leuen
C þat non ne miȝt leuen him
H þat no man ne miȝt louen him
B þ*a*t no myȝte reuen hym

R þat no*n* myȝt reue hy*m*
Har. þat noman miȝt reuen him
Miroir Mais une vice male aveit,
Ke nuls hom creire nel poeit (Aitken, p. 144, 5090–1)

It seems that the English translator misunderstood the French as meaning 'that no man might believe him' rather than 'that no one could believe it'. The original English mistranslation was the reading at β and continues to C. P retains 'leuen' but alters the wording and the sense to 'do hym leuen'—i.e. 'make him abandon'. H alters 'leuen' to or misreads it as 'louen'. (The letters 'e' and 'o' are easily confusable in full rounded hands such as those found in H and C.) B, R, and Har. in error share the reading 'reue(n)', presumably with the sense 'that no man might take away from him'.

(iii) Aitken, V

P þe king corouned went hym þan þennes
C þe king conred went him þa*n* þe*n*nes
H þe kinge tourned & went þennes
B þe kyng wente hym þan þennes
R þenne þe kyng went forth
Har. þe kinge went hi*m* þennes wepinge
Miroir Li reis Conred dunc s'en partist

(Aitken, p. 147, 5318)

The H reading 'tourned' probably derived from a corruption of the king's name as seen in P and C. (The initial letters, 't' and 'c', are so easily confusable as readily to lead to a misreading.) B, R, and Har. omit the king's name. This may be looked upon as a shared error although the tendency to omit the name in this tale is common throughout the MSS.

(iv) Aitken, XIV

P, C, H whi lesestou so many soules
B, R, Har. why slest þou so many soules
Miroir Tantes almes purquei perdez

(Aitken, p. 171, 16326)

(v) Aitken, XIV

P, C, H	to nempne god in þi mouþe for þi grete folye
B, R, Har.	to nempne god i*n* þi mouþ for þe gret folye
Miroir	De Deu numer pur ta folie

(Aitken, p. 173, 16376)

The following evidence supports β:

(i) Aitken, XI

P, C, H	& held hi*m* þ*er*for a fole & auisard (P auisad)
B, R, Har.	& holden for a fool a musard
Miroir	A fol le tenent e a musard

(Aitken, p. 161, 12540)

'Musard' is recorded from the fourteenth and fifteenth centuries, in some instances in collocation with the word 'fool'.[12] The error 'uisard' in P, C, and H is surprising. It is presumably a form of 'wizard', first recorded for *c.* 1440.[13] The instance here is certainly earlier, towards the end of the fourteenth century at latest.

(ii) Aitken, XIII

P, C, H	þ*a*t he nas per*e* to an angel
B, R, Har.	þat he ne was pere to au*n*gels
Miroir	Ke il as angles per n'esteit

(Aitken, p. 166, 15440)

(iii) Aitken, XIII

P, C, H	as schipp doþe whan it is vnder wiþ outen helpe
B, R	as þe schip doþ whan it is vn tyed wiþ outen helpe
Har.	as þe schipp doþ whan it is vnstered wiþouten help
Miroir	Cum fait la nef desatachée (Aitken, p. 167, 15479)

P, C, and H are in error with the reading 'vnder'. Har. has its own independent alteration to 'vnstered'.

(iv) Aitken, XIII

P, C, H	þat vnneþe ne myȝth helde hym

[12] See *OED*, s.v. *Musard*. [13] See *OED*, s.v. *Wizard*.

B, R, Har.	þat vnneþes he wiþ held hym
Miroir	Ke il a peine se detient

(Aitken, p. 167, 15495)

(v) Aitken, XIII

P, C, H	and opon þe þrid day was he at*ra*uailed
B, R, Har.	& vpon þe þridde day he was so traueyled
Miroir	A tierz jur tant fut traveillé

(Aitken, p. 168, 15507)

(vi) Aitken, XIV

P, C, H	forto chastise ȝou of ȝoure synnes
B, R, Har.	forto chastyse ȝou of ȝoure folye(s)
Miroir	Pur vus chastier de folies

(Aitken, p. 172, 16348)

(vii) Aitken, XIV

P, C, H	do it where þou wilt
B, R, Har.	do it i*n* þi celle
Miroir	En ta celle met tun escleir

(Aitken, p. 173, 16371)

(viii) Aitken, XIV

P, C, H	ne þine honden liften vpp toward god
B, R, Har.	ne þin honden liften vp to ward heuene
Miroir	Ne de tes mains el ciel lever

(Aitken, p. 173, 16377)

(ix) Aitken, XIV

P, C, H	he dude come tofore hym his deciples
B, R, Har.	he dide comen to forn hym alle his disciplis
Miroir	Ses disciples tuz venir fait

(Aitken, p. 173, 16390)

Granted α and β, alternative readings where four MSS agree against two should establish shared error for the latter. In the case of γ the evidence noted so far is inconsistent. The tendency is for R and Har. to agree (presumably in error) against B, P, C, and H. For example:

Aitken, I

B, P, C, H	fot is eu*er* þe lengur þe wors
R, Har.	fote was (euer) þo lenger þe wers
B, P, C, H	his legge
R	þe legge (Har. fote)

Aitken, II

B, P, C, H	of wycked lyf
R, Har.	of yuel lif
B, P, C, H	ac he nold no more
R, Har.	and said þat he wolde no more
B	& a mesel come þer
P	& a mesel com þan þer
C	& a mesel com þer þan
H	& a mesel come þer þan
R	then þer come a mesel
Har.	and þan com a mesel

Aitken, XII

B, P, C, H	& seyde to þe abbot
R, Har.	& spake to þo abbot

On the other hand there is conflicting evidence as, in the first place, where B and Har. agree against R, P, C, and H. For example:

Aitken, XIII

B, Har.	talent for to eten
R, P, C, H	talent to mete

Aitken, XIV

B	and leyd it al vpon an hep
Har.	& bren it al opon an hep
R, P, C, H	& leyde it opon an hepe

Aitken, XIV

B, Har.	& schet þe dore harde
R, P, C, H	& schette þo dore faste

Secondly, support for a special affinity between B and R, though slight, does also arise, as in the following instance:

Aitken, VII

B, R	go & fecch he seyde
Har. P, C, H	go & seche he saide

By contrast, the weight of evidence for δ is convincing. A significant lacuna occurs in Aitken, XVI:

H, C	to lyue & be nouȝt in doute
R	to life for to make us stedefaste in þo bileue þat we schuld rise fro ded to life & not to be in doute

P, B, and, with slight alterations, Har. all contain the material omitted by mechanical error in H and C. Agreements of C and H against P, B, R, and Har. are fairly frequent. For example:

Aitken, IV

C, H	þe lawe
P, B, R, Har.	her lawȝe

Aitken, XI

C, H	despeplen
P, B, R, Har.	despoilen
C, H	þe corseintes
P, B, R, Har.	þe holy corseintes
C, H	he seide to him
P, B, R, Har.	vnto hym he seide

Aitken, XII

C, H	þat held him longe
P, B, R, Har.	þat longe helde hym

C, H to swich point come als
P, B, R, Har. come vnto swiche a poynt as

C, H schewed
P, B, R, Har. schewed hym

C, H forsake þat
P, B, R, Har. noman forsake þat

Aitken, XIII

C, H þat he bi come negligent
P, B, R, Har. þat he bicom more necligent

C, H he seide psalmes
P, B, R, Har. he seide his psalmes

C, H þe litel harm he fel in a gretter harme
P, B, R, Har. þe litel he fel in a grete harme

Aitken, XIV

C, H sy*n*ned hou
P, B, R, Har. ysynned wiþ me hou

C, H what wiltþou
P, B, R, Har. whare wiltou

C, H repented nouȝt
P, B, R, Har. repented hir nouȝth

C, H telde hit antone
P, B, R, Har. telde it to antoyne

Aitken, XVI

C, H arise to lyue
P, B, R, Har. arise fram deþ to lyue

C, H after seide
P, B, R, Har. after he seide

C, H soule wend fro þe body
P, B, R, Har. soule wende out of þe body

C, H ne bi leue y nouȝt
P, B, R, Har. ne bileue ich riȝth nouȝth

C, H y schal leue agayn
P, B, R, Har. it schal lyuen aȝein

C, H	maistrie is
P, B, R, Har.	maistrie it is

The weakest point in the stemma, then, is γ. Further evidence, arguments for independent rather than shared error, considera-tion of the possibility of contamination—all might lead to a more persuasive conclusion. Thus, in support of γ, the reading quoted linking B and R might convincingly be dismissed. The full sentence as found in P reads:

And þis large broþer bade þat oþer ȝiue hym su*m* bred. & he ansuered þe*r* nys non. goo & seche he seide. & he went jn & fonde þe hucche ful of bred.

That B 'fecch' and R 'fecche' are in error is confirmed by the French 'quere',[14] but it is in no way difficult to see how this mistake could have occurred independently in two MSS: 'f' and the long form of 's' are confusable, often virtually identical, in many hands so that 'seche/secche' could easily have been read by different scribes as 'feche/fecche'—and all the more readily so in view of the similarity of meaning not only in the context but especially in the phrase 'go and . . .', whereby 'go and fetch' could so plausibly have been taken as the required sense. However, the problem of γ is less than urgent, since on other grounds the relative importance of B, R, and Har. for an edition of the *Mirror* is not in doubt. B is not without imperfections: it has suffered something of that linguistic revision which is the common legacy of Middle English copyists and it has its own crop of careless and usually small errors from which none of the *Mirror* MSS is free. Yet R and Har. are of a different order. The version in Har. is partly the product of re-writing, at times remarkably maladroit; sometimes the text runs parallel to that of the other MSS, sometimes it differs considerably. Furthermore, the gospel versions in Har. are different in origin from the translations of the Anglo-Norman text of the *Miroir* in the other MSS. R also presents a markedly corrupt text, though it might more aptly be described as frequently re-worded and re-phrased than as re-

[14] Aitken, p. 151, 5971.

written, a point which may conveniently be illustrated from the R version of the sentence quoted above from P. R reads:

And þe large broþ*er* bad þat oþ*er* ryse & gyf hy*m*. And he grocched agayne & saide. þ*er* is no*n*. þu has wasted alle. Go & fecche þ*a*t oþ*er* saide. And he ȝede inne o scorne. & he fonde þe cofer ful of brede.

Thus, P 'ansuered', 'he', 'went', and 'hucche' are altered in R to 'grocched agayne (& saide)',[15] 'þ*a*t oþer', 'ȝede', and 'cofer'; R omits 'sum bred';[16] R adds 'ryse &', 'þu has wasted alle', and 'o scorne'. In all these points the other MSS essentially agree with P.[17] Moreover R, as already mentioned, is by far the most damaged and incomplete of the English MSS.

In other respects, despite inconsistent and problematic variants, the stemma is well supported by the weight of the evidence as a whole. It may therefore be concluded that an edition of this substantial though hitherto unpublished Middle English text should be based on P or B, the choice depending on evidence from comparison with the Anglo-Norman *Miroir* as to which, on balance, offers the more faithful version of the original English translation. A minimal, though adequate, textual apparatus would normally need to record only substantive variants and only where P and B differed.

[15] As R, B, and Har. also have '& saide' as against P, C, and H, which have only 'ansuered'.

[16] Only P and B have 'sum'. Often the Anglo-Norman reading offers inconclusive testimony *vis-à-vis* the English text. This is a typical instance. Although the Middle English translation is sometimes close even to the point of unidiomatically calquing on the Anglo-Norman, from the French 'Dun li pain' (see n. 17) one could not justify a choice between 'bred' and 'sum bred' as the original reading in the Middle English. Thus, independent error may have arisen in B and P with the addition of 'sum', or at γ (R and Har.) and δ (C and H) by the omission of 'sum'.

[17] The corresponding lines from the *Miroir* are:

E li larges al altre dist:
'Dun li pain', e li respundi:
'N'i ad point, frere', il dit a li:
E la huche pleine i trovat.

(Aitken, p. 151, 5968–72)

A Poem Presented to William Waynflete as Bishop of Winchester

EDWARD WILSON

THE poem printed below, unrecorded in the *Index of Middle English Verse* and its *Supplement*, occurs only in BL Add. MS 60577, ff. 22^{v}–24.[1] The principal scribe, who copied this item, also set down two lines of Latin which may reasonably be taken as scribal autobiography and which state that he was a monk of St. Swithun's Priory, Winchester:

> Omnibus apertum fiat fiat quoque certum
> Sancti cenobij veteris me esse swythuni. (*Front pastedown*)

Other items in the manuscript, and the evidence of the earliest ownership, indicate clearly that its provenance was St. Swithun's Priory, Winchester, and the present poem has two references to Winchester: 'The chyrche of Wynchester (l. 33) ... My lorde of Wynchestre (l. 40).' Addressed to the Bishop of Winchester, the reference to the lily as 'your floure' (l. 61) identifies him as William Waynflete, bishop of Winchester 1447–86.[2] There is nothing in the poem which is inconsonant with the provenance of the manuscript, and the probability is that the author, like the scribe, was a monk of St. Swithun's. The date of

[1] For the full evidence for the provenance, ownership, and date of this manuscript, briefly summarized in this paragraph, see my Introduction to *The Winchester Anthology: a Facsimile of British Library Additional Manuscript 60577 with an Introduction and List of Contents by Edward Wilson and an Account of the Music by Iain Fenlon* (Cambridge, 1981); the poem is no. 74 in the List of Contents (p. 22), and is hitherto unprinted.

[2] On the lilies in Waynflete's arms see W. K. Riland Bedford, *The Blazon of Episcopacy* ... (Oxford, 1897), p. 122, no. 20, and R. Chandler, *The Life of William Waynflete* ... (London, 1811), 30–1.

copying of the bulk of the manuscript can be placed after 1477. The fragment of Earl Rivers's translation of *The Dictes and Sayings of the Philosophers* (ff. 38–44^{v}), a work of which the manuscript presentation copy is dated 24 December 1477 and of which Caxton's first edition is dated in one copy as 18 November 1477, establishes that this part of the manuscript onwards cannot have been begun earlier than the end of 1477; another item in the manuscript bears a colophon dated 1487 (f. 107^{v}). Although, as I have noted elsewhere,[3] there are codicological features, concerning watermarks and letter forms, peculiar to ff. 1–37, in which the Waynflete poem occurs, we need not assume a significantly prior date for the copying of these folios. However, there is a linguistic feature peculiar to ff. 1–37^{v}. After comparing the spellings of this manuscript with those in the archive for the forthcoming *Atlas of the Dialects of Later Middle English*, Mr Michael Benskin has informed me (private communication) that up to f. 37^{v} the English is clearly localizable as East Leicestershire, on the Rutland border; villages in the likely area of origin include Thorpe Satchville, Twyford, Lowesby, Tilton, Withcote, Owston, and Knossington. From f. 38 onwards, however, the scribe abandons most but not all of the distinctive features of his East Midland dialect.[4]

The date of composition of the poem addressed to Waynflete can be established with reasonable certainty as *c.*1451. It relates how, after the death (l. 17) in April 1447 of Waynflete's predecessor, Cardinal Beaufort, the speaker and some companions went overseas (l. 20) and returned 'a foure yere and more' (l. 26) later. It is puzzling, however, that on their return the announcement of Waynflete's election to the see of Winchester seems to be news to them (ll. 32–40 and 42). Waynflete's election had, in

[3] Facsimile edition (n. 1, above), p. 2.

[4] Mr Benskin discusses briefly the language of this manuscript in his article 'A Linguistic Atlas for Late Mediaeval English', *Mediaeval English Studies Newsletter* [Tokyo], iv (July 1981), 5–13, on p. 12. The Winchester manuscript belongs on the western fringe of a complex of manuscripts which includes the Middle English *Rosarium Theologie*; see further the article by Professor McIntosh elsewhere in this volume (pp. 235–44).

fact, gone ahead with remarkable speed. Beaufort died at Wolvesey Palace, Winchester, on 11 April 1447, and the very same day Henry VI, at Windsor Castle, granted a *congé d'élire* with the request that

oure right trusty and welbeloved clerc and concellour' maistre William Waynflete Provost of oure College Royal of oure Lady of Eton [be elected] in all the haste that ye goodly may ... and cause us to have bothe you and the sayd chirch [of Winchester] in the more special favour of oure good grace in tyme to come.[5]

A second royal letter was sent from Windsor on 13 April with instructions to proceed to the election of Waynflete on 15 April and telling the prior and convent not to wait upon

eny lettres under oure grete seel for we have in such wise ordeined that ye shal not nede theym at that tyme but have theym in goodly haast after bering date before.[6]

The electors complied with Henry's request on 15 April; Waynflete was consecrated at Eton on 30 June, and enthroned at Winchester on 19 January 1448. There are no records of any Winchester monks going abroad 'as pylgrims' (l. 20) for the period 1447–51, and their ignorance of Waynflete's election until their return when the news made them 'ryght merye' (l. 42) implies that, if their exile and ignorance are historically autobiographical, they left Winchester within hours (or a day or two at the most) of Beaufort's death. Alternatively, it may be that the exile is a poetic invention, made in order to magnify the sorrow at Beaufort's death and the horror at the 'seduciouse rebellyons' (l. 22) in England: i.e. a way of saying that both the sorrow and the horror were so great that they would reasonably (even if they actually did not) drive one into exile.

[5] J. Greatrex, *The Register of the Common Seal of the Priory of St. Swithun, Winchester 1345–1497*, Hampshire Record Series, 2 (1978), pp. 99–100, no. 314. This must have crossed with the petition for a licence to elect a bishop sent by the prior and convent to the King on 12 April (ibid., p. 99, no. 313). Henry's licence and request that Waynflete be elected were exhibited in the chapter house on 14 April (ibid., p. 100, no. 316).

[6] Ibid., p. 100, no. 315.

The probable date of composition, 1451, is a particularly interesting one in Waynflete's life. First, there seems to have been a move in that year to dispossess Waynflete of his see. In Waynflete's Register is a document dated 7 May 1451, with the marginal title 'Prouocacio domini', which relates how 'In quadam alta camera le peynted Chambre vulgariter nuncupata' in his manorhouse at Southwark, in the presence of a notary public, Thomas Gyan, and of John [Stanbury], bishop of Bangor, and James [Blakedon], bishop of Achory, who were asked to be witnesses, Waynflete appeared

holding in his hands a writing, which he read before them, and in which he alleged that his bishopric was obtained canonically; that he had peaceable possession of it; that his reputation was without blemish [*fui et sum integri status, bone fame, opinionis illese, et conuersacionis honeste*]; that he laboured under no disqualification, and was ever ready to obey the law; but that probable causes and conjectures [*causis probabilibus et verisimilibus coniecturis*] made him fear some grievous attempt to the prejudice of himself and see; and to prevent any person from giving him disturbance in the premises, in any manner, on any pretext, he appealed to the apostolic seat, and to the Pope, and claimed the protection of the court of Canterbury; putting himself, his bishopric, and all his adherents, under their defence, and protesting in the usual form.[7]

The next day, 8 May, in a document with the marginal title 'Procuratorium generale et personale in causis Appellacionis', he appointed fourteen [not nineteen as Chandler states] proctors:

to manage, jointly or separately, any business respecting himself or his see, at Rome or elsewhere.[8]

---

[7] This English summary is from R. Chandler, op. cit., pp. 66–7, but I have inserted quotations from the original Latin in Waynflete's Register (Hampshire Record Office, Winchester), i, f. 11*. In quotations from the Register the manuscript's spellings and capitalization are preserved, but abbreviations are silently expanded and modern punctuation points are provided. The 'causes' (legal—'subjects of litigation', 'actions', 'pleas') and 'conjectures' are 'probable' and 'likely' in the sense that they are the ones most likely to be advanced and made.

[8] Chandler, ibid., p. 67; Register, i, f. 11*v.

Secondly, the sequelae of the 'seduciouse rebellyons' (l. 22) of 1449–50, notably, but by no means only, Jack Cade's rebellion which had begun towards the end of May 1450 in south-west Kent, Waynflete's diocese being, as Dr Griffiths has remarked, 'perilously close to the infected region',[9] were still being felt in Winchester in 1451. It was in Winchester, at the third session of the 1449 parliament held between 16 June and 16 July, and attended by Waynflete, that

> The Lord Sturton thinketh that ther wold be certein comyssioners of oyer and terminer to enquiere of murders and ryottes don ageinst the peace and also of lyveries and that every shireve certify therof.[10]

Only months later, Adam Moleyns, bishop of Chichester and keeper of the privy seal, was murdered at Portsmouth on 9 January 1450 by mutinous soldiers; his murderers were indicted at the sessions of oyer and terminer at Winchester on 14–17 July 1451.[11] After Moleyns's murder 'many sowdeours at portesmouth' had 'soor pilled and enpoured the contray'.[12] Winchester itself had evidently been a seat of disaffection, for in June 1451 one quarter of the traitor 'John Rammesey wyne drawer' was to be sent to Winchester for exhibition there.[13] Indeed, according

[9] R. A. Griffiths, *The Reign of King Henry VI: the Exercise of Royal Authority 1422–1461* (London and Tonbridge, 1981), 611. For accounts of the disturbances and uprisings of 1449–50 and earlier see notes to ll. 21–2 and 79–80.

[10] Huntington MS 202, f. 30v; quoted in R. A. Griffiths, 'The Winchester Session of the 1449 Parliament: a Further Comment', *Huntington Library Quarterly*, xlii (1978–9), 181–91, on p. 189.

[11] J. H. Ramsay, *Lancaster and York: A Century of English History (A.D. 1399–1485)* (Oxford, 1892) ii. 113; R. L. Storey, *The End of the House of Lancaster* (London, 1966), 62; B. Wolffe, *Henry VI* (London, 1981), 221; Griffiths, op. cit., p. 519; L. E. James, 'The career and political influence of William de la Pole, 1st Duke of Suffolk, 1437–1450', University of Oxford B.Litt. thesis (1979), 189.

[12] Robert Bale's Chronicle in R. Flenley, *Six Town Chronicles of England* (Oxford, 1911), 128.

[13] N. H. Nicolas, *Proceedings and Ordinances of the Privy Council of England* (London, 1837), vi. 108. According to Bale's Chronicle (ed. cit., p. 129), on 29 March 1450 'oon John Ramsey servaunt to a vynter in london was drawe hanged and quartered be cause he seid london shall put þe kyng from his crown'. Despite a slight difference in name this must be the same incident in a

to Miss Helen Lyle, Waynflete's 'palace at Winchester was looted' in 1450.[14] However, I can find no reference to this in any primary sources (Miss Lyle gives no citation on this point), and both Dr Wolffe and Dr Griffiths (although the latter adopts Miss Lyle's statement on p. 645 of his book) have suggested to me that Miss Lyle may have conflated evidence of unrest at Winchester with the sacking of Bishop Aiscough's palace at Salisbury after his murder on 29 June 1450 at Edington in Wiltshire.[15] A commission of oyer and terminer appointed on 20 May 1451 was to include Hampshire,

> touching all treasons, insurrections, rebellions, felonies, trespasses, lollardries, conspiracies, confederacies, false allegiances, riots, routs, congregations, unlawful gatherings, maintenances, ambidextries, champerties, extortions, oppressions, misprisions, offences, negligences, falsities, robberies, homicides, murders and deceptions since 8 July last.[16]

It was against this background that Waynflete issued his *mandatum*, at his palace of Wolvesey in Winchester, on 2 July 1451,

> at the requisition of the archbishop, for supplications to be made in his diocese, with litanies on certain days, for the peace and tranquillity of the church, the king, and realm of England [*pro pace et tranquillitate ecclesie, Regis et Regni Anglie*]; no one being ignorant what whirlwinds of adversity, what violent gusts of party, and what grievous perils the nation had lately encountered [*Quanti quidem aduersitatum turbines*,

---

trial record cited by R. Virgoe, 'The Death of William de la Pole, Duke of Suffolk', *Bulletin of the John Rylands Library*, xlvii (1964–5), 489–502, on p. 491 n. 3: 'The anger of the Londoners at Suffolk's escape [from the Tower on 17 March 1450] was clearly the main cause of the abortive rising in the city on 21 March led by John Frammesley, a vintner's servant, who proclaimed "By this toun, by this toun, for this array the king shall lose his crown", and was executed for it (P.R.O., Ancient Indictments, K.B. 9/73/1).' Since Storey (p. 62 n. 2) cites both Bale and the same trial record, his date of 12 January must be a slip.

[14] H. M. Lyle, *The Rebellion of Jack Cade 1450*, Historical Association Pamphlet, General Series, G. 16 (London, 1950), 15.

[15] Ramsay, ii. 129; Storey, p. 66; Wolffe, p. 119; Griffiths, pp. 644–5. However, Miss Lyle does also note the sacking of Aiscough's palace (op. cit., p. 15).

[16] *Calendar of the Patent Rolls, Henry VI*, v (A.D. 1446–1452), 477. See also Wolffe, pp. 240 and 248; Griffiths, p. 649.

quam graues scissurarum procelle, et quanta pericula hijs diebus inuolunt [sic] *anglicos*]; exhorting persons of every rank, to study to please God effectually by fasting, prayer, processions, and good works, in order to avert the impending calamities; and granting indulgence as usual.[17]

Thirdly, 1451 also saw the resolution of a conflict between Waynflete and the Mayor and Commonalty of Winchester over St. Giles' Fair. An indenture dated 3 July 1451, executed by Waynflete at Winchester, relates how

'debate' has been between the Bishop of Wynchestre and the Maire and the Commune of the city of Wynchestre, upon the franchises and customs of the Fair of 'Saint Gile'.[18]

It may be, as the *Dictionary of National Biography*'s account of Waynflete suggests, that the 'debate' was exacerbated by the exhibition of a quarter of the remains of John Ramsey in a town where discontent must have run high.

From the historical context of the period around 1451, when Waynflete seems not to have been held in quite such unanimous esteem as the poem states (ll. 1–8 and 39–40), it would seem that the poem may have been intended as both propaganda on Waynflete's behalf and welcome evidence for him that he had his supporters.

The poem was clearly recited in Waynflete's presence: it allegorizes the properties of the lily 'the whiche in your presence ye may beholde and see' (l. 59), and concludes with the presentation of the lily branch:

> Thus I beseche your lordeshyppe to be mery thys nyght
> And take thys lytyl braunche of a chylde of youres. (ll. 127–8)

The reference to a 'chylde' just might indicate that the presenter (though not the author) of the poem was one of the *pueri eleemosynariae* of St. Swithun's who are recorded as taking part

[17] Chandler, op. cit. (above, n. 2), pp. 67–8; Register, i, ff. 13*ᵛ–14*.

[18] *Sixth Report of the Royal Commission on Historical Manuscripts*, part 1, (London, 1877), 603. The full text is printed in *City of Winchester: Calendar of Charters*, intro. by J. A. Herbert (Winchester, 1915), Appendix IV (no. 21).

in various dramatic activities in the fifteenth century;[19] St. Swithun's also had an *episcopus iuvenum*,[20] and at some churches at least there is evidence that it was the custom of the boy bishop to deliver (though not write) a sermon.[21] The boy bishop sermon might, at first blush, seem to offer some analogue with the Waynflete poem delivered by a 'chylde'. However, unlike the poem, the two surviving boy bishop sermons written in English—admittedly too small a number from which to draw safe conclusions—both exploit the theme of childhood and the fact that the speaker is a child.[22] Further, the bishop was the spiritual 'fader' (ll. 1, 10, etc.) of adults, too, and the alleged autobiography with its reference to a four-year exile as pilgrims and to the speaker and his companions being joined by 'straungers of tendere yeres' (l. 105) would sound odd in the mouth of a literal child. It appears more likely that the speaker is an adult who is the spiritual child of his bishop.

No record of the 'performance' of this poem survives, and nothing wholly like it is known for any other bishop. However, some parallel for verse composed and performed in honour of a bishop is provided by the moral stanzas which accompanied the subtleties at the feast for the enthronement of John Morton as

[19] See E. K. Chambers, *The Mediaeval Stage* (Oxford, 1903), i. 361, and ii. 396.

[20] Chambers, i. 361.

[21] Chambers, i. 355–6; K. Young, *The Drama of the Medieval Church* (Oxford, 1933), i. 110.

[22] Both the sermons are edited by J. G. Nichols (with an introduction by E. F. Rimbault), 'Two Sermons Preached by the Boy Bishop at St. Paul's, Temp. Henry VIII., and at Gloucester, Temp. Mary', *Camden Society Miscellany*, vii (1875), 1–29. The first (pp. 1–13) is attributed by *STC* (282) to Bishop John Alcock (d. 1500), but J. W. Blench, *Preaching in England in the late Fifteenth and Sixteenth Centuries* (Oxford, 1964), 351, says that 'it is probably not by him'; the second (pp. 14–29) was delivered at Gloucester in 1558 and is by Richard Ramsey (on whom see A. B. Emden, *A Biographical Register of the University of Oxford* (Oxford, 1957–74), iv, s.v. Ramsey *alias* Hallynge, Richard). Erasmus' *Concio de puero Iesu*, English translation printed by Robert Redman (?1540; *STC* 10509), is not said to have been delivered by a boy bishop but simply delivered by a boy in St. Paul's School (cf. Chambers, ibid., i. 356 n. 3); it, too, exploits the theme of childhood and the fact of a boy speaker.

bishop of Ely on 29 August 1480 (*Supplement* to *The Index of Middle English Verse*, 3563. 5);[23] there was a certain dramatic interplay as one stanza headed 'Responcio episcopi' was evidently spoken either by Morton himself or by someone playing the part of Morton. The feast was attended by laity as well as clergy, and in the Waynflete poem the address to all three estates (ll. 73–96) suggests that all three may have been present.

The presentation of the lily 'braunche' at the end of the last stanza links the Waynflete poem in type with other poems which accompany the sending or presentation of a gift: (i) a seven-line poem (*Index* and *Supplement*, 932) sent with a ring from a lover to his lady;[24] (ii) a seventy-seven-line poem (*Index* and *Supplement*, 3604) by Lydgate accompanying the gift of an eagle and 'gyven vn-to þe kyng henry þe vj and to his moder, þe qweene Kateryne, sittyng at þe mete; vpon þe yeris day, in þe Castell of hertford'.[25] Although not apparently accompanying a material

[23] The earliest text is in Arnold's *Chronicle* (?1503; *STC* 782), sig. Qiv^{v}–Qv. J. Bentham, *The History and Antiquities of the Conventual and Cathedral Church of Ely* ...^{2} (Norwich, etc., 1812), Appendix, no. xxix, pp. 34*–35*, prints an account of Morton's installation from BL MS Harley 3721, and in no. xxx, pp. 35*–36*, reprints the subtlety verses 'from an old Book ... printed in the old black character'; see also p. 179 n. 11. W. Stevenson, *A Supplement to the Second Edition* ... [of Bentham] (Norwich, 1817), Notes, pp. 141–3, adds notes on the subtlety verses. I owe the reference to *Supplement*, 3563. 5 to Professor A. F. Johnston of the University of Toronto. Bentham (followed by *Supplement*, 3563. 5) mistranscribes MS Harley 3721's 'M° CCCC lxxx' (f. 64), for the date of Morton's installation, as '1479'; the date is correctly given in le Neve's *Fasti Ecclesiae Anglicanae 1300–1541*, iv, revd. by B. Jones (London, 1963), 15.

[24] R. H. Robbins, *Secular Lyrics of the XIVth and XVth Centuries*^{2}, (Oxford, 1955), p. 87, no. 95.

[25] R. H. Robbins, ibid., pp. 88–90, no. 96. Since Henry's mother, Katherine of Valois, died on 3 January 1437, Robbins's date for the poem as 1446 is impossible (and his use of the date of Henry's marriage to Margaret of Anjou in 1445 as a *terminus post quem* an irrelevance); the *Supplement*, without evidence, re-dates the poem to 1428. W. F. Schirmer, *John Lydgate: a Study in the Culture of the XVth Century* (London, 1961), 133, dates the poem as '?1429', but gives no evidence. Henry was at Hertford Castle for Christmas in December 1423 (see M. E. Christie, *Henry VI* (London, etc., 1922), Appendix I ('Itinerary of Henry VI'), 375–89, on p. 375 (and see also p. 38); and Wolffe, p. 34), and from the fuller evidence of the itineraries of his later years (see

gift, clearly related to this genre is a twenty-line poem (*Index* and *Supplement*, 2267) by Dunbar addressed to James IV 'In hansill of this guid New ȝeir', expressing the wish that God will send the king good things, including 'many Fraunce crownes' (the French gold *écu*), no doubt in the hope that the king will be as generous to his servants.[26] Two other poems, *Index*, 1496 (*Supplement*, 837. 5), by Lydgate, and *Index* and *Supplement*, 1789, refer to the metaphorical gift of a lover's heart on New Year's Day.[27] The genre of the mumming is also relevant, since it is particularly associated with the giving of gifts.[28] Lydgate's May-day mumming at Bishopswood (*Index*, 2170), 'sente by a poursyvant to þe Shirreves of London, acompanyed with þeire breþerne ... at an honurable dyner, eche of hem bringginge hys dysshe', provides a close parallel with the Waynflete poem's gift

Wolffe, pp. 361–71) it appears that Henry spent New Year where he had spent Christmas. Born on 6 December 1421, he would have been only just two years old on 1 January 1424; there are many gaps in the published itineraries for Henry's earlier years and doubtless there were other New Years before his mother's death which he spent at Hertford Castle. Some of the presents, though neither an artificial eagle (cf. J. Evans, *A History of Jewellery 1100–1870*² (London, *1970*), *51* and *64;* and *MED*, s.v. *Egle* (n.), 2 (a)) nor a signet ring or seal manual bearing an eagle (as Schirmer suggests; for an account of the signet of the eagle see J. P. Collier, *Camden Soc.*, lxvii (1857), 77–80), received by the infant Henry are noted by Wolffe, pp. 37–8, and Griffiths, p. 53; in a poem of 1449–50 Henry is symbolized by an eagle (*Index* and *Supplement*, 3455/24). *Pace* Robbins, p. 258, on no. 96, *Index* and *Supplement*, 886 is not a presentation poem but a 'compleynt' with no mention of a gift.

[26] J. Kinsley, *The Poems of William Dunbar* (Oxford, 1979), p. 69, no. 18. See also I. S. Ross, *William Dunbar* (Leiden, 1981), 65 and 203.

[27] J. Stevens, *Music and Poetry in the Early Tudor Court*², (Cambridge, etc., 1979), 210 and 228 n. 12, suggests that these poems may have accompanied the gift of heart-shaped jewellery. R. F. Green, 'Hearts, Minds, and Some English Poems of Charles d'Orléans', *English Studies in Canada*, ix (1983), argues that *Index* and *Supplement*, 922, and *Index*, 2030, 2204, and 2278, should also be considered in the context of heart-shaped jewellery (for discussion and illustrations of which see also J. Cherry, 'The Medieval Jewellery from the Fishpool, Nottinghamshire, Hoard', *Archaeologia*, civ (1973), 307–21, referred to by Green). *Index* and *Supplement*, 932 (above, n. 24) may also belong in this context.

[28] G. Wickham, *Early English Stages 1300 to 1600*², *i (1300–1576)*, (London, Henley, and New York, 1980), 195 and 204.

of a lily branch since the personifications described may have 'presented actual or artificial May boughs and flowers intended as '"sotleties" (place favours) to be placed on or near the diners' plates'.[29]

In the text printed below the spelling of the manuscript is reproduced except for the correction of scribal errors; editorial expansions of scribal abbreviations are in italics; scribal insertions appear between the marks \ /; emendations are in square brackets; *y* and *þ* are distinguished in the printed text though not in the manuscript; initial 'ff' is printed as 'F' at the beginning of a line but preserved elsewhere; word-division, capital letters, and punctuation are as in modern English. The manuscript punctuation is limited almost entirely to the *virgula suspensiva*, which is used regularly to indicate the caesura, but twice (l. 14, after both *fortune* and *chaungeynge*; l. 118, after both *wele* and *dysese*) it is found twice in a line. The caesura is once (l. 16, following *oure*) indicated by a *punctus elevatus*. The *punctus* occurs twice only, at the end of ll. 4 and 9. There is no gap between stanzas, which are indicated at each opening line by a scribal form of the paraph identical with the abbreviation used for *-ra-*.

I am indebted to the British Library for permission to publish the poem, and to the Hampshire Record Office (Diocese of Winchester) for permission to quote from Waynflete's Register. Professor R. B. Dobson, Dr J. G. Greatrex, Dr R. A. Griffiths, Dr G. L. Harriss, and Dr B. Wolffe fully and generously answered my historical queries. Professor I. Lancashire discussed the performance context of the poem with me and gave valuable references. Other aid on specific points is acknowledged as they arise.

f. 22v

Ryght noble *and* blessede fader, to whom of excellence
The flo*ur* ys p*ro*clamed thoroweought thys realme wyde,

[29] J. Norton-Smith, *John Lydgate: Poems* (Oxford, 1966), 123.

Whos p*er*fyghtnesse *and* trouthe stant i*n* suche reue*r*ence
That fame hathe ou*er*spradde in euery syde
Youre grete laboure for co*m*mun wele at thys tyde,
That thorowoute þe contre where men ryde or goo
Thys ys the co*m*mune voice (what nedythe to hyde?):
'God save þ*a*t lorde from grevau*n*ce *and* from woo'.

Sum tyme we servede a lorde of ful worshypful mynde,
A fader of wysdam, as openly hathe ben p*re*vede:
We meene yo*ur* p*re*decesso*ur*, the verrey rote *and* rynde
Of all our*e* weele *and* hono*ur*, whos blode neu*er* yitt
myschevede,
Ne thys reame in hys dayes reprooched ne rep*re*vede.
But age *and* fortune, chau*n*geynge neuer in oon,
Hathe hym ou*er*throwe þat vs all relevede.
Hadd he lyvede thys oure wee hadde been gladde ychoon.

But he ys passede *and* goon; ther*e* ys noo mor*e* to saye.
Thus rennethe þe cours *and* faate of our*e* mortalyte.
For sorowe of þe whiche iche of vs went hys weye
To strange co*n*treys as pylg*r*ims byyonde þe q*ui*ke see
Vnder drede *and* shame ffor þe foule c*ru*eltee
And seduc*i*ouse rebellyons that i*n* thys lande aroose,
Soo *con*fusede *and* mate for verrey sorowe *and* pytee
That byfore noo strau*n*ger we durste our*e*selfe vnclose.

Endurede thus in sorowe *and* woofull tourment
Our*e* carefull hert*is* a foure yere *and* more,
And by p*ro*cesse after, our*e* teeres somwhate stente
For oure lord*is* dethe, that Y rehersede byfore.
Our*e* treso*ur* faylede faste, *and* spente was all our*e*
stoor*e*,
For the whiche vs thought to reto*ur*ne agayne.
Thus drawynge homewarde to þe co*n*trey we were i*n* boor*e*,
Oon tolde vs tythyng*is* of whiche we were ryght fayne:

f. 23
'The chyrche of Wynchest*er*', *quoth* he, 'hathe a fayre g*ra*ce
And grete fortune to rewle *and* to sett folk*is* at reste.
Howe many noble p*re*latys haue occupyed that place!
Were neu*er* bett*er* p*re*stys then haue ben there p*ro*fessyde,
As wele in covnsell as in corage of breste,
To wythestande all rancor*e*, malice, *and* adu*er*syte.
Off all our*e* lordys that nowe ben trustyde beste
My lorde of Wynchestre men seyn that hitt ys he.'

Be gladde than, my lorde, in v*er*tue for to sprede,
For wee were ryght merye whan wee hadde suche relacyou*n*,
And as ye haue bygune sparythe not to p*ro*cede,
For oonly p*er*seuerau*n*ce deseruethe coronacyou*n*.
Fye on gaderynge of good! Haue hitt i*n* abhominacyou*n*!
Yee see what sorowe hit causythe, robbry, thefte, *and* stryff.
And veyn hit ys in thyes dayes to vse suche occupacyou*n*
Whan at the laste therfor*e* a man shalle leese hys lyff.

I speke i*n* noo p*ro*uerbys; my speche ys open *and* clere.
Beholde the lylyes off the felde, that neyther*e* carde ne spy*n*ne.
What avaylethe rychesse mor*e* tha*n* nedythe vs here?
All þ*a*t ys to myche reboundethe into synne.
Off evell getyn good, the thryde heyre couthe neu*er* wy*n*ne.
Wer hit not spedfull to kepe thys in reme*m*brau*n*ce?
Hadde so*m*me me*n* of thys avysede themsylfe wit*h*ynne
Fortune hadd not shewyde them þe vysage of hyr varyau*n*ce.

But Y retourne agayn to þe noble p*ro*pu*r*te
Off þe lyly reme*m*bryde a lytyll herebyfore,
The whiche i*n* yo*ur* p*re*sence ye may beholde *and* see,
And rehersede in Script*ur*e in plac*is* nyghe a scoore.
And for hit ys yo*ur* flour*e* syttynge hytt ys ther*e*foor*e*

As for your*e* plesau*n*ce to be hadde i*n* co*m*mendacyou*n*.
And yff [Y] tryppe i*n* sentence I beseche to be forbore;
For lake of auctoryte Y folowe ymagynacyou*n*.

f. 23[v]
Fyrste, the lyly growethe streight vpwarde to heven,
As hytt apperethe by the stalke to eu*er*i mans sight.
Cutt hit fro roote, hitt kepythe the colour*e* even,
W*ith*ought fadyng a whyle—suche v*er*tu hit hathe *and* myght.
The roote ys medicinable, as phisik can hit dyght,
To rype an empostem engendryde in a man.
Loo here thre p*ro*pu*r*tees aft*er* myn ensight
Rehersede of þe lylie, rudely soo as Y can.

Lat prest*is* be streight *and* straite of lyvynge w*ith*yn
As þe lylie growethe, nott crokede in consciens.
They shall haue a forhede than to repreve synne
And to telle the trouthe w*ith*ought fere or offens.
Wolde God eu*er*i prest wolde folowe thys sentence,
Reme*m*brynge hys office on Godd*is* worde to worche.
Hadd oure faders eschewede suche maner*e* i*n*co*n*ue*n*ie*n*s
The peple hadde nott be sett soo sore agayn þe Chyrche.

Secundlye I referre to knyghthode *and* chyvalrye
Off thys noble lylye the secunde propurte:
Thoff hit be kytt for a tyme yitt lat natt þe flo*ur* dye.
Remembrethe your*e* auncyent strenght, yo*ur* olde humanyte.
Thoff hitt fade for a whyle dyspeyre natt all yee;
Thynke, syrs, yo*ur* nobleye co*m*mythe of Allmyghty God;
Yelde yow to hym lowelye, for t[r]ustethe wele þ*a*t He
For to punysshe yo*ur* p*ri*de hathe shewyde yow Hys rodde.

The p*ro*purte of þe rote, and þe medycyne w*ith*all,
I remitt i*n* gen*er*all to þe peple all abowte
That wel-nyghe wythe empostymes ys i*n*fecte ou*er*all,

And whan synne ys roten hitt wyll be casten oute.
The s*er*uaunt agayne hys soueraigne bygy*n*nythe to strout,
And yonge men agayn olde takene parcyalyte.
But yff we be r[e]formede, I put yow out of dowte,
The lylye wyll avoyde vs that we shall hytt neu*er* see.

f. 24
Butt alas the lylye growethe ˋnoweˊ amonge thornes
That whilome was ˋatˊ large in þe felde ful playn.
Wolde the faders of þe Chyrche oones sharp her*e* hornes
To restore thys flo*ur* to the astaat agayne,
The erthe shulde be fecundius þ*a*t now ys full barreyn,
And burgeon lilies *and* roosez to þe sowles sustenance.
Now, blessed lorde, reforme vs—þ*er* ys no mor*e* to sayn—
And graunte vs to fulfylle þ*a*t ys vnto thy plesau*n*ce.

Here than we apperd w*ith* strau*n*gers of tender*e* yeres
That for to lerne *and* see haue fervens *and* desyre,
And bisought vs of co*m*panie for to ben oure feres.
To they sawe yo*ur* lordeshyppe ther her*tis* ˋwereˊ sett on fyre
And yave to theyr guides grete rewarde *and* huyre
To garde *and* co*n*duct theym to yowr*e* high p*re*sence
And prayede me full hertelye yo*ur* lordeshypp to require
To shewe theym the fauoure of yo*ur* magnifycence.

Nowe sethe yee bee the verreye lanterne *and* lyght,
A ffader of þe Chyrche, co*m*forte in our*e* dystresse,
Accepte our*e* good wyll, thoff lytyll be oure myght,
þ*a*t wol peyn vs as we can to doo your*e* herte gladnesse.
For youre heele ys oures—thys we knowe exp*re*sse—
And trustethe wele yo*ur* dysese were to vs a peyn.
Lat our*e* werk*is* to our*e* word*is* bere verrey wytnesse,
That to yo*ur* dysporte our*e* myght we woll co*n*streyn.

And lyke as by Seynt Cecile co*n*uertede was Valeryau*n*
And crownede wi*th* þe lylye by the hond*is* of þe aungell
  bryght,
Soo enspire your*e* herte as wele as eu*er* was man
I beseche oure Lorde for Hys myche myght,
And graunt yowe i*n* heuene even þe same syght
And to smelle the sauour*e* of eu*er*lastynge flowres.
Thus I beseche yo*ur* lordeshyppe to be mery thys nyght
And take thys lytyl braunche of a chylde of youres.

Finis

NOTES TO THE TEXT

1. *Ryght*] A space two lines in depth has been left for a large *R*; a 'lower case' *r* is in the scribe's hand.

Ryght . . . fader] For this form of address to a bishop cf. a letter from Robert Hungerford, Lord Moleyns, 13 June 1448, 'To the worschpful fadyr in God and my ryth gode lord the Bysshop of Wynchestyr [Waynflete]', *inc.* 'Worshypful fadyr yn God and my rythe gode lord', and *expl.* 'rythe worschypful fadyr yn God and my rythe gode lord' (N. Davis, *Paston Letters and Papers of the Fifteenth Century*, part II (Oxford, 1976), no. 873; cf. also no. 912, William Worcester to Waynflete, 17 May 1470: 'To the ryght reuerent fader yn God my full worshypfull Lord Bysshop of Wynchestre'). Cf. also *MED*, s.v. *Fader* (n.), 7 (c).

2. *flour*] A common Middle English usage denoting perfection, but given particular literary point here by the later allegorizing of the lily on Waynflete's arms, by the reference to the 'euerlastynge flowres' (l. 126), and by the physical presence of the lily which is given to Waynflete at the conclusion of the poem.

4. *ouerspradde*] = 'disseminated, made known' (Waynflete's 'grete laboure'); this particular use is not known to *OED*.

5. This could well be a reference to Waynflete's part in the negotiations with Jack Cade in his revolt of 1450 (see Wolffe, pp. 235 and 237–8; Griffiths, pp. 611–12 and 616). After the collapse of Cade's revolt, Waynflete was one of sixteen commissioners of oyer and terminer appointed on 1 August 1450 sent into Kent 'not as used to be supposed further to suppress rebellion, but genuinely to inquire into grievances' (Wolffe, p. 239; Griffiths, p. 641). Probably after the date of this poem, in March 1452, Waynflete was one of Henry's negotiators in a settlement reached with Richard, Duke of York who wished

by armed force to coerce Henry into removing the Duke of Somerset from his presence (Wolffe, p. 255; Griffiths, pp. 696–7).

9. Henry Beaufort, bishop of Winchester 1404–47; for his life cf. A. B. Emden, *A Biographical Register of the University of Oxford* ... (Oxford, 1957–74). Such strong praise, though doubtless owing partly to local patriotism, has its echoes elsewhere. As G. L. Harriss has noted, 'Even in his lifetime Henry Beaufort was a controversial figure. The Londoners envied his wealth and detested his policies; Humphrey, duke of Gloucester, denounced him as an ambitious schemer and a traitor; both pope and king punished him for his disobedience. Yet more than once he was extolled in parliament for his generosity, loyalty, patriotism and wisdom in affairs of state' ('Cardinal Beaufort—Patriot or Usurer?', *Trans. Royal Hist. Soc.*, 5th series, xx (1970), 129–48, on p. 129). His death is regretted in another poem (*Index* and *Supplement*, 3455): 'I-closid we haue oure welevette hatte, | That keueryd vs from mony stormys brown' (R. H. Robbins, *Historical Poems of the XIVth and XVth Centuries* (New York, 1959, p. 202, no. 84/7–8).

10. *A fader of wysdam*] Either, 'An ecclesiastical superior (a sense *MED*, s.v. *Fader* (n.), 7 (a), records twice, first *c.*1445 in Pecock ('fadris of þe chirche')) of sound judgement'—Beaufort had been both a bishop and a cardinal; or, 'A spiritual protector (cf. *MED* 4 (a) and *OED*, s.v. *Father* (sb.), 4 a and c) of sound judgement'. Cf. also ll. 79, 99, and 114.

11. *rote and rynde*] = 'source'. B. J. and H. W. Whiting, *Proverbs, Sentences, and Proverbial Phrases from English Writings Mainly before 1500* (Cambridge, Mass. and London, 1968), R 193, and *OED*, s.v. *Rind* (sb.[1]), 2, record the collocation from the fourteenth to the sixteenth centuries. To speak of Beaufort as a source of wealth was no merely decorative compliment: 'over practically half a century, Cardinal Beaufort, whether dead [i.e. through his executors] or alive, supported the Lancastrian dynasty to the tune of a quarter of a million pounds, about half of it during the critical years 1428–45' (Griffiths, p. 392); for the benefactions to Winchester see L. B. Radford, *Henry Beaufort* ... (London, 1908), 292–3.

12. *blode ... myschevede*] = 'family never yet transgressed'. Probably a covert defence of the Cardinal's nephew, Edmund Beaufort, Duke of Somerset, whose involvement in the English disasters in Normandy and France had made him notably unpopular. A mob of more than 1000 retainers had attacked him in London on 1 December 1450 (Storey, p. 80; Wolffe, p. 244; Griffiths, p. 647), and a bill in Parliament demanded his dismissal (with others) from the king's entourage as from 1 December 1450 (Storey, p. 81; Wolffe, p. 244; Griffiths, p. 691). Probably after the putative date of this poem, the Duke of York, in February–March 1452, made bitter attacks on Somerset (Storey, pp. 95, 101; Wolffe, pp. 253–5; Griffiths, pp. 694–7). A poem of 1450 (*Index* and *Supplement*, 1555) includes Somerset amongst those criticized (Robbins, op. cit. (l. 9 n.), p. 189, no. 76/61–4).

13. *reproochede*] = 'brought into reproach or discredit'; *OED*, s.v. *Reproach* (v.), first records the verb *c.*1489 (although the rare variants *reproce* and *repruce* are found earlier, as is the substantive), but the sense required here is not recorded before 1593 (s.v. 4).

reprevede] = 'impaired or diminished', a sense *OED*, s.v. *Reprove* (v.), 6, first records 1450–80, describing it as rare.

14. *in oon*] = Either, 'individually, one without the other' (though *in one* is not known to *OED* in this sense), i.e. both age and fortune change for the worse, and one cannot get old without experiencing bad luck at the same time; or, 'in unison' (*OED*, s.v. *One* (numeral a., pron., etc.), 30 d (b)), i.e. advanced years and good luck are never in step either because good fortune will depart with advancing years or because old age prevents one from exploiting the good fortune one does have. Alternatively, one could emend *neuer* to *euer*; for the idiom *ever in one* = 'continuously' cf. *MED*, s.v. *Ever* (adv.), 9 (m), and *OED*, s.v. *Ever* (adv.), 3, and s.v. *One* (numeral a., etc.), 30 d (c). Beaufort's retirement from national politics in June 1443 (cf. Emden, op. cit.), at the age of *c.*68, was by his choice (in which his age may have been a factor), and was not an 'overthrow' (cf. l. 15) by fortune; indeed, his counsel was still sought informally and he continued to exert privately an influence on public affairs (Griffiths, p. 281). However, it would not be surprising if a monk-poet of St. Swithun's were unaware of his bishop's continuing power behind the scenes, and he doubtless assumed that Beaufort's retirement to Winchester was the result not only of age but of a fickle fortune.

15. *þat*] = 'who'.

17. Beaufort died on 11 April 1447.

20. *quike*] = 'running, flowing' (cf. *OED*, s.v. *Quick* (adj.), 9).

21–2. As the House of Commons put it in 1449, 'many Murdres, Manslaughters, Rapes, Roberies, Riottys, Affrayes and othur inconvenientes, gretter than afore, nowe late have growen within this your Roialme' (*Rotuli Parliamentorum* ..., v. 200). For details up to 1451, see Ramsay, ii. 103–4, 113, 120–41, 146–7; Storey, pp. 8–9, 34–5, 40, 43–4, 45–6, 53–60, 61–8, 77–82, 84–92; Wolffe, pp. 17, 104–5, 116–34, 215–45, 248; Griffiths, pp. 286–8, 304–10, 562–665, 684–92. For Hampshire and Winchester in particular see introductory paragraphs to this article. Cf. also note to ll. 79–80.

22. *seduciouse*] First recorded by *OED* in 1447 (although *sedition* is well attested from *c.*1375 onwards).

44. *coronacyoun*] *MED* records *Coronacioun* (n.), of the crowning of a sovereign or his consort and once each applied to the Virgin and to Christ. For the sense here, 'rewarding with honour and bliss', cf. *OED*, s.v. *Coronation*, 1 b (quotation of 1612) and *MED*, s.v. *corounen* (v.), (1), 6 ('*Theol.* To "crown" or reward (the virtuous), bestow eternal life and bliss upon') and 7 (a) ('to

bestow or reward with honour, glory, happiness, etc.'). The poet nicely returns to the idea in the final stanza (l. 122).

45–8. A perennial topic of preachers, but one which would be notably appropriate in Henry VI's reign when many exploited first the king's youth and then his incompetence to their financial advantage (Wolffe, pp. 106–16; Griffiths, pp. 83–8, 94–104, 329–75) and when the murders of the Duke of Suffolk, Lord Saye, and bishops Moleyns and Aiscough, all in 1450, would serve as a vivid reminder that in 'thyes dayes' in particular 'at the laste' might be sooner than expected. The charge of 'gaderynge of good' might not unfairly have been laid against Cardinal Beaufort, but the poem's praise of him (stanza 2) shows that it is not made here.

49. *prouerbys*] = 'riddles, enigmas', a sense *OED*, s.v. *Proverb* (sb.), 3, records exclusively from biblical use, its first example being 1382, Wyclif, *John* xvi. 25: 'I haue spokun to ȝou thes thingis in prouerbis [*gloss* or derke saumplis; Vulgate *in proverbiis*]; the our cometh, whanne now I schal not speke to ȝou in prouerbis [Vulg. *in proverbiis*], but opynly [Vulg. *palam*].'

50. In the margin the scribe gives the reference '*con*side*r*ate lilia agr*i*'. Matthew 6: 28.

52. *reboundethe*] = 'overflows'. *OED*, s.v. *Rebound* (v.), notes that in early usage it was often confused with *Redound* (v.), and that Wyclif used it to translate Latin *redundare* (see 1, d).

53. Whiting and Whiting, op. cit. (l. 11 n.), G 333 first record this proverb *c.*1303 in Mannyng.

55–6. *somme men*] The poet might have had the murders in 1450 of the rapacious Duke of Suffolk and Lord Saye in mind, but such a comment is always topical.

58. *remembryde*] = 'mentioned', a sense *OED*, s.v. *Remember* (v.), 3, notes as common between c.1430 and 1660.

61. *your floure*] On the lilies in Waynflete's coat of arms see n. 2 to introductory paragraphs above.

syttynge] = 'befitting, appropriate'; see *OED*, s.v. Sitting (ppl.a.), 2.

63. *Y*] omitted in MS.

tryppe] = 'make a false step, fall into error'; *OED*, s.v. *Trip* (v.), 9, first records this sense in 1509; even the literal, physical sense 'stumble' is not recorded before *c.*1425 (trans.) and *c.*1440 (intrans.), senses 6 and 8.

64. *auctoryte* (here = 'an authoritative source [as, a written tradition]' for the following interpretation of the properties of the lily) is usually in the Middle English period opposed to experience. For the opposition to *ymagynacyoun* cf. Nicholas Love's *The Mirrour of the Blessed Lyf of Jesu Christ*: 'Wherfore we mowen to sterynge of deuocioun ymagine and thynke dyuerse wordes and dedes of hym [Jesus] and othere that we fynde not writen so that it be not aȝenst the byleue' (ed. L. F. Powell (London, etc., 1908), p. 9; I owe this

reference to Dr A. J. Minnis). See further A. J. Minnis, 'Langland's Ymaginatif and Late-Medieval Theories of Imagination', *Comparative Criticism*, iii (1981), 71–103.

67–8. Cf. Trevisa's translation of Bartholomaeus Anglicus' *De Proprietatibus Rerum*, XVII, cap. 91: 'And if þe stalk be ykutte al fro þe roote, for al þe kynde humour of þe stalk is yclosed in þe piþ, kynde hete þat is in þe piþ torneþ to þe ouer party of þe stalk and makeþ digestioun in mater of þe flour, and þanne þe flour sprediþ and is white whanne þe humour is ful digeste. Þerfore þere it is yseyde þat versifiours likned þe lilye to mannes inwitte þat is besy atte laste to þenke on þinges þat euer schal laste. ... þe lilye stalk wiþ floures newe ykutte ypyȝte in a clotte of clay kepith þe floures freisshe long tyme. (edd. M. C. Seymour *et al.* (Oxford, 1975), ii. 981/26–32, 982/1–2), and *Index* and *Supplement*, 3945: '... the lylie that faire flowre | that many yeres shall kepe his color' (ed. V. J. Scattergood, *Politics and Poetry in the Fifteenth Century* (London, 1971), 383/11–12; the poem, probably to be dated 1424, is discussed on pp. 77–9).

67. *even*] = 'completely' or 'uniformly'.

70. *rype an empostem*] = 'bring an abscess to a head'. Cf. Trevisa, ed. cit. (above, ll. 67–8 n.): 'Þe vertu of þe lilye rypiþ bocchis and sores; þerfore it helpiþ aȝeins postemes and bocches ...' (ii. 980/16–17), and *Agnus Castus*: 'Þe vertu of þis herbe [lilium] is ȝef þu stamp it with talwȝ and frye it with olye and leye it as a playster to þe place quere is a cold gowte or a posteme it schal rype hym and breke hym' (ed. G. Brodin (Uppsala, 1950), pp. 167–8). On impostumes see R. von Fleischhacker, *Lanfrank's 'Science of Cirurgie'*, EETS 102 (1894), 204 ff.; M. S. Ogden, *The Cyrurgie of Guy de Chauliac*, i, EETS 265 (1971), 72 ff.

71. *ensight*] = 'understanding, knowledge'.

73. *streight and straite*] A nice play on words: (1) *streight*, though a possible spelling of Mod. Eng. *strait*, is here presumably Mod. Eng. *straight* (< pa.ppl. of *stretch*) and is itself a play on senses: (*a*) lit. both 'nott crokede' (l. 74) and also 'direct, undeviating', as the lily, in both these senses, grows 'streight vpwarde to heven' (l. 65); (*b*) 'honest', a sense *OED*, s.v. *Straight* (adj.), 6, first records in 1530; (2) *straite*, though a possible spelling of Mod. Eng. *straight*, is here Mod. Eng. *strait* (< OF *estreit*, Latin *strictus*), with the sense 'severely regulated'.

75. *forhede*] = 'assurance, boldness'. This sense is unknown to *MED*, and *OED*, s.v. *Forehead*, 2, first records this usage, which it compares with Latin *frons* (cf. *Oxford Latin Dictionary*, s.v. *frons*², 3), in 1560.

76. *offens*] i.e. [*withought*] *offens* = 'without causing offence'; *MED*, s.v. *Offens(e* (n.), 3 (a), records *withouten offens(e* in this sense once, *ante* 1450. The preaching of priests who were 'crokede in consciens' would give offence to congregations by its hypocrisy.

78. *on ... worche*] = Either, 'to preach (speak or write; cf. *OED*, s.v. *Work* (v.), 4 and 24 b) according to (*or* upon) God's word'; or, 'to act according to God's word' (cf. *OED*, s.v. *Work* (v.), 21). Although the poet has been concerned about upright living (which would favour the latter interpretation), his statement that if priests live righteously 'than' (l. 75) they will have the courage to preach suggests that neglect of preaching is a result of crooked lives and one which particularly troubles him. The ideal priest combines the duty of preaching with the obligation to perform good works: cf. *CT Gen. Prol.* I. 496–7, and *Sec. N. Prol.* VIII. 64–5. It may be that, like the narrator of the *Gen. Prol.* (498), in his exhortation to act according to 'Goddis worde' the poet means not the message of the gospels in general but in particular Matthew 5: 19's statement about the man who 'fecerit et docuerit'. Cf. also note to ll. 79–80.

79. *faders*] = Either, 'ecclesiastical superiors'; or, 'bishops' (as at l. 99); or, 'spiritual protectors'. Cf. also l. 10 n.

inconueniens] = 'transgression', a sense *MED*, s.v. *Inconvenience* (n.), (c), records from *c.*1440 onwards.

79–80. Although the poet's comments on the transgressions of 'oure faders', both in their lives and in their failure to preach, can be paralleled in other periods (cf. G. R. Owst, *Preaching in Medieval England* ... (Cambridge, 1926), 25 ff.), they may have reference to contemporary controversy. Reginald Pecock, bishop of Chichester, in at least two sermons on episcopal preaching delivered in 1447 and 1449 (there was possibly a third sermon between these dates or after 1449) had argued that 'a bishop as such is not bound to preach in person to the people of his diocese' (E. F. Jacob, 'Reynold Pecock, Bishop of Chichester', *PBA* xxxvii (1951), 121–53, on p. 132; cf. also Emden, op. cit.). Save amongst bishops, according to Thomas Gascoigne, this aroused furious hostility in both clergy and laity, and almost everyone cried out 'Vae episcopis! ... aut enim nesciunt praedicare episcopi, aut non possunt praedicare, negociis saeculi aut deliciis corporis impediti, aut quia non possunt vere praedicare, nisi praedicent illa mala in quibus vel pro quibus ipsi episcopi sunt rei, nec bona opera praedicant, quae episcopi non faciunt, sed negligunt, et talia bona operantes derident, vel non ponderant' (*Loci e Libro Veritatum* ..., ed. J. E. Thorold Rogers (Oxford, 1881), p. 41). Like the poet, Gascoigne attributes the current anti-clericalism to such attitudes: 'et de die in diem surrexerunt plurimi in populo; et occiderunt episcopum Cicestrensem, Adam Molens, et episcopum Sarum, Willelmum Asku, et persecuti sunt episcopum Cestriae, Buthe nomine, et episcopum Norwicensem, Walterum Lyart, et rectores et vicarios diversos in Cancia, et juxta Sarum et Hungyrforth spoliaverunt' (pp. 41–2; cf. also pp. 44–5). It was doubtless the bishops' roles in national government (with unsuccessful and unpopular policies) and as landowners which provided the main motives for the murders and assaults on them, but local clergy, too, were subjected to violence: see Storey, pp. 9, 62, 66, 225; Wolffe, pp. 119, 221, 241; Griffiths, pp. 129, 140, 418, 519, 566, 568–9, 577–9, 639–40, 644–55. For topical poems *c.*1450 attacking specific clerics see *Index* and *Supplement*, 544 (in *Suppl.* for 'LVII' read 'LXVII'), 1555 (discussed by Griffiths, pp. 639–40), 2338, 4261, and *Supplement*, 556. 5. As Waynflete was both a bishop and a statesman, and one who had been the object of some hostility (see introductory paragraphs, above), the lines are notably candid.

81. *referre*] = 'submit for consideration', a sense *OED*, s.v. *Refer* (v.), 6, first records in 1456.

84. *humanyte*] = 'courtesy, graciousness'.

86. The notion is perhaps now most familiar from *The Wife of Bath's Tale* (*CT* III. 1109 ff.), especially ll. 1117 ('Crist wole we clayme of hym oure gentillesse') and 1162 ('Thy gentillesse cometh fro God allone'). For further references see notes to ll. 1109 ff. in F. N. Robinson's edition.

87. *trustethe*] MS *teustethe.*

88. The poet may have in mind the English humiliations in Normandy and France.

90. *remitt*] = 'refer for consideration'.

93. An old preaching commonplace (e.g. Chaucer, *Pars. T.* X. 506: 'Murmure eek is ofte amonges servauntz that grucchen whan hir sovereyns bidden hem doon leveful thynges'; cf. also 392 and 402) given particular topicality by the events of 1449–50 (see references in notes to ll. 21–2 and 79–80); *soueraigne* = '(any) superior or lord'.

strout] = 'strut, strive'.

94. For the commonplace of 'rebelle and unbuxom' youth see G. R. Owst, *Literature and Pulpit in Medieval England*[2], (Oxford, 1961), 461–4.

takene parcyalyte] = 'make faction', a collocation unknown to *OED*; s.v. *Partiality*, 2, it first records the sense 'rivalry, factiousness' in 1480.

95. *reformede*] MS *roformede.*

put ... dowte] = 'assure you'.

95–6. = 'Unless we are reformed (i.e. mend our ways through our own efforts) I assure you that the lily (its root being used in medicines which are maturative or cause suppuration; cf. ll. 69–70 and 89) will have to be used as part of the process of removing (cf. *MED*, s.v. *Avoiden*, (v.), 2 (c)) the sin/pus so that we shall never see it [the sin/pus] again'; l. 96 parallels l. 92. The point is that self-reform is less painful and unpleasant than delaying until moral/medical intervention is inevitable (on the details see Lanfrank, pp. 210 and 336 ff., and Guy de Chauliac, pp. 86 and 590 ff. (note the 'lily rote' at p. 591/33); edd. citt., above, l. 70 (n.)). The lily here must = an aggressively therapeutic and improving agency of Virtue.

97. An echo of Cant. 2: 2, 'lilium inter spinas'. For other vernacular glosses on this text see (i) W. N. Francis, *The Book of Vices and Virtues*, EETS 217

(1942), 254/32–255/21, where the lily is the chaste soul that 'kepeþ his fairenesse amonges þe þornes of temptacion of þe flesch'; (ii) an unpublished text, *c.*1400, cited by *MED*, s.v. *Lilie* (n.), 2 (a), as *Bk. Mother* 11/21, where the lily is Christ dwelling 'among synful men, prickynge with here synnes'. See further the references given at l. 102 below. The sense of l. 97 is that virtue (the lily) is being choked by sinful men (thorns).

98. *þe*] MS *þe fle* (*fle* expuncted).

99. *faders*] here (as perhaps also at ll. 79 and 114) = 'bishops' specifically, as the reference to 'hornes' (see note) makes clear. Cf. also l. 10 n.

hornes] *MED*, s.v. *Horn* (n.), records the sense 'the apex of a bishop's miter' once (6 a (a)), and the sense 'one of the peaks of a bishop's miter' twice (6 d (c)); the sense 'horn of a mitre' is quite common for Medieval Latin *cornu* (cf. *Dictionary of Medieval Latin from British Sources*, s.v. *cornu*, 7 g). For the use of the bishop's 'horns' to cut down wrong-doers (the thorns) cf. *MED*'s quotations s.v. 6 d (c).

101. *fecundius*] = 'fertile'; in neither *MED* nor *OED*, although the latter s.v. *Fecundous* (a.), records *fecundious* as the first (1630) of its two quotations.

102. *lilies and roosez*] Lilies and roses are often linked in both religious and secular contexts (cf. *MED*, s.v. *Lilie* (n.), and *lilie-flour* (n.)). Although roses, unlike lilies, are not mentioned as such in Cant. 2: 1–2 (cf. l. 97 above) they are sometimes mentioned in commentary on that passage, and this may account for the mention of roses here; for such commentaries cf. (i) Ambrose, *PL* 15. 1871 (in addition to the lilies Ambrose mentions 'spinae rosarum, quae sunt tormenta martyrum'); (ii) Alanus de Insulis, *PL* 210. 64 ('viola humilitatis, patientiae rosa, lilium castitatis'); (iii) the unpublished text, *c.*1400, cited by *MED*, s.v. *Lilie* (n.), 2 (a), as *Bk. Mother* 11/13: 'In þe secunde chapitele of þis bok [Cant. 2:1], Gods Sone ... syngeþ his song: "I floure of þe feld", þat is most rede, brennynge in charite', where the red *flos campi* might suggest a rose. On the virtues symbolized by the lily and the rose see further F. N. Robinson's edn. of Chaucer (references given s.v. ll. 220 ff. of the Second Nun's Tale), and D. W. Robertson, Jr., *A Preface to Chaucer* ... (Princeton and London, 1963), 225 n. 138.

sustenance] = 'support'.

103. *reforme*] probably in the sense 'restore' (cf. *OED*, s.v. *Reform* (v.[1]), 2, and cf. l. 100), but the sense 'lead out of wickedness into righteousness' is also relevant.

105. The young strangers, whoever they were, seem also to have been wealthy (line 109).

106. *fervens*] = 'ardour'.

108. *To*] = 'until'. I cannot parallel *to* in this sense beginning a sentence.

109. *huyre*] = 'recompense'. The spelling with medial *-uy-* (rhyming on *fyre*) looks like a southernism and could not reasonably be assigned to East Leicestershire, the area indicated by the spellings of the rest of the poem (and the folios up to 37[v]; see opening paragraph of this article).

110. *garde*] *MED*, s.v. Garde (v.), has two quotations only: (i) 1448-*ante* 1500, a French exclamation ('Deue me garde!'); (ii) Chaucer, *CT* I. 4101, where one MS reads 'garderere' for other MSS' 'warderere'. *OED* first records the verb in 1500 (sense 7), but the sense 'escort' (1 d) is first recorded in 1597.

111. *require*] = 'ask, request'.

114. *A ffader of þe Chyrche*] cf. ll. 10 n. and 99 n.

117. *expresse*] = 'for certain'.

121–2. In the versions of the life of St. Cecilia known to me, the angel bore two crowns, one of roses and one of lilies; thus Chaucer's Second Nun's Tale: 'This angel hadde of roses and of lilie | Corones two' (*CT* VIII. 220–1), one being given to Cecilia and one to Valerian (222–4). For other English versions see T. Wolpers, *Die englische Heiligenlegende des Mittelalters* (Tübingen, 1964), 437 (Index, s.v. *Caecilia*). Although reference to crowns of both flowers would have picked up the lilies and roses of l. 102, the poet no doubt mentions the lilies alone partly because of their particular applicability to Waynflete, whose flower they were (l. 61), and who was about to receive (l. 128) an earthly prefiguring of the heavenly crown of lilies, but also because the crown of roses symbolized martyrdom (as the lilies symbolized purity). The poet might properly hope that Waynflete would receive a crown of lilies for his purity, but would hardly wish that his bishop would obtain the roseate crown of martyrdom (the murders of bishops Moleyns and Aiscough in 1450 showed that this might not be a remote possibility).

125. *even*] MS *even to* (*to* expuncted).

126. *sauoure*] The scent of the lilies and roses had been a feature in the Cecilia story; see Chaucer's version, ll. 242–59.

128. Either a real lily or a piece of jewellery featuring a representation of one. Mr J. P. Fuller, of the Victoria and Albert Museum, London, has informed me (private letter) that he has been 'unable to find conclusive evidence that artificial flowers are known in English art in the fifteenth century. I have consulted with my colleagues in the Department of Metalwork and we feel that this could be a reference to a ring or brooch featuring such a flower as these certainly are known from this period', though the interpretation as a real lily 'still bears credence'. A well-known instance of a jewel incorporating a lily is William of Wykeham's Founder's Jewel, perhaps bequeathed to New College, Oxford, in 1404 (see J. Evans, *A History of Jewellery*, pp. 60–1 and Plate 19 a; for heraldic jewels see pp. 64–7). Professor R. F. Green has pointed out to me a passage in a letter of John Paston III to John Paston II, 21 September 1472, in which there is a reference to a flower which must obviously be in the form of a jewel: 'forget not in all hast to get some goodly ryng, pryse of xx s., or som praty flowyr of the same pryse and not vndyr, to geue to Jane Rodon . . .' (ed. cit. in l. 1 n., part 1 (Oxford, 1971), no. 354, p. 579/56–8). For poems accompanying a gift of jewellery see notes 24, 25, and 27 (and cf. also notes 28 and 29) to the Introduction above.

ADDENDA

Since the despatch of the typescript of this article the following items have been noted:

1. To note 14 to the Introduction add: For other evidence of unrest in Winchester itself see J. N. Hare, 'The Wiltshire Risings of 1450: Political and Economic Discontent in Mid-fifteenth Century England', *Southern History*, iv (1982), 13–31, on p. 26: 'Men from Newbury were also involved in an incident in Winchester [in 1450], when they sought to extort £100 from the abbot of Hyde.'

2. The text (Jolliffe, A. 5) cited in the notes to ll. 97 and 102 as *Bk. Mother* has now been published: A. J. McCarthy, *Book to a Mother: an Edition with Commentary*, Salzburg Studies in English Literature, Elizabethan and Renaissance Studies xcii, Studies in the English Mystics i (Salzburg, 1981); the quotations will be found on p. 11, ll. 22–3 and 11–13 respectively.

'No newe thyng': The Printing of Medieval Texts in the early Reformation Period

ANNE HUDSON

IT is well known that there are a number of English Wycliffite texts that were printed in the early Reformation period during the reigns of Henry VIII and Edward VI. Equally familiar is the fact that a group of texts found their way into print then that claim or imply Lollard origins, but which are untraceable in manuscripts of the early Lollard period.[1] Best known of these are *Wycklyffes Wycket* and the *Ploughman's Tale*, the latter foisted upon Chaucer; less notorious is the *Praier and Complaynte of the ploweman*. These works, attested and unattested in the medieval period, raise a number of interesting questions. Why did the sixteenth-century reformers resort to these old texts? How did they regard the ideas of an earlier reforming movement? How did they treat the texts—respectfully, or in cavalier fashion, interpolating their own preoccupations and altering the medieval terms to accord with sixteenth-century ideas? Most importantly for a literary critic, can the claims of the unattested works to be medieval compositions be sustained, or are they forgeries? There is not space here to answer fully the

[1] Many of these texts were described by Margaret Aston in her two papers, 'Lollardy and the Reformation: Survival or Revival?', *History*, xlix (1964), 149–70 and 'John Wycliffe's Reformation Reputation', *Past and Present*, xxx (1965), 23–51. It should be noted that Wyclif's *Trialogus* was printed in Basel in 1525, and that a version of the Wycliffite *Opus Arduum* appeared with a preface by Luther on Wittenberg in 1528; I have discussed the latter in 'A Neglected Wycliffite Text', *Journal of Ecclesiastical History*, xxix (1978), 257–79.

first two questions; what I hope to do is to answer the third, and by so doing to throw some light on the last.

The texts with which I shall be dealing were printed within the period 1525 to 1550. Many of them were reprinted during the following sixty or seventy years, a time which saw also the issue of other Lollard texts. But the motives of the later editors were more complicated by antiquarianism, an interest in history as apart from theology.[2] The earlier prints, as the prefatory epistles to many make clear, were direct contributions to an ongoing, contemporary debate; they were directly polemical in the intent of their printers, just as they had been polemical in the purpose of their original authors. This contemporary relevance is demonstrated by the fact that many of them were printed abroad on the same presses that issued the texts of Tyndale, William Roye, Simon Fish, and George Joye.[3] Several of them appeared on the various lists of proscribed books that were issued before 1560;[4] the names of George Constantine and William Tyndale were associated with the editorship of one of them.[5] These books, like the works of contemporary reformers, were confiscated and held as evidence of heresy. Because of their dangerous nature, many of the bibliographical details about them are obscure: the printers concealed their own names and the place of publication, and many carry no date of imprint. Few survive in more than five copies, many in only one or two. It is quite possible that other Lollard texts were printed, but have not

[2] See, for instance, Thomas James's edition of *Two Short Treatises, against the Orders of the Begging Friars* (Oxford, 1608; *STC* 25589). It is, of course, impossible to make a firm distinction between antiquarian and theological interest, as the works of Bale and Foxe make very clear.

[3] See Anthea Hume's 'English Protestant Books Printed Abroad, 1525–1535: An Annotated Bibliography', in L. A. Schuster *et al.* (edd.) *The Confutation of Tyndale's Answer*, (New Haven and London, 1973), ii. 1065–91. There is an illuminating account of the context of these editions in W. A. Clebsch, *England's Earliest Protestants 1520–1535* (New Haven, 1964).

[4] See *Concilia Magnae Britanniae et Hiberniae*, ed. D. Wilkins (London, 1737), iii. 707, 719–20, 739 and John Foxe, *Actes and Monuments* (London, 1563), 573–4; also Clebsch, pp. 262–9.

[5] See Hume, pp. 1077–8, but cf. Clebsch, pp. 265–7.

survived; the titles under which the existing editions are found do not always correspond to their medieval titles, and many Lollard texts are in any form without title. My concern here is not bibliographical, and I have accepted the views of others on details of date and place of publication. For ease of reference, however, I give here a list of the texts with which I shall be dealing and the basic bibliographical details about them.[6]

A. The editions for which medieval manuscripts survive fall into two subgroups, the first published abroad, the second in England:

A proper dyaloge, betwene a gentillman and an husbandman . . . ([Antwerp, 1530?]; *STC* 1462. 3); this contains part of the Lollard treatise entitled in its modern edition *The Clergy may not hold Property*.[7]

A compendious olde treatyse, shewynge, howe that we ought to haue ye scripture in Englysshe (Hans Luft, Marburg [i.e. Johannes Hoochstraten, Antwerp] 1530; *STC* 3021); another edition appeared under the same title printed by Richarde Banckes in London [*c.* 1538?], *STC* 3022; both include a version of a short Lollard text defending biblical translation.[8]

The two treatises above were issued together, in an extended frame of the first (for which see below), with the title of the second (Hans Luft, Marburg [i.e. Hoochstraten, Antwerp], 1530; *STC* 1462. 5, formerly 6813).[9] In the following discussion I have used the earliest, separate versions.

[6] I have used, save in individual cases noted below, Hume's list together with *STC*. I am grateful to Miss Pantzer for providing me with a xerox of the revised entries for the first two texts described below.

[7] See *The English Works of Wyclif hitherto unprinted*, ed. F. D. Matthew (EETS 74, 1880; 2nd revd. edn. 1902), 362–404.

[8] The text has been printed twice, by M. Deanesly, *The Lollard Bible* (Cambridge, 1920), 437–45 and by C. Bühler, 'A Lollard Tract: on Translating the Bible into English', *MÆ* vii (1938), 167–83; I have used the latter. The comments of both editors on authorship should be ignored. Foxe printed it *Actes* (1563), 452–5.

[9] It was this version that was reproduced in facsimile by F. Fry (London, 1863) and appeared in the Arber Reprints (London, 1871).

The examinacion of Master William Thorpe ... [with] *The examinacion of ... syr Jhon Oldcastell* ... ([Antwerp, 1530]); *STC* 24045); the first part of this survives in a fifteenth-century manuscript, Bodleian Rawlinson c.208, and the second part will be discussed below.[10]

The Lanterne of Lyght (Robert Redman, [London, 1535?]; *STC* 15225); the medieval text survives in two manuscripts.[11]

Jack vp Lande (John Gough, [London, 1536?] *STC* 5098); this is found in two medieval forms, Latin and English.[12]

The dore of holy scripture (John Gowgh, London, 1540; *STC* 25587. 5, formerly 3033); an edition of the text now known as the General Prologue to the Wycliffite Bible translation.[13]

The true copye of a prolog wrytten ... by J. Wycklife ... (Robert Crowley, London, 1550; *STC* 25588); the text is the same as the last, but the print was an entirely new one from a different manuscript.

B. The texts for which no medieval evidence survives are the following:

The praier and complaynte of the ploweman vnto Christe ([Antwerp, 1531?]; *STC* 20036); this was reprinted in London and issued [*c.* 1532?], *STC* 20036. 5.[14]

[10] Foxe, *Actes* (1563), 143–72 reprinted the 1530 edition; a modern reprint appeared in *Fifteenth Century Prose and Verse*, ed. A. W. Pollard (Westminster, 1903), 97–189; a facsimile of the British Library copy was produced recently (Amsterdam and Norwood, N. J., 1975).

[11] It was edited by L. M. Swinburn (EETS 151, 1917); Swinburn did not use the print.

[12] See the edition of *Jack Upland, Friar Daw's Reply and Upland's Rejoinder* by P. L. Heyworth (London, 1968); Heyworth did not know of the Latin form, whose significance will be discussed below. For the date of the edition, and the possibility that there was another separate printing, see the same author's paper 'The Earliest Black-letter Editions of *Jack Upland*', *Huntington Library Quarterly*, xxx (1967), 307–14. Foxe reprinted Upland in *Actes*[2] (1570), i. 341–5.

[13] See *The Holy Bible .... made from the Latin Vulgate by John Wycliffe and his Followers*, edd. J. Forshall and F. Madden (Oxford, 1850), i. 1–60.

[14] The earlier version was reprinted in *Harleian Miscellany* (London, 1744–6), vi. 84–106. The later altered the preface heading from 'To the christen reader' to 'W.T. to the reader', which may be why both Bale, *Illustrium Maioris Britanniae scriptorum summarium* (Ipswich, 1548), f. 221, and Foxe, *Actes*[2] (1570), 494–501 ascribed the edition to Tyndale.

The examinacion of ... syr Jhon Oldcastell; see above.

[*The ploughman's tale*] (Thomas Godfrey, London, [1536?]; *STC* 5099. 5); the tale was also incorporated into the reprint of William Thynne's edition of Chaucer's work issued in 1542, and subsequently appeared in all sixteenth-century editions of Chaucer.[15] Another separate edition was produced by William Hyll ([1548?]; *STC* 5100), and an edition with a commentary was issued in 1606 (*STC* 5101).

Wycklyffes wycket ... (Norenburch, [i.e. London, John Day?], 1546; *STC* 25590); there is a variant version apparently issued the same year and place (*STC* 25590. 5), two editions probably published two years later (*STC* 25591 and 25591a), and a much later edition (London, 1612; *STC* 25592) declaredly based on an earlier printed copy.[16]

With two exceptions, one of which may be the result of accidental loss of the title page in the single surviving copy, all these texts acknowledge their early origins. Some are specific about their date: Thorpe's trial is dated 1407 (sig. A1), the *Proper Dyaloge* is said to have been written in the 'tyme of kinge Rycharde the secounde' (sig. B4) and the *Compendious treatyse* about 1400 (sig. A1^{v}). The antiquity of the *Praier and complaynte*, alleged to derive from 'not longe after ...' 1300 (sig. A1), and of the Prologue to the Wycliffite Bible, in both editions stated to

[15] See A. N. Wawn, 'The Genesis of *The Plowman's Tale*', *Yearbook of English Studies*, ii (1972), 21–40 and 'Chaucer, *The Plowman's Tale* and Reformation Propaganda: the Testimonies of Thomas Godfray and *I Playne Piers*', *Bulletin of the John Rylands Library*, lvi (1973), 174–92. A modern print of Thynne's text appears in W. W. Skeat, *Chaucerian and other Pieces* (Oxford, 1897), 147–90. There is a copy of Thynne's 1532 edition of Chaucer (*STC* 5068) now in the University of Texas library in which appears inserted a sixteenth-century manuscript copy of the *Ploughman's Tale*; see A. S. Irvine, 'A Manuscript Copy of *The Plowman's Tale*', *Texas Studies in English*, xii (1932), 27–56. Irvine did not know of *STC* 5099. 5, but suggested that the manuscript did not derive directly from either *STC* 5100 or Thynne's 1542 edition.

[16] Appended to the *Wycket* in the early editions was *The testament of maister Wylliam Tracie esquier, expounded by Wylliam Tyndall* (*STC* 25590, sigs. B3^{v}–C3^{v}). There have been various modernizations of the *Wycket*, for which see E. W. Talbert in *A Manual of the Writings in Middle English 1050–1500*, ii, revd. J. Burke Severs (Hamden, Conn., 1970), 523.

have been written 'two hondred yeares past' (1540, sig. A3; 1550, sig. A1), is overstated—in the 1550 edition of the latter despite the attribution to Wyclif himself. The title of the *Wycket* indicates Wyclif's authorship and alleges the date, impossible for the ascription, of 1395 (sig. A1); the print of *Jack vp Lande* claims Chaucer's paternity (sig. A1), though, perhaps surprisingly, this was not taken up by editors of Chaucer until Speght's second edition of 1602.[17] The surviving copy of the *Ploughman's Tale* lacks an original title page, but the implied authorship of the text, which may originally have been explicit, was accepted by 1542.[18] The only text which is completely opaque about its origins is the *Lanterne of Lyght*, a work which in many ways presents the fullest picture of Lollard beliefs. This opacity is interesting: presumably it implies that those responsible for issuing the edition thought that it could stand without apology or explanation, as a statement of opinions that would appeal to men of a reforming cast of mind in the 1530s without the excuse of antiquity. As such it is to be compared with those trial documents of the 1520s and 1530s where it is now unclear, and plainly was in some instances to the enquiring authorities, whether the suspect was old Lollard or new Lutheran.[19]

Turning to the way in which the sixteenth-century editors treated their medieval texts, the simplest cases are very easy to state. The latest edition, the second printing of the General Prologue, claimed to derive from 'an olde English Bible bitwixt the olde Testament and the Newe. Whych Bible remaynith now in ye Kyng hys maiesties Chamber' (sig. A1). Forshall and Mad-

[17] *STC* 5080 and 5081, ff. 348–50^v^; Speght's head-note to the text makes the unfortunate suggestion 'This is thought to bee that Crede which the Pellican speaketh of in the Plowmans tale', confusing Upland with *Pierce the Ploughmans Crede* (ed. W. W. Skeat, EETS 30, 1867).

[18] In William Thynne's second edition of Chaucer's works, *STC* 5069 and 5070, ff. 119–126^v^ at the end of the *Canterbury Tales*; in the third edition, *STC* 5071–4 ([1550?]), it was moved to a position before the Parson's Tale (ff. 93–100), a position it retained in all subsequent sixteenth-century editions.

[19] See A. G. Dickens, *Lollards and Protestants in the Diocese of York 1509–1558* (London, 1959), *passim*, and C. Cross, *Church and People 1450–1660* (Edinburgh, 1976), 31–80.

den in their edition of the Wycliffite Bible identified this manuscript as that now classified as Mm.2.15 in the Cambridge University Library, in which the Prologue stands between the testaments.[20] Collation of six chapters confirms this view, and reveals that Crowley's print is an extremely accurate version, preserving even some of the linguistic eccentricities of its exemplar. Somewhat more interesting because the precise exemplar has disappeared is the case of the *Proper Dyaloge* in both its separate and combined forms. The frame, the dialogue of the title, is a wholly sixteenth-century device, though many of the complaints voiced, against clerical interference in secular life and the temporal claims of the clergy, are, as the speakers acknowledge, of long standing. The Husbandman produces the medieval text, 'aboue an houndred yere olde', in the following words (sig. B4):

> halfe the boke we want
> Hauynge no more left than a remenant
> From the begynnynge of the .vi. chapter verely

This accuracy is roughly confirmed by the one surviving manuscript of this version of the text, now Lambeth 551, in which the opening words of the print are found near the beginning of chapter VII.[21] In fact, were Lambeth the only medieval version of this text to survive, it might be difficult to establish that the print did not derive straight from Lambeth—so close is the agreement between the two. But another longer version is found in three medieval manuscripts (CUL Dd.14.30(2), BL Egerton 2820, and Huntington Library HM 503) and one sixteenth-century manuscript (CUL Ff.6.2). Though the precise relation between the two medieval versions is hard to ascertain, there are a handful of agreements between the *Proper Dyaloge* and this better attested medieval version and against Lambeth 551, agreements which can only be explained on the assumption that the print

[20] Forshall and Madden, i, pp. liv–lv.

[21] In Matthew's edition, p. 382/25. The print continues to Matthew 396/10 including what Matthew regarded, without justification in the Lambeth manuscript, as an appendix but omitting the Latin authorities.

derives from a manuscript very close to Lambeth but not identical with it.[22] Such a conclusion also, of course, accounts for the alleged incompleteness of the Husbandman's exemplar and for the apparent discrepancy in chapter numbering.[23] Apart from these few agreements against Lambeth, the print is entirely faithful to the text as attested in Lambeth. The reason for the fidelity may perhaps be inferred from the Gentleman's response to the text (sig. C6^{v}):

> Nowe I promyse the after my iugement
> I haue not hard of soche an olde fragment
>   Better groundyd on reason with scrypture.
> Yf soche auncyent thynges myght come to lyght
> That noble men hadde ones of theym a syght
>   The world yet wolde chaunge perauenture.
> For here agaynst the clergye can not bercke
> Sayenge as they do/ thys is a newe wercke
>   Of heretykes contryued lately.
> And by thys treatyse it apperyth playne
> That before oure dayes men dyd compleyne
>   Agaynst clerckes ambycyon so stately.[24]

The third instance of almost complete faithfulness to a medieval exemplar is, however, the text which nowhere proclaims its antiquity: the *Lanterne of Lyght*. Two medieval copies survive, Harley 2324, used by Swinburn, the editor of the EETS text, and Harley 6613, not known to Swinburn and defective because of loss of leaves. A third copy is known to have existed in the possession of John Claydon in 1415; the second folio incipit is

[22] The full evidence will be set out in the edition of the longer version I am preparing for EETS; the best evidence is the print's inclusion of three lines after Matthew 386/26 (sig. B7^{v}) and of two after Matthew 387/12 (sig. B8), in both cases supported by the longer version.

[23] The chapter numbering is quite clear in Lambeth, and the edition's numbering is not a simple omission of a minim since it is given both as a numeral and as a word. It seems likely that the edition's exemplar had a different chapter division.

[24] The search for precedent, for evidence that the reformers were in a tradition of thought, is obvious in many of these texts and was taken up by Bale; see especially L. P. Fairfield, *John Bale, Mythmaker for the English Reformation* (West Lafayette, 1976).

given in the trial proceedings in Chichele's register, an incipit that does not agree with either Harley manuscript.[25] The print is in some respects superior to each of the manuscripts separately, and in a few cases appears to derive from an exemplar better than either.[26] The format of this exemplar can be precisely determined from the one large omission in the print, where it is clear either that the printer inadvertently turned over two leaves or that his model lacked one folio; there is no conceivable ideological reason for the omission, an omission which locally produces nonsense and which leaves chapter IV without an opening or marking in the text, despite being called for in the final *tabula*.[27] The printed text is considerably shorter than the version in the extant manuscripts, because it has omitted the Latin quotations pedantically included in the earlier versions before the English translations. At the beginning of the text there is a good deal of minor re-wording that makes little difference to the sense; at the end there is some sign of abbreviation, probably to ensure that the text concluded within the quire, an aim effected somewhat over-zealously. There is some modernization of vocabulary, sometimes done with greater regard for the look of the individual word than for the overall sense of the passage.[28] But in general the sense is so well kept that use of this print, together with Harley 6613, would allow a number of corrections to be

[25] Harley 6613 lacks Swinburn's 14/24–17/1, 21/3–29/8, 31/13–37/18, 48/24–50/19, and 128/13 to end. For the Claydon trial see the edition of the Chichele register by E. F. Jacob (Canterbury and York Society, 1938–47) iv. 132–8; no doubt Claydon's copy was destroyed immediately after the trial.

[26] For instance, the print agrees with Harley 6613 in adding 'nonnes, systers and spytlers' in 38/17 and in reading *dystynctly* rather than *diligentli* at 56/17; on the other hand Harley 6613 alone omits 79/30–80/1; the print has a fuller translation of the Latin quotations, which are omitted from the print itself, than the available manuscripts at 127/2 and 137/2.

[27] The loss is from 13/19 to 15/5 of the modern edition and is on sig. A8^{v} of the print. The amount of text lost, some 46 lines, is a very credible content for one folio or, if the error were the printer's, one opening; Harley 2324 contains some 36 lines to a folio, recto and verso, Harley 6613 approximately 58 lines.

[28] For instance, 57/2 *style* for *poyntel*, 51/15 *tarynge* for *terren*, and less happily 93/22 *nowe* for *wowe*, 16/15 *verefyed* for *waried*, and 108/5, etc. *wyll* for *nile*.

made to Swinburn's edition. References to affairs of the early Wycliffite period are hardly changed, though the term *Lollardis* (11/11) is changed to *heretyckes* (sig. A7); the description of the persecution of those favouring vernacular scriptures (100/1 ff., sig. G5), the account of penance (104/21 ff., sig. G7) and of Antichrist, the court of Rome its head, the archbishops and bishops its body, and 'þise (patched and) cloutid sectis . as mounkis chanouns . and freris ... þe venymous taile' (16/10 ff., sig. B1), remain unaltered. As Swinburn said (p. x), the fifteen points assembled by the trial lawyers at Claydon's investigation give a fair survey of the heresy in the *Lanterne*; none of these are mitigated or altered in the print. The only significant change clarifies an obscure passage, suppressing an allusion to the Eucharist and substituting a clearer exhortation to preaching.[29]

Somewhat further removed from extant medieval English manuscript versions are the prints of Upland and Thorpe, but in each case there is good evidence that points towards the authenticity of most of the material introduced. In each case there are both English and Latin versions surviving from the pre-Reformation period, each preserving slightly different textual traditions; this enables an assessment to be made of the later edition, and this later edition in turn can be used to remedy defects in the earlier vernacular version. For the autobiographical account of Thorpe's trial in 1407 there are three medieval witnesses, the English account in Bodl. MS Rawl. c.208 (R), and two Latin versions in Vienna 3936 (V) and Prague Metropolitan Chapter O.29 (P); there are a number of sixteenth-century versions, Latin and English, apart from the edition here under discussion (A),

[29] The two Harley manuscripts agree in reading (Swinburn 12/7–9) 'What is to be sett biforne þe bodi of Crist þat prestis sacren? And siþen þei treten Cristis bodi. miche raþer seiþ Ierom þei schullen preche & blesse þe peple. Hec dist. 99.' The print (sig. A7[v]) substitutes 'And Seyncte Jerom commendyth in prestehode prechynge the gospel and blessyng the people before the sayeng of masse. And Seynct Paull sayth that Christ sent hym to preche & not to baptyse. So by this it apereth that prechynge the gospel is the hyghest seruyce that may be done to god.' A marginal note supplies the references 'Dist. 56. I Corin. 1 Non me misit christus baptizare sed euangelizare.'

but they are all derivative, directly or indirectly, from this edition and have no independent value.[30] V and P fairly clearly derive from a common exemplar, presumably the single copy taken abroad to the Hussite area. Whether the original of the text was in English or Latin is not immediately clear, but does not affect the present issue. In general R is much closer to VP than is A. But in cases where error can be established, the value of R against A is more evenly balanced; there are, furthermore, a number of cases where the agreement of A with VP shows that R's apparently acceptable version is probably unoriginal.[31] The main text of the Antwerp print is not modified for doctrinal reasons save possibly in two minor cases: first where the statement 'þe worschipful sacrament of þe auter is *verri Cristis fleisch* and his blood in forme of breed and wyne' (R, f. 41) is amplified by the expansion of the italicized words to 'the sacramente of Christis flesche' (sig. C8^v^), and secondly where the less extreme 'it stierith god to take greate vengeaunce both vpon lordis and vpon comons which suffer thes priestes charitably' (sig. E7) is substituted for the interventionist 'it terriþ God to take greet veniaunce boþe vpon lordis and vpon comouns whiche suffren þese prestis to lyuen as þei now done and wolen not bisien hem to amende þese prestis charitabli' (R, f. 66). But the latter, like a number of even more minor changes, is probably a case of inadvertent haplography. However, though the main text is authentically medieval, the same cannot be proved for material that stands after it. The preface (sig. A1^v^–A2^v^) is declaredly

[30] Again full evidence for these assertions will be given in my edition of the text. A Latin version (now incomplete) in Bale's handwriting was entered into the manuscript of the *Fasciculi Zizaniorum*, Bodl. e Mus. 86, f. 105^v^ and following five inserted and unnumbered leaves; this was reprinted by Foxe in *Commentarii Rerum in Ecclesia Gestarum* ... (Strasburg, 1554), ff. 118–156^v^ and in *Rerum in Ecclesia Gestarum* ... (Basel, 1559), pp. 79–96. In his *Actes* Foxes substituted the English from the 1530 print (1563 edn. pp. 143–72).

[31] For instance, in my edition of an extract from R in *Selections from English Wycliffite Writings* (Cambridge, 1978), no. 4/53–4 I should have emended the text in the light of agreement between A and VP to read 'I schulde herþoruȝ first [wounde and defyle myn owne soule, and also I schulde herþoruȝ] ȝeue occasioun to many men and wymmen of ful sore hurtynge.'

editorial, and refers to the burning of Thomas Hitton in Maidstone 'now thys yere'. After the trial account appears (sigs. G6–H2) Thorpe's *testamente*, of which there is no trace in R (nor any indication that that manuscript is now defective). The *testamente* is dated in the print 20 September 1460, some fifty-three years, as it observes, after Thorpe's trial. This in itself casts doubt upon the authenticity of the *testamente*, or at least its attribution to Thorpe: Thorpe appears to have been instituted to the vicarage of Marske, Cleveland, in 1395, and would therefore have been at least eighty-five by 1460.[32] In fact, the *testamente* has no connection with the trial or with the interests shown in it; it deals, after an introduction concerning Christ as the foundation of all faith, with the evils of the clergy in general terms. It could be a medieval text, but there is nothing in it to connect it specifically with Thorpe. The editor of the Thorpe trial is unusually forthcoming with his comments on his treatment of the language (sig. A2^{v}):

> This I haue corrected and put forth in the english that now is vsed in Englande / for ower sothern men / nothynge thereto addynge ne yet therfrom mynysshyng. And I entende hereafter with the helpe of God to put it forthe in his owne olde english which shal well serue / I doute not / bothe for the northern men and the faythfull brothern of scotlande.

If he carried out his intention, all trace of it has been lost.[33]

The position with regard to Jack Upland is in detail complicated, but in the last resort there seems little evidence that the print put out by Gough shows substantive sixteenth-century

[32] See *Selections*, pp. 155–7, for some details about Thorpe.

[33] The identity of the editor is a question of considerable obscurity. Foxe, though he printed the 1530 version in his *Actes*, added a comment to his introduction in the second edition of this work (1570, i. 629): 'Although for the more credite of the matter, I rather wished it in his own naturall speache, wherin it was first written. Notwithstandyng, to put away all doubt and scruple herein, this I thought before to premonishe and testifie to the reader touchyng the certeintie hereof: that they bee yet a lyve, which haue seen the selfe same copy in his own old Englishe, resemblyng the true antiquitie both of the speache and of the tyme.'

interference. Again, the printed versions of the sixteenth century that survive are all dependent upon Gough (G).[34] But the evidence for the earlier tradition is more varied. In the first place there are two manuscripts, Harley 6641 and CUL Ff.6.2, of which Heyworth provided an edition (E); secondly, there is the indirect evidence of Daw's *Rejoinder* (D), found only in Bodl. MS Digby 41, which, as Skeat perceived and Heyworth confirmed, points to a different version of the questions from that found in E.[35] Unknown to Heyworth, there is a third medieval witness: in MS Bodl. 703 is a text by William Woodford, the Franciscan opponent of Wyclif, setting out a series of 65 questions and answers, the questions being those of Upland, the responses those of Woodford (W).[36] In general G and W agree with each other and against E (D's evidence is only partial, and its text sometimes agrees with E, sometimes with GW).[37] There are a few places where G can be shown to be defective by agreement between E and W, and equally a few places where W can be detected in error by agreement between G and E.[38] W because of its textual proximity to G provides a check on the possibility of G's alterations, suppressions, or additions. In fact in many cases W confirms G's authenticity: G and W contain material not found in E, whilst conversely both G and W omit material found only in E.[39] There are a few instances where W

[34] See Heyworth's paper, (above, n. 12), and edition, p. 29 n. 3.

[35] Skeat, pp. xxxv–xxxvii, and Heyworth, pp. 29–35.

[36] Ff. 41–57; the discovery was made by E. Doyle and is reported in J. Catto, 'William Woodford, O.F.M. (*c.* 1330–*c.* 1397)', University of Oxford D.Phil. thesis (1969), 31.

[37] The fuller comparison allowed by the discovery of W bears out Heyworth's observation that D departs from E principally after l. 285 and that there may have been three versions of Upland (pp. 32–3 and n. 2). G's idiosyncrasies begin at almost exactly the same place, suggesting that there may have been a break in the textual tradition at that point.

[38] For the first instances are at E 371 *causis*, W *causas*, G *cause* or E 390–400, lacking in G; for the second most notably the surviving manuscript of W lacks E 237–43, though it appears in G.

[39] In Skeat's print of G, sections 7–8, 27, 29, 31, most of 37, most of 41, 47, and 50 are all present in W but not in E; in Heyworth's edition of E, ll. 169–73, 182–6, 244–62, 277–81, 291–4 are peculiar to E and missing in both W and G.

does not confirm G's text. One case seems plainly a sixteenth-century sophistication: this is the omission of question 65 (E, 390–400) on the Eucharist, found in both W and E. There are some seven extra questions in G, where the issue is much less clear: after W question 62, E 378, are inserted two questions (sigs. B4–B5), one on the legitimacy of fraternal habits and leaving them and the other on letters of fraternity, whilst at the end are five extra questions (sigs. B5ᵛ–B8). But in all these cases the material added goes over ground that has been covered elsewhere in all versions. The only possibly topical issue is that of the lawfulness of leaving an order, but this, whilst obviously relevant at the time of the disendowment of monastic and fraternal communities by Henry VIII, was a question discussed by the Lollards earlier.[40] Since no good motive can be found for supposing that the independent material in G was supplied by the sixteenth-century editor, it seems wiser, in the light of the evidence where G's text is supported, to withhold condemnation and to conclude that Upland, like Thorpe, is substantively a reliable transcript of a lost medieval exemplar.

John Gough, in his edition of the General Prologue in 1540, asks his readers for an even higher degree of faith. In his long address to the readers he draws their attention to the old-fashioned language 'þe which auntyant wrytynge dyffereth farre from the termys and sentence þat is now in our tyme wryten and spoken' (sig. A3ᵛ). More surprisingly he also draws attention to the more contentious parts of the text (sig. A7):

I humbly requyre you in case ye fynde ony thyng in this boke that shall offend you in the x chapiter or in the xiij I praye you blame not me though I haue folowed myne orygynall and olde copy in worde and sentence. Yet I wrote it not blamyng no person nowe lyuyng, I trust

[40] The suppression of the friaries was not effected until 1539, but the matter of dissolution of religious houses had been under discussion for a number of years before the act against the monastic houses gave clear warning to the friars; see S. E. Lehmberg, *The Reformation Parliament, 1529–1536* (Cambridge, 1970), 223–9, and references given. For Lollard discussion see, for instance, T. Arnold, *Select English Works of Wyclif* (Oxford, 1869–71), i. 403/34, ii. 299/5, iii. 432/35.

there be no suche abuses in rulers, gouernours, pastours, curates and preachers, as was in the Romysh church in those dayes (two hundred yeares paste and gone) God forbyd that there shulde be ony suche poysoned stomakes in this Realme.

No doubt, with the *Kynges preuylege* on the title verso, some such disclaimer was prudent.[41] But it is not clear that Gough played entirely fair with the text or his readers. Gough's rewording of the text, largely no doubt in the cause of modernization of the language, makes it difficult to discover which, if any, of the extant manuscripts of the Prologue he used as his exemplar. None of the ten, however, justify some changes in chapter x, one of those whose text Gough was most anxious to authenticate.[42] Towards the end of the chapter his version removes a criticism that linked *lordis* with *prelatis* as indulgers *in wakingis and pleyingis bi niȝt, and in rere-soperis and othere vanites* (I. 34), and, perhaps more dangerously, as the inflicters of inordinate taxes and other extortions on the commons; the sentence is abbreviated and only prelates and curates named (sig. L4^{v}). Two sentences later again changes are made that eliminate lords from condemnation of the practice of offering to *dede stockes or stones* rather than to *the lyuely ymage of God whiche is a christen man* (sig. L5). That Gough himself was responsible for these alterations is suggested by the wording of this sentence: men 'in tymes past kneled and prayed, and offred fast to dead

[41] Gough was also the publisher of Upland, and again there had the royal privilege, though the terms of it are not set out in full in Upland. Heyworth argued (art. cit., pp. 313–14) that Upland was issued as part of Henry VIII's 'calculated campaign of printed propaganda against Rome in his attempt to justify and to secure his claims for royal supremacy'. Heyworth did not mention Gough's 1540 Prologue, and it would be more difficult to argue the king's involvement with this: even though the Prologue is less consistently outspoken than Upland, Henry's conservatism had by that time come to the fore and it is not clear that he would by then have sympathized even with the more moderate work's advocacy of vernacular scriptures for all. It would seem wiser to take the privilege here, at any rate, as 'a perfunctory and permissive formula'. Gough was imprisoned in January 1541 for printing and selling seditious books (see Aston, *Past and Present*, xxx (1965), n. 28).

[42] To the list in Forshall and Madden, i, p. xxxvii, should be added MS 12 in the Scheide collection, Princeton.

ymages, as I am certayne some yet do preuyly' (sig. L5). Rather earlier in the same chapter the editor intrudes more blatantly: after an original comment on the proclamation of papal indulgences at the instigation of secular lords (I. 30), is added 'this hath bene euydently sene of late dayes in our tyme in Englond (for the redresse) laude we God and praye we for our moste noble kynge, that he maye prosperously lyue and fynysshe the werkes that he hath begonne in God' (sig. K3). In fairness to Gough, it does not appear that his text is consistently unreliable, and it must be admitted that the attentive reader would pick up the contemporary reference from the wording in some cases. But Crowley was wise in 1550 to go back to a manuscript for his edition of the Prologue, rather than reissuing Gough's text.[43]

The remaining text from the first part of my list, the *Compendious treatyse*, is difficult to assess. Bühler in his edition of the medieval tract listed seven manuscripts, to which can be added an eighth; but five of these are post-medieval transcripts, all apparently derived from the same exemplar that seems originally to have been in the library of Worcester Cathedral, and one of the medieval texts is a fragment only consisting of the first thirty-one lines.[44] However, these witnesses, essentially four at best, are in agreement in the version they offer; the only serious discrepancy concerns the position of a passage of twelve lines, at

[43] It is not clear whether Crowley knew of the earlier edition: he does not mention it, but, though he observes (sig. A2^{v}) 'Many men bistowed muche to haue it copied out to the intent thei might enioye ye frutes of it, in the tyme of errowre and ignoraunce: but thou hast it now offered vnto the for little coste, in a time when true religion biginnith to floryshe. It was at þ^{e} fyrste made common to fewe men y^{t} wolde and were able to optayne it. But nowe it is made commen to all menne, that be desyrouse of it', he does not claim his text as the first print.

[44] To Bühler's list may be added Corpus Christi Coll. Cambridge, MS 100, pp. 227–33, a Parkerian collection like 298 and derived from the same source as that, though unlike it corrected from some other source. The other transcripts are Lambeth Palace 594, BL MSS Harl. 425 and Cotton Vitellius D.vii; the incomplete text is in Trinity Coll. Cambridge, MS B.1.26, f. 143^{v}, where it appears in the inner margin of the final leaf. The only complete medieval texts are Trinity Coll. Cambridge, MS B.14.50, ff. 26–30^{v} and Pierpont Morgan Library, New York, MS 648, ff. 142–43^{v}.

the end or in the middle of the text.[45] The printed version, in all three issues, omits almost a third of this text, rearranges some, and adds further material of greater length than that left out.[46] Some of the omissions could well be accidental, occurring by haplography either by a medieval scribe or by the printer. The puzzle derives from the similarity in nature of material omitted and added: biblical and patristic justifications for scriptural translation are found in both categories. It is certain that some revision of the text had occurred: the version found in the manuscripts must be dated before 1414, since it refers to archbishop Arundel as still alive; on the other hand the printed text alludes to the *cruell dethe* of Richard Flemyng, bishop of Lincoln, which occurred in 1431.[47] Some of the added material would have considerable relevance in the 1520s and 1530s:

And therfore it were good to the Kyng and to other lordes to make some remedy agaynst this constitucyon of Antechrist that saythe it is vnlawfull to vs englyshe men to have in englyshe goddes lawe / and therfore he brennythe and sleythe them that maynteyne thys good deade / and that is for default that the kyng and lordes knowen not ne wyll not knowe ther owne office in meantenance of god and hys lawe. (sig. A5v)

... it lyethe neu[er] in Antichristes power to destroye all englysshe bookes / for as fast as he brennethe / other men shall drawe / and thus the cause of heresy and of þe people that dyethe in heresy is the frowardnes of byshoppes that wyll not suffer men to haue opyn comounyng and fre in the lawe of gode ... And nowe they turne his lawe

[45] Trinity B.14.50 formed the basis of Bühler's edition; ll. 229–41 of that text are found in the Morgan manuscript and all the later transcripts (Trinity B.1.26 lacks everything after l. 31) at the end.

[46] Omitted from Bühler's text are ll. 1–3, 35–9, 45–57, 62–80, 95–9, 207–9, 213–16, 228–76, 299–301; the most substantial additions occur after Bühler's ll. 62, 305, 210, and 213, the last by rearrangement standing at the end of the treatise.

[47] The earlier text was itself a reworking of part of a Latin tract which I have argued elsewhere to be by Richard Ullerston ('The debate on Bible translation, Oxford 1401', *EHR* xc (1975), 1–18), and the reference to Arundel was added in that revision. The printed version (sig. A5) omits the words *þat nowe is* (291) from the story about the archbishop and adds the comment that 'he became the most cruell enemy that myght be agaynst englyshe bookes' (sig. A5v).

by ther cruell constitucyons into dampnacion of the people. (sig. A6–A6^{v})

But similar comments had been made from Wyclif's day onwards, even before Arundel's Constitutions had given them full justification.[48] What is clear is that if the additions in the printed edition are editorial then they were made within the same tradition as produced the original tract: a tradition which regarded the precise citation of biblical, patristic, scholastic, and canonistic passages as the best way of arguing a question.

Something in transition must be said about the *Examination* of Oldcastle that is appended to the trial of Thorpe. This text was used in turn by John Bale in *A brefe chronycle concernynge the Examinacyon and death of ... Syr Johan Oldecastell ...* ([Antwerp?], 1544; *STC* 1276; reprinted in [1545?] and [1548?], *STC* 1277–8), a work that I have not considered here because it does not purport to be a simple reprinting of one medieval text but declaredly draws on many sources.[49] The text is an abbreviated and chronologically obscure account of the long process of investigation that Oldcastle underwent, a process interrupted by his escape from custody and by the rising of 1413. Parts of it apparently derive from the same source as the documents recorded in the *Fasciculi Zizaniorum* and Arundel's register.[50] But

[48] With the second compare the *Opus Arduum*, dated between Christmas 1389 and Easter 1390 (Brno University Library, MS Mk 28, f. 174^{v}) where the prophecy of Revelations 12:4 is said to be fulfilled 'per generale mandatum prelatorum ad comburendum, destruendum et condemnandum omnes libros, scilicet omelias ewangeliorum et epistolarum in lingwa materna conscriptos, suggerendo quasi non liceat nobis Anglicis legem diuinam habere in nostro vulgari ... Sed quamuis ad hec quantum potuit per se et per suos laborauit diabolus, non tamen profecit, quia non omnes libri tales sunt destructi, sed loco eorum alii iam de nouo conscripti sunt ut in breui, Domino fauente patebit, ipsis multum forciores.'

[49] Mrs Aston (1964), p. 155 n. 19, suggested that Bale in 1543 did not know the *Examination*; but side-notes in the *Brefe chronycle* make it plain that he had used it fully by the following year. For Bale's work on Oldcastle see L. P. Fairfield, 'John Bale and the Development of Protestant Hagiography in England', *Journal of Ecclesiastical History*, xxiv (1973), 145–60. A reprint of the *Brefe chronycle* is in the *Harleian Miscellany*, ii. 233–64.

[50] *Fasciculi Zizaniorum*, ed. W. W. Shirley (Rolls Series, 1858), 438–9 and 441–2; the material from Arundel's register is printed in Wilkins, iii. 354–5.

no precise parallel is known to the arguments recorded between Oldcastle and Arundel (sigs. H7^{v}–I4), though it is credible enough that such occurred. Bale maintained (sig. A3^{v}) that the *Examination* was issued by Tyndale, but observed. 'The which examinacyon was wrytten in the tyme of the seyd Lordes trouble / by a certen frynde of his / and so reserued in copyes vnto this our age. But sens that tyme I haue founde it in theyr owne wryttynges (which were than his vttre enemyes) in a moche more ample fourme than there.' Notwithstanding his reservations about brevity, Bale used the text extensively and treated it as carefully as he did his others, Arundel's register, Netter's *Doctrinale*, and the *Fasciculi Zizaniorum*, and more. Properly, this text belongs with the next group, though it appears as an appendix to one of those for which a medieval exemplar is known. More investigation of the Oldcastle revolt, and of the sources of evidence about it, may throw further light on this enigmatic text;[51] but there is little or nothing in it to suggest a sixteenth-century forgery.

Can any generalizations be made from this mass of detail? It seems to me that it would be fair to say that, with very few exceptions, all the evidence points to a remarkable conservatism in the sixteenth-century handling of the medieval material. There is some variation in the extent to which archaic linguistic forms are retained, but in substantive readings fidelity to the older exemplars can in many cases be established with a high degree of certainty. The fidelity is such that, where material is locally found that has no model, as for instance the extra questions in Upland or the added authorities of the *Compendious treatyse*, it would seem reasonable in default of positive contrary indication to accept that the sixteenth-century editor had an exemplar that differed from those surviving, but an exemplar that was medieval. The exception to this is obviously where the wording of

[51] Though there are references to a book about Thorpe that antedate the printed text (see Foxe, *Actes*, ed. S. R. Cattley (London, 1837–41), iv. 235, 259, 679 and v. 39), I have not come across comparable allusions to a text about Oldcastle.

the edition explicitly refers to contemporary events, or appeals to a contemporary audience—as in the case of the intrusions in Gough's edition of the General Prologue. Where the editors may not be so faithful is over omissions: in particular the topic of the Eucharist produced omission in Upland and re-wording in the *Lanterne of Lyght*. On the other hand, discussion of the Eucharist did not always provoke alteration: the longest treatment of the subject in the texts so far considered is in Thorpe (sigs. C7^{v}–D2^{v}), a passage that is unchanged from the version in the surviving manuscript.

In the light of these conclusions we may look briefly at the remaining three texts, the *Ploughman's Tale*, Wyclif's *Wycket*, and the *Praier and complaynte of the ploweman*. The first of these has been examined recently by Andrew Wawn, who concluded that all of the *Tale*, apart from the opening fifty-two lines and ll. 205–28, had 'an early fifteenth-century date of composition'.[52] Whilst I am not entirely convinced by Wawn's dissection of that early poem into a basic debate and a revised version with interpolation, his arguments for an early Lollard origin for the work seem to me entirely persuasive. The evidence that Wawn used was both ideological and linguistic. With regard to the second, the case in the *Ploughman's Tale* is happier than in either of the other two texts: the verse form of the *Tale* makes it possible to argue on strong grounds for the originality of vocabulary in rhyming position. The balance of probability is against the likelihood that the strongly archaic language of the *Praier and complaynte* was composed by a sixteenth-century forger,[53] but this cannot formally be proved. Even less would it be legitimate to dismiss the claims of the *Wycket* to antiquity on the grounds of the more modern language of its editions. In subject matter there seems to me nothing in the *Praier* that would be out

[52] Wawn (1972), 39.

[53] The morphology is noticeably archaic, especially in the frequent use of the past participial *y*-prefix; as instances of obsolescent or obsolete vocabulary note *bynemen*, *dysparpled*, *fulleden* 'baptised', *gylteth* 'sins', *herynge* 'praise', *sythe* 'afterwards' adv., *vnworshypped*, *yerners* 'runners'.

of place in a Lollard tract of the early fifteenth century. The case with the *Wycket* is to my mind rather less clear: the terms in which the Eucharist is discussed are not altogether those found in Lollard treatments of that subject and, though biblical passages are amply quoted, there is not the usual Wycliffite citation of patristic proof texts. The *Wycket* was, however, notorious before it was printed: it is mentioned in numerous trials from 1518 to 1532.[54] Bale records that William Grocyn had written a tract against it, and gives the incipit; Bale himself owned a copy of this lost work. This would put the date of composition of the *Wycket* certainly before 1518 and more probably well before this.[55]

From the viewpoint of Robert Crowley, the printer of the latest edition considered here, there is an inexplicable omission from my discussion. The issue of the General Prologue must have been a relatively simple task, and the preparation of the text can have occupied only a small amount of Crowley's time before its appearance in 1550. For in the same year Crowley produced three editions of *Piers Plowman*, editions which, as Kane and Donaldson have been able to deduce from their collations, show successive modifications made as the result of conflation with new manuscripts that came to hand.[56] There is not space here to examine in full Crowley's side-notes, let alone to consider whether any of the idiosyncrasies of his texts reflect his editorial tampering. But it is clear that Crowley linked *Piers Plowman* with the earlier reforming movement: he dated the poem between 1350 and 1409, and most probably in the reign of Edward III, 'In whose tyme it pleased God to open the eyes of many to se hys truth, geuing them boldenes of herte, to open their mouthes and crye oute agaynste the worckes of darckenes, as did John

[54] See the registers used by Foxe, *Actes*, iv. 207–8, 226, 234–6, v. 39–40.

[55] Bale, *Scriptorum Illustrium Maioris Brytanniae ... Catalogus* (Basel, 1557–9), i. 707 and ii. 164.

[56] *STC* 19906, 19907, and 19907a; see G. Kane and E. T. Donaldson, *Piers Plowman: the B Version* (London, 1975), 6–7 and ensuing discussion of textual relations.

Wicklefe, who also in those dayes translated the holye Bible into the Englishe tonge ...' (sig. *ii). The modern reader of the B version might be surprised to learn that passus v contains proof by Reason that 'Abbayes shoulde be suppressed', a subject also argued, we are told, in passus x; but it is clear from Crowley's comment on the second of these that he regarded the whole as a tract for his times: 'Loke not vpon this boke therfore, to talke of wonders paste or to come, but to amende thyne owne misse, which thou shalt fynd here moste charitably rebuked' (sig. *2^{v}). Modern critics may see a world of difference between *Piers Plowman* and, for instance, Jack Upland or Thorpe's disputations with archbishop Arundel.[57] To the reformers of the sixteenth century all of these texts, along with passages from Chaucer or Gower, were grist to the mill of their argument: to support their own contentions on theological and ecclesiastical questions, and to show that the ideas they put forward were supported by 'a witness preordained by God, so many years before us, for the confirmation of our doctrine'.[58]

[57] I hope to trace elsewhere the fortunes of the ploughman figure, influenced by *Piers Plowman* and by Chaucer's *Canterbury Tales*, in the fifteenth and sixteenth centuries, and to consider the justification for subsequent interpretations in Langland's text. Pamela Gradon has examined the position of Langland in regard to Wyclif's thought in 'Langland and the Ideology of Dissent', *PBA* lxvi (1980), 179–205.

[58] Quoted by Margaret Aston (1964), p. 157, from Luther's preface to the 1528 edition of the Lollard *Opus Arduum*.

Jocelin of Brakelond, Abbot Samson, and the Case of William the Sacrist

P. L. HEYWORTH

IN a reflective passage at the close of his *Domesday Book and Beyond* F. W. Maitland expressed the conviction that a century hence (he wrote in 1896) the materials available to the medieval scholar would not be in the shape in which he found them then. Maitland spoke confidently of the advances in scholarship that would be made possible by the work of philologist and palaeographer, annalist and formulist, cartographer and (prophetically) photographer, and of the opportunities such advances would present. What above all else he looked forward to was a time when 'by slow degrees the thoughts of our forefathers, their common thoughts about common things, will have become thinkable once more'.

No one in his generation in Middle English studies has done more than Norman Davis to encourage this ideal of historical knowledge. If the common thoughts of common people about common things in England of the later Middle Ages are more accessible to us than they were to scholars of Maitland's generation credit must go to the patient and unforgiving labour Norman Davis has spent over a period of more than thirty years on the letters and papers of an obscure fifteenth-century Norfolk family. And while he himself refuses to claim more for his work on the Pastons than that it enables us to see a little more clearly the kind of linguistic attainment that laymen of comparatively modest social standing had been able to acquire by the middle of the fifteenth century, we can fairly add, by way of a supplementary gloss, another view: when Chaucer lived he must have heard this very language—matter-of-fact, unmetaphorical, capable of religious solemnity or of broad humour, even if far better fitted for narrative than for analysis. That is Virginia Woolf's view, and though a limited view it nudges us towards the recognition that there is no better aid to the understanding of Chaucer's language and hence of his poetry than a reading and a re-reading of the Paston Letters.

Maitland ends his book with a sentence that pupils of Norman Davis may be forgiven for believing they have heard—or have heard something very like—before: 'There are discoveries to be made; but also there are habits to be formed.' Discoveries take care of themselves, lying in wait in unexpected places, though they tend to ambush those best prepared to wrestle them to the ground. What most of us have learned from him is a habit, one indispensable to the vernacular medievalist: the habit of confronting individual and particular words (and not always the most obviously problematic words) and asking the right questions of them and their history—palaeographical, phonological, etymological, grammatical, semantic, idiomatic; what, in short (though often at length) at this place in this text does the word signify and, beyond that, what are its ramifications?

In what follows the method is employed to illuminate a dark place in perhaps the best known and most widely read book to come down to us from the English Middle Ages, the twelfth-century Chronicle of Jocelin of Brakelond—a book which owes its latter-day fame to Thomas Carlyle's brilliant vulgarization of it in his *Past and Present*—in the conviction that it helps explain a puzzling episode in the life of the hero of Jocelin's chronicle, Samson, abbot of the Benedictine monastery of St. Edmund at Bury, Suffolk, and in the history of the house he ruled.

And since Abbot Samson was, as it happens, a Norfolk man—he was born at Tottington near Thetford and used to preach eloquently in his native dialect (*Anglice sermocinare solebat populo, set secundum linguam Norfolchie, ubi natus et nutritus erat*)[1] that, on the present occasion, is apt too.

[1] *The Chronicle of Jocelin of Brakelond*, ed. and trans. H. E. Butler (London, 1949), 40. All references are to this edition and this translation.

I

The St. Edmundsbury of the last decades of the twelfth century, as preserved for us in the narrative of Jocelin of Brakelond, is a house deeply tainted with materialism, and a community in which (in the words of Dom David Knowles) the purely spiritual ideal of the monastic life had been lost to view. It provided the conditions in which scandalous mismanagement and casual venality flourished, and its characteristic mode of life may be best described as a debilitating and inefficient worldliness.

In Jocelin's account much of the blame for this is laid at the door of Samson's predecessor. Abbot Hugh, he declares, using the words of Genesis about the ageing Isaac, was grown old and his eyes waxed somewhat dim. Pious, kindly, and a strict monk; but in the business of this world he was neither good nor wise. While zealous for discipline and for religious observance within the monastery, during his last years the management of the abbey's land and properties went from bad to worse, and the monks did not what they ought but what they would. Hugh found only one remedy and one consolation: he borrowed money. His infirmity spread, as such infirmities will, to others. And so it came about that each obedientary had his own seal and bound himself in debt to Jews and Christians as he pleased. The treasures of the house—rich copes and gold vessels and other church ornaments—were placed in pawn without knowledge of the rest of the convent. Debt was piled on debt and in foolhardiness bred by desperation interest was turned into capital.[2]

The enormity of the financial problems which beset the house may be illustrated by a single episode—a transaction which led the convent to saddle itself with a debt of £880 to Benedict the Jew of Norwich. It began with a secret loan of 40 marks at interest taken by the Sacrist from Benedict the Jew to cover the cost of some building repairs. When this debt had increased to £100 Benedict appeared at the abbey to demand payment.

[2] *Chron. Joc.*, pp. 1–2.

Instead the bond was re-negotiated in the amount of £400 to be paid in four years. At the end of four years there was still no money to clear the debt and a new bond was entered into for £880 to be paid off at the rate of £80 a year. Benedict also held a number of bonds for smaller debts—one of them of fourteen years' standing—and in total the convent owed him £1,200, not counting the accumulated interest.

This is a monumental piece of thriftlessness, but it is matched by the devious behaviour and the calculated self-interest of the various parties to it. In the first place, the original loan was entered into without the knowledge either of the abbot or of the rest of the convent. It was secretly negotiated by the Sacrist and the bond was sealed with a seal removed by him without authority—hence sacrilegiously—from the shrine of St. Edmund where it was kept. The loan's existence was revealed only when Benedict, armed with letters from the king, arrived to claim the money due to him. In his anger Abbot Hugh threatened to dismiss the Sacrist but instead was persuaded to allow the debt to be re-negotiated and compounded.

No doubt the compounding weighed heavily with the abbot in his change of heart. The sum added to the original debt was £100 lent by Benedict to the Sacrist on Abbot Hugh's behalf and the Sacrist publicly undertook to repay the whole debt—the convent's and the abbot's—at the end of four years, and a bond was given which the abbot took care to have sealed with the convent's seal rather than with his own.[3]

But more vividly than anywhere else the moral bankruptcy of St. Edmundsbury under Abbot Hugh appears in a subsequent turn the affair took, an episode which demands to be described in Jocelin's own words.[4]

And R. the almoner of our lord the King came and made it known to the Abbot that a rumour had reached the King concerning these great debts. So after the Abbot had taken counsel with the Prior and a few others, the Almoner was brought into the Chapter; and, while we sat

[3] *Chron. Joc.*, pp. 2–3.
[4] Ibid., pp. 3–4.

by in silence, the Abbot said: 'Here is the King's Almoner, my lord and friend and yours also, who led by his love of God and of St. Edmund, has told us that our lord the King has heard something untoward concerning us, and that the affairs of our Church are ill-managed both within and without. Wherefore it is my will, and I charge you on your obedience that you should say and openly acknowledge how matters stand.' The Prior therefore arose, and speaking as it were on behalf of us all, he said that the Church was in good state, and that the Rule was well and religiously observed within our house, while without our affairs were well and wisely handled, though none the less we had incurred some small amount of debt, like others of our neighbours; but that there was no debt of sufficient magnitude to be a burden to us. Hearing this the Almoner replied that he was very glad to have heard the testimony of the Convent—that is to say, the Prior speaking as he did.

Here is a society which has lost the will to knowledge of truth and falsehood and any conviction of its importance.

II

The burden of Jocelin of Brakelond's narrative is, of course, how St. Edmundsbury was roused from its moral torpor and restored to spiritual health by the efforts of one man, Abbot Samson, who against all odds was elected to succeed the feckless Abbot Hugh. Those odds included the opposition of the Sacrist William Wiardel, who was himself a candidate for the abbacy—opposition which must subsequently have been sharpened by Wiardel's sense of humiliation at having been passed over in favour of a younger man who had twice served under him as sub-sacrist.[5] Samson's experience in that office must have convinced him that the removal of Wiardel was indispensable to any serious reform of the house, but it must also have made it clear to him how difficult his dismissal would be to achieve.

[5] The anger or at least the discomfiture of Samson's superiors at learning, in the presence of the king, that Samson was the candidate preferred by the convent to succeed to the abbacy is plain from a single detail in Jocelin's account: they blushed (*Erubuerunt inde fratres qui maioris dignitatis erant*, *Chron. Joc.*, p. 21).

The sacrist was an important official in any house: he was in charge of the service of the altar, the vestments, hangings, and lighting of the church; he was also sometimes (as at Bury) responsible for building operations and repairs. At Bury, a monastic borough, his authority was much enhanced by virtue of his position as lord of the borough. Thus, among other rights, he had the power to levy taxes and to appoint the reeve or reeves of the borough, to whom he farmed the town, and thus effectively controlled the government of the place; and as archdeacon of the exempt *banleuca*—a large area including the town and suburbs from which the episcopal as well as the royal jurisdiction was expressly excluded by royal grant—he also possessed jurisdiction in the abbot's ecclesiastical court and the profits arising from it.[6]

Hence Wiardel's power, arising from the scope of his jurisdiction and his long exercise of it, was very deeply entrenched. It must have been reinforced by the influence which accrued to him as a natural reward for his amiable generosity: he 'gave and spent as he pleased, a kindly man, giving away both that which should be given and that which should not, and "blinding the eyes of all with gifts" '.[7] Wiardel also had influential friends, as is shown by his success in avoiding, through the intervention of one of them, dismissal over the matter of the secret loan he had taken from Benedict the Jew during the abbacy of Samson's predecessor;[8] and after Abbot Hugh's death, though he persevered in his spendthrift ways and (as Jocelin relates) buildings went unrepaired and debts unpaid, the Prior, *ex officio* head during the vacancy, thought it wise to shut his eyes to his misdemeanours.[9] Wiardel's personal authority within the convent was considerable enough to win toleration for his permissive treatment of the Jews of Bury; by his express leave the Jews of the town were made free of the monastery and of the church

[6] See David Knowles, *The Monastic Order in England* (Cambridge, 1940), 446.

[7] *Chron. Joc.*, p. 9.

[8] Ibid., p. 3.

[9] Ibid., p. 9.

even during divine service, their money was kept in the treasury in the Sacrist's custody, and in time of war their wives and children were given refuge in the pittancery. Not surprisingly the Jews called him their father and their patron.[10] His popularity among his brother monks is clear from the conspiracy threatened by some members of the house following Samson's dismissal of Wiardel.[11]

The justice of Samson's action in deposing the Sacrist need not be argued. What is surprising is not that he moved against him but that he moved against him so quickly. The newly-elected abbot had every reason for postponing a confrontation with such a man.[12]

Samson's position was in any case seriously undermined by his subscription to an oath agreed to by the convent in full chapter on the eve of the departure of the delegates to the royal court to proceed to the election of a successor to Abbot Hugh, that on whomsoever the choice fell, he should refrain from changing obedientiaries without consent of the convent. And in Samson's case the explicitness of the directive would be reinforced by the irony that he was himself author of it, and prime mover in persuading the convent to accept it.[13] Thus, what was probably intended as an attempt to safeguard his own position as sub-sacrist in case of the succession of one ill-disposed to-

[10] 'Iudei, inquam, quibus sacrista pater et patronus dicebatur' (*Chron. Joc.*, p. 10).

[11] *Chron. Joc.*, p. 30.

[12] Jocelin's chronology is far from clear, but the sequence of events at Samson's accession seems to be this: he entered the monastery on Palm Sunday, 1182 (p. 24); he summoned all the barons, knights, and free men to do homage to him on the fourth day of Easter (p. 27); he held his first Chapter, appointing Hugh sub-sacrist and at the same time suspending Wiardel's direct control over the finances of the house (pp. 29–30); after this, 'but not on the same day', he transferred some officials to other posts (p. 30); 'last of all' he deposed Wiardel himself (p. 30). How closely Wiardel's dismissal followed his loss of financial control is uncertain. But after his account of the dismissal Jocelin remarks that 'after the close of Easter [sc. the next Monday after Easter week] the Abbot visited all his manors and ours' (p. 31), which suggests that it followed very closely indeed, and was one of the events of that same Easter.

[13] *Chron. Joc.*, p. 18.

wards him, proved to be an embarrassing constraint after his election as abbot. Quite apart from this impediment to action, moderation might be looked for from one who had himself suffered (unjustly, as he always claimed) imprisonment and exile at the hands of Abbot Hugh twenty years before.[14] Samson would be unlikely either to underestimate the authority with which he found himself suddenly vested, or to wield it lightly, especially in such a grave matter as the summary deposition of an obedientary.

His decision to proceed against Wiardel is therefore not easy to explain, even allowing due weight to Jocelin's remarks that he was said to exalt justice above mercy.[15] The simple view, that it proves merely that Samson was neither a respector of oaths nor of obedientaries is hard to defend. It ignores the shrewd political sense which is so characteristic of Samson throughout his career. As a monk he had known when it was advisable to shut his eyes, leaving it to the Lord to judge.[16] As abbot, neither in his dealings with the convent nor with the world outside, did he ever forget the limits of his real, as distinct from his theoretical, power. He was capable of making peace in public over an issue on which he later insisted in private;[17] and in the interests of the house he was not beyond tempering justice with discretion.[18] Nor does this view begin to account for one of the most extraordinary episodes in Jocelin's account of Samson's abbacy—his violence in following up Wiardel's dismissal with the razing of the Sacrist's houses in the cemetery.[19]

There is little reason to believe that Samson would be unaware of the gravity of his oath-breaking, or blind to the dangers of

[14] *Chron. Joc.*, p. 4.

[15] Ibid., p. 34.

[16] Ibid., pp. 4–5.

[17] The conflict between him and the convent over the corody of Ralph the Gatekeeper (*Chron. Joc.*, pp. 117–20).

[18] Witness the case of Geoffrey Ruff, monk of Bury, who was long tolerated by Samson despite a reputation for worldliness and other reports of evil behaviour, because, Jocelin suggests, he was useful in the custody of four of the manors of the house (*Chron. Joc.*, p. 122).

[19] *Chron. Joc.*, p. 31.

confrontation with a man as powerful and popular as the Sacrist. Either of these would have been seriously damaging to his recently assumed authority; together they were potentially disastrous. That he saw the risks is clear from his tactics: he first appointed a sub-sacrist and gave orders that Wiardel should do nothing in respect either of revenues or expenses, save with his assent; next he transferred some minor obedientaries to other offices; finally he deposed the Sacrist. This must represent a careful attempt to assess the strength of the opposition by minor encroachments before proceeding against Wiardel. That he was also aware of the possible consequences, and had taken thought for avoiding them, is clear from his prompt and effective response to the conspiracy threatened against him by Wiardel's friends in the convent.[20]

It is in Samson's defensive action to this conspiracy, and in its aftermath, that the explanation of the episode is, I believe, to be found. Jocelin relates how, on the morning after the first news of the opposition reached him, Samson appeared in Chapter armed with evidence against Wiardel: bonds sealed with Wiardel's seal and without the convent's leave, in which were pledged church vestments, ornaments, and service books, as well as money, all cancelled and redeemed by Samson.[21] He added much else to show why he had deposed the Sacrist but, says Jocelin, 'the chief cause he did not mention, not wishing to make a scandal of him.'[22] This 'chief cause' emerges in Jocelin's account of Samson's final action after appointing a new sacrist: his destruction of Wiardel's houses, 'as being unworthy to stand upon the earth, on account of the frequent wine-bibbing and other things of which it is best to say nothing, which willy-nilly he had witnessed when he was sub-sacrist' (*Abbas uero domos*

[20] Ibid., pp. 30–1.

[21] Ibid.

[22] 'multa alia adiecit, ostendens quare deposuerat W.; precipuam tamen causam subticuit, nolens eum scandalizare' (*Chron. Joc.*, p. 31). For the sense of *scandalizare* see n. 48. The Bury *Gesta Sacristarum* says only that Wiardel 'non sine causa a domino Sampsone abbate amotus fuit ab administratione' (*Memorials of St. Edmund's Abbey*, ed. T. Arnold, ii (Rolls Series, 1892), 291).

sacriste in cimiterio funditus precepit erui, tanquam non essent digne stare super terram, propter frequentes bibaciones et quedam tacenda, que nolens et dolens uiderat quando fuit subsacrista).[23] It is concealed in the phrase *quedam tacenda*, 'other things of which it is best to say nothing'.[24]

III

The *tacenda*-formula is a variant of the rhetorical figure apophasis, a figure which conveys meaning by the device of affecting to deny that which it is really intended to affirm. It is widely used in the Middle Ages in a form which derives from two related texts in Ephesians: 'But fornication, and all uncleanness, or covetousness, let it not even be named among you' (5:3), and 'have no fellowship with the unfruitful works of darkness, but rather even reprove them; for the things which are done by them in secret it is a shame even to speak of' (5: 11–12). In their original contexts the passages are part of St. Paul's elaboration of his doctrine on marriage and married love and in particular the sexual responsibilites (amounting to duties) one to the other, of wives and husbands.

The pejorative sense, evident enough in the Pauline texts, is intensified in the Middle Ages, and the association of the formula with sexual practices persists. With other verbal usages of a similar kind the *tacenda*-formula belongs to the technical vocabulary of theologians and canonists in their treatment of the doctrine of marriage, specifically in discussions of contraception, whence it finds its way into the manuals of confessors and the sanctions of the penitentials.

Characteristic of such vocabulary is a predisposition to vagueness, a careful preference for not calling a spade a spade. Thus,

[23] *Chron. Joc.*, p. 31.

[24] Carlyle made ironical play with the phrase: 'Failing all else, what gossip about one another! This is a perennial resource. How one hooded head applies itself to the ear of another, and whispers—*tacenda*. Willelmus Sacrista, for instance, what does he nightly, over in that Sacristy of his? Frequent bibations, *frequentes bibationes et quaedam tacenda*,—eheu!' (*Past and Present*, II, VI).

the term universally employed in the medieval church for artificial contraceptives (then as now forbidden by ecclesiastical law) is 'poisons of sterility' (*sterilitatis venena*). Similarly, the related sin of non-procreative intercourse is described as 'what is done against nature' (*contra naturam*).[25] Such vagueness does not mean that those using the terms lacked explicit and detailed knowledge of the practices referred to. Quite the contrary—the vagueness is employed because canonists and confessors were all too familiar with them but thought it prudent to avoid public disclosure of sins unknown to the innocent.

Bartholomew of Exeter (1140–84) advises the confessor not to ask specifically about sins 'against nature' because men and women, by the express naming of crimes unknown to them, may fall into sins they had been ignorant of,[26] and in cases where penitents confess to unlawful coition Alan of Lille (d. 1202) enjoins the priest to inquire whether it is fornication, adultery, incest, or the sin against nature, but not to descend more minutely lest he gives occasion of sin to the penitent.[27] The canonist Hostiensis (Henry of Segusio), in his influential *Tractatus de poenitentia et remissionibus* (written between 1250 and 1261), sums up what had long been established practice: the ways in which the sin against nature is committed, he says in his advice to confessors, 'I neither wish to write nor do I advise you to reveal'.[28] In this way a convention of calculated vagueness in

[25] Both circumlocutions derive from passages in Augustine: *sterilitatis venena* from his treatise on *Marriage and Concupiscence*, I xv 17, CSEL 42. 229–30, *contra naturam* from *The Good of Marriage*, xi. 12, CSEL 41. 203–4. Under the headings *Aliquando* and *Adulterii malum* respectively they are taken into two of the most influential ecclesiastical texts of the medieval church—the *Decretum* (*c.*1140) of the canonist Gratian (= 2. 32. 2. 7 and 2. 32. 7. 11) and the *Sentences* (1154–7) of the theologian Peter Lombard (= 4. 31. 3 and 4. 38. 2). See John T. Noonan's comprehensive work *Contraception: a History of its Treatment by the Catholic Theologians and Canonists* (Cambridge, Mass., 1965), 131, 136, 174–5.

[26] Noonan, op. cit., p. 271.

[27] Ibid., p. 271.

[28] *Summa aurea*, v. 49; Noonan, op. cit., pp. 223–4, 271–2.

such matters was established and one so powerful that it has survived to the present day.[29]

The interpretation of a figure, apophasis, the effect of which is to conceal rather than to reveal meaning, is not without difficulties; but there is no doubt that from the late twelfth century at least the *tacenda*-formula (things 'of which it is best to say nothing', 'which ought not to be named among you', 'which it is a shame even to think of') signifies vice *contra naturam*, for it is in conjunction with the charge of indulging in practices *contra naturam* that the *tacenda*-formula is regularly found.[30]

For the Middle Ages the association was already present in the Pauline text. Ephesians 5:6 looks back to the sins referred to in the preceding verses, including the 'unspeakable' vices of v. 3, and declares 'because of these things cometh the wrath of God upon the children of disobedience'. This passage (frequently linked with the Old Testament story of the destruction by fire and brimstone of Sodom, Gomorrah, and the cities of the plain, Gen. 19:24–5) is perennially identified with vice *contra naturam*, as for example in canon 11 of the third Lateran Council (1179) and again in canon 14 of Lateran IV (1215). From these two authoritative citations the passage found its way into the law of the church as a result of its insertion into the *Liber extra* (*Decretum Gratiani*) of Gregory IX in 1234.[31] Although the association of the *tacenda*-formula with vice *contra naturam* ante dates these official promulgations, they must have powerfully reinforced the association and must have greatly increased awareness of it

[29] See n. 32.

[30] This use is, of course, quite separate from the *taceat*-formula employed when a person or thing is to be eulogized, called by Curtius the 'outdoing' topos (*European Literature and the Latin Middle Ages*, trans. W. R. Trask (New York, 1953), 162–5). Context makes confusion of the topoi impossible.

[31] For Lateran III, see J. Alberigo *et al.*, *Conciliorum oecumenicorum decreta*[3] (Bologna, 1973), 217 (canon 11); for Lateran IV, Alberigo, p. 242 (canon 14); for the codification of 1234, see c. 4. *x*. v. 31 (Lateran III) and c. 13. *x*. iii. 1 (Lateran IV). See further Michael Goodich, *The Unmentionable Vice: Homosexuality in the Later Medieval Period* (Santa Barbara and Oxford, 1979), 43–4.

within the church and beyond and may be held to account in part for the extraordinary longevity of the idea of 'the unmentionable vice' and for its subsequent verbal fossilization.[32]

The conciliar ordinances of Lateran III and IV and subsequent codification in the decretals of 1234 certainly lie behind the ubiquitous presence of the idea in the systematic penitential manuals which flowed directly from Lateran IV and its attempt to impose a firmer moral discipline on the life of the church and its members—the *summae* and *summulae* of the thirteenth century and their successors.

Representative examples in France in the thirteenth century are the *Summa de virtutibus et vitiis* (before 1261) of William Peraldus, Dominican 'bishop' of Lyons, who quotes Pope Symmachus (498–514), to the effect that unnatural vice is *ineffabile* and adds the gloss *non debet homo loqui de peccato isto*, and *La Somme le Roi* (1279) of Friar Lorens of Orléans, confessor to Philip the Bold, king of France, which declares 'cel pecchie est

[32] Some examples may be of interest as illustrating the later history of the topos. A medical treatise much admired in Victorian public schools has this to say in a passage describing the dangers to schoolboy morals resulting from the common nineteenth-century habit of sleeping two in a bed: 'Most emphatically I condemn this system, which is still unhappily in existence, as distinctly conducing, *without the need of my entering into further details*, to a flagrant species of immorality and depravation of character' (Clement Dukes, *Health at School*[3] (1894), 108). The convention also infiltrated Victorian hymnody. A hymn, 'Lift up your hearts! We lift them, Lord, to Thee', composed by H. M. Butler, Headmaster of Harrow School (later Master of Trinity College, Cambridge), for school confirmations, includes this verse: 'Above the level of the former years | The mire of sin, the slough of guilty fears, | The mist of doubt, the blight of love's decay . . . | Above the swamps of subterfuge and shame, | *The deeds, the thoughts, that honour may not name,* | *The halting tongue that dares not tell the whole.*' Butler was at the time active in founding the Church of England Purity Society, the work of which in relation to public schools was discussed at the Headmasters' Conference in 1884 *in camera* and without record being kept. See J. R. de S. Honey, *Tom Brown's Universe: the Development of the English Public School in the Nineteenth Century* (London, 1977), 180 n., 182 n.

Cf. for a more recent example Mr David Niven's memory of a schoolboy encounter: 'It was a very dreary experience and the laws on homosexuality being what they still are, *I am certainly not going into it in any great detail here*' (*The Moon's a Balloon* (1972), 30).

contre nature, e en mout de manieres qui ne font a nomer por la matire qui est trop abhominable'; in England in the fourteenth century (1340) one of Friar Lorens's translators,[33] Michael of Northgate, Benedictine of St. Augustine's, Canterbury, denounces unnatural vice as the sin of Sodom and Gomorrah, the 'mest uoul an lodlakest þet ne is naȝt to nemny', and Chaucer's Parson fifty years later describes it as 'thilke abhomynable synne, of which that no man unnethe oghte speke ne write'.[34]

These examples are also representative in the way they practise the reticence they preach—and, rhetorical convention apart, reticence is what one would expect from compendia of orthodox morality intended for the guidance of confessors and spiritual directors. An earlier, fuller, and much less constrained handling of the subject occurs in a text which is of special interest since it is exactly contemporary with Jocelin's chronicle and purports to describe an actual event. It is found in a chapter headed 'Of the vnclene and foule vyce and synne of sodemytys' in an account of a vision of purgatory seen by a monk of Eynsham on the Thursday before Easter 1196:

Sothely, alle thoo that were there ponyssht and peynde were in thys worlde whyle they leuyd doers of that foule synne the whiche oughte not to be namyd, not only of a crystyn man but also of none hethyn man. Certen grete monsturs—that ys to seye grete bestys onnaturally schapyne—schewyd hem selfe in a fyrye lykenesse, horrabulle and gastfulle to sight, and oftyn tymes vyolently came apone hem and also in a fowle damnable abusion compellyd hem to medylle with hem, howe be hyt that they refusyd and wulde hyt not—I abhorre and ame asschamed to speke of the fowlnesse and vnclenes of that same synne. Thanne betwene her peynfull and cursyd clepynges they roryd and yellyd and cryed owte and afterward they fylle done to gedyr, lyke as yf they hadde ben gonne and ded and anon takyn vppe ageyne and so

[33] Lorens's work was very popular in England: at least six translations appeared before Caxton's print (*The Royal Book*) of 1486.

[34] Peraldus, *Summa*, 2. 3, *de Luxuria*, pars 2, cap. 3; Lorens of Orléans, *La Somme le Roi*, cited from BL MS Cotton Cleopatra A.v. by W. Eilers, Chaucer Society, Second Series, Part XVI (1882), 565; Michael of Northgate, *Ayenbite of Inwyt*, EETS 23 (1866; revd. P. Gradon, 1965), 49; Chaucer, *Canterbury Tales*, I. 909.

forth putte vnto newe peynys. Trewely y remembryd not wele at that same tyme the seyyng of the holy postle sent powelle in hys pystylle of seche persons, where he condempnyth the foule vyce and synne agaynest nature bothe of men and wemen.

This is a usefully explicit treatment of a topic in the discussion of which, as we have seen, explicitness is habitually avoided, and it is distinguished by a freedom we are more accustomed to associating with imaginative literature. Yet Roger of Wendover (d. 1236) whose *Flores Historiarum* (which he started to write shortly after 1215) is a first-hand authority at least from 1201, accepted the monk's vision as an authentic description of an actual event: he inserts an abridgement of it in his chronicle under the year 1196.[35]

While the sin against nature may be invested with a slightly different range of meanings by different writers and may be used to signify different actions in different circumstances (depending upon whether it is practised within or outside of marriage, between male and female, or homosexually), in the circumstances described by Jocelin—'unspeakable' acts in the male and celibate society of a Benedictine convent—Wiardel's must have been the common failing of the inhabitants of Sodom and Gomorrah, the sodomitic vice.

IV

We know from the vehement attacks made on it by Anselm, archbishop of Canterbury (1093–1109), that it was a fashionable vice in England by the late eleventh century. Anselm's biographer Eadmer records a conversation between Anselm and the King in

[35] There are more than two dozen MSS of the Latin version of the work extant; the English version is known only from the early print by William de Machlinia, 1485 (E. G. Duff, *Fifteenth Century English Books* (Oxford, 1917), no. 357), quoted here—with amended punctuation—from the reprint of E. Arber, 1901. For a Latin text and full discussion of authorship, etc., see *Eynsham Cartulary*, ii, ed. H. E. Salter, Oxford Historical Society Publications, 51 (Oxford, 1908), 257 f. For the suggestion that the vision was known to Dante, see *Analecta Bollandiana*, xxii (1903), 232.

1094, in the course of which Anselm expressed the wish to hold a synod of the English church. The King asking what such a council would discuss, Anselm replied, 'That most shameful crime of sodomy ... that crime, I say of sodomy, but lately spread abroad in this land, has already borne fruit too abundantly and has with its abomination defiled many. If it be not speedily met with sentence of stern judgement coming from you and by rigorous discipline on the part of the Church, the whole land will, I declare, become little better that Sodom itself.'[36]

The King, of course, was William Rufus, who was not one to encourage Anselm's appetite for reformation of the nation's morals,[37] and he dismissed his request for a synod. But early in the reign of Rufus's successor Henry I, who was no admirer of his brother's profligacies, Anselm moved swiftly and acted decisively to check the spread of the vice: at the Council of Westminster in 1102 it was decreed that any member of a religious order found guilty of the crime was to be denied advancement in the church and if he already held a preferment he was to lose it, while laymen were to be degraded from the status that lawfully belonged to their rank.[38]

The vice had become established early in England. Elsewhere in Europe adultery, consanguinity, and clerical marriage all re-

[36] 'Nefandissimum Sodomae scelus ... scelus, inquam, Sodomae noviter in hac terra divulgatum, jam plurimum pullulavit, multosque sua immanitate foedavit. Cui, fateor, nisi districti a te prodiens sententia judicii, et ecclesiasticae vigor disciplinae celerius obviet, tota terra non multo post Sodoma fiet' (*Eadmeri Historia Novorum in Anglia*, ed. M. Rule, (Rolls Series, 1884), p. 49).

[37] Cf. Freeman's judgement of William Rufus: 'Into the details of the private life of Rufus it is well not to grope too narrowly. In him England might see on her own soil the habits of the ancient Greek and the modern Turk' (E. A. Freeman, *The Reign of William Rufus and the Accession of Henry the First* (Oxford, 1882), i. 159).

[38] *Eadmeri Historia*, pp. 143–4. The *Summa aurea* of the thirteenth-century canonist Hostiensis identifies the common vice of the clergy as that of Sodom and Gomorrah, warning that if a clerk boasts publicly of his vice he will incur suspension on account of the scandal and infamy. (*Sed nec debet clericus de sua incontinentia publice gloriari: alias propter scandalum et infamiam ortam ab officio et beneficio suspendetur* (*Summa aurea*, 5, *de Excess. praelat.* 2).

mained more serious issues during the twelfth century. Anselm's is the first ecclesiastical legislation against sodomy; the first ecumenical council at which notice was taken of it was Lateran III in 1179. It is impossible to estimate how far Anselm's reforms were successful, but it would be unwise to take too sanguine a view. The English bishops continued to be troubled by the issue throughout the thirteenth century. Statutes of the bishops of London (1245–59), Coventry and Lichfield (1224–37), and Exeter (*c.* 1287) all direct diocesan clergy to seek out and punish those guilty of the offence.[39] In the rest of Europe it is popular from the end of the twelfth century: when that impetuous but orthodox cleric Alan of Lille (1128?–1202) wrote his *De planctu Naturae* in emulation of Bernard Silvestris and Claudian and had to produce a fresh cause of complaint he found it in sodomy, denounced by him in an elaborate play of grammatical metaphor.[40] Those who claim that the vice became naturalized in England can point to the certainty that among the successors to William Rufus Richard I and Edward II were addicted to it while many of his contemporaries believed Richard II to be so. The idea of sodomy remained a very familiar one in the later Middle Ages and in England it formed an extremely damaging political charge.[41]

Anselm's open attack is testimony to the prevalance of the vice among the religious at the turn of the eleventh century. By the close of the Middle Ages it is part of the armoury employed

[39] *Councils and Synods with other Documents relating to the English Church, II. A.D. 1205–1313*, edd. F. M. Powicke and C. R. Cheney, in 2 parts (Oxford, 1964): London, pt. i, p. 632; Coventry and Lichfield, pt. i, p. 219; Exeter, pt. ii, p. 1069. The Coventry and Lichfield statute is representative: 'Ut breviter dicam, omnis coitus est contra naturam qui non est inter virum et mulierem, et debet appellari vitium sodomiticum, propter quod deus destruxit illas civitates de quibus satis notum est vobis omnibus.'

[40] 'The sex of active nature trembles shamefully at the way in which it declines into passive nature. Man is made woman, he blackens the honour of his sex, the craft of magic Venus makes him of double gender. He is both predicate and subject, he pushes the laws of grammar too far' (*The Complaint of Nature*, trans. D. M. Moffat (New York, 1908), p. 3, metre 1, ll. 16 f.).

[41] See Gervase Mathew, *The Court of Richard II* (London, 1968), 139.

in the strident anti-clericalism of the late fourteenth and fifteenth centuries, especially favoured by the Lollards in their attacks on the religious orders. 'Let us rout these murderers, burn these sodomites, hang these traitors,' Thomas of Walsingham, the St. Alban's chronicler, records a London crowd as howling during a riot provoked by the Austin Friars in 1387.[42] And as this episode suggests it is a popular commonplace of the period, cropping up in literary satire,[43] religious polemic[44] and political manifestos. It is with a wholly satisfying predictability that, for example, there appears as the third of the twelve Lollard Conclusions nailed to the doors of Westminster Hall and St. Paul's during the Parliament of 1395 the charge 'þat þe lawe of continence annexyd to presthod þat in preiudys of wimmen was first ordeynid inducith sodomie in al holy chirche'—accompanied by the equally predictable disclaimer that 'we excusin us be þe bible for þe suspecte decre þat seyth we schulde not nemen it.'[45]

[42] 'Disperdamus homicidas, incendamus sodomitas, suspendamus Regis et Angliae proditores' (*Historia Anglicana*, ed. H. T. Riley, ii (Rolls Series, 1864), 158).

[43] Cf. 'Lat a freer of sum ordur *tecum pernoctare*, | Odur thi wyff or thi doughtour *hic vult violare*; | Or thi sun he weyl prefur, *sicut furtam fortis*; | God gyffe syche a freer peyne *in inferni portis!*' (*Political Poems and Songs Relating to English History*, ed. T. Wright, ii (Rolls Series, 1861), 249–50. There is a history of coarse humour on the subject long before the 'Lollards': see for example, from the twelfth century, Walter Map's scandalous anecdote about St. Bernard, *De nugis curialium*, I. xxiv.

[44] Cf. 'ȝour freres ben taken alle day with wymmen & wifes, | Bot of ȝour priuey sodomye speke I not here' (Jack Upland's *Rejoinder*, ed. P. L. Heyworth, (Oxford, 1968), 103/58–9); and on monks, lines from Wilfrid Holme of Huntington's poem *The Fall and Evill Success of Rebellion*, written in 1537: 'And as for their chastitie the visitours knoweth wel, | For Sodome and Gomor had never such ordinance, | Their polution and wayes, I ashame for to tell', quoted by A. G. Dickens, *Lollards and Protestants in the Diocese of York 1509–1558* (Oxford, 1959), 120.

[45] Printed by H. S. Cronin, *English Historical Review*, xxii (1907), 297. I cannot identify the 'suspecte decre'. Knowles, *The Religious Orders in England*, ii (Cambridge, 1955), p. 103, n. 2, points to Wyclif's own habit of making accusations of immorality by way of apophasis: 'taceo autem de corporali incontinencia'. The Lollards had no monopoly when it came to accusations of depravity: see the anti-Lollard poem 'Gens Lollardorum gens est vilis Sodomorum', printed in T. Wright, *Political Poems and Songs*, ii (Rolls Series, 1861), 128.

Whether such accusations (which are, as Dom David Knowles once remarked, the first refuge of calumny) are generally true, need not concern us; polemicists are not upon oath. But there can be little doubt that in a historian as sober and scrupulous as Jocelin is recognized to be, and with no discernible motive for falsification, the form of words 'things of which it is best to say nothing' reveals that which it pretends to conceal—an imputation of sodomy.

V

If this interpretation is allowed, many things otherwise puzzling become clear. It explains why Samson acted against Wiardel despite the powerful discretionary arguments there were for avoiding a contest. It explains why, in dismissing the Sacrist ostensibly for financial malpractice he did not also act against others who, on the basis of the evidence produced by Samson in Chapter—a bag full of cancelled bonds with their seals still hanging from them, some given by his predecessor Abbot Hugh, some by the Prior, some by the Sacrist, some by the Chamberlain and other officials, the total amounting to three thousand and fifty-two pounds and one mark of capital alone, apart from interest—were also guilty.[46] If the real reason for sacking Wiardel was that he negotiated loans without authority it is not easy to see what limits Samson could set to prosecution: that the practice was widespread is implied by his discovery on another occasion that there were thirty-three personal seals owned by members of the convent.[47]

Indeed, Samson's decision to suppress the chief cause of Wiardel's dismissal bears vivid witness to the force of the pragmatic considerations which moved canonists to recommend and confessors to practise the reticence inculcated by the *tacenda*-

[46] *Chron. Joc.*, p. 30.

[47] Ibid., p. 38. In 1213, novices and absentees apart, there were only sixty-seven monks in the house all told (Knowles, *The Monastic Order in England* (1940), Appendix XVII).

formula. As abbot his chief responsibility lay in the spiritual welfare of his house, and that thought for this lay behind his silence is clear from the only reason given by Jocelin to account for it. Samson did not, he says, wish 'to make a scandal' of Wiardel. The ecclesiastical definition of scandal is that which gives occasion to sin to others. In the words of St. Thomas Aquinas, a man's spiritual downfall may be brought about by another in so far as he may be drawn to sin by the persuasion or example of that other person; and this, says St. Thomas, 'is scandal properly so called'.[48]

Above all, it explains the apparently gratuitous destruction of Wiardel's houses in the precincts 'so that within a year, in the place where a fine building had stood, we saw beans sprouting, and nettles in abundance where once had lain jars of wine';[49] they were destroyed because polluted and in their destruction received that recompense of their pollution which was due.[50]

[48] 'in processu viae spiritualis contingit, aliquem disponi ad ruinam spiritualem per dictum vel factum alterius: inquantum scilicet aliquis sua admonitione, vel inductione, aut exemplo alterum trahit ad peccandum; et hoc proprie dicitur scandalum' (*Summa theologica*, II. II. xliii. I). Cf. Du Cange, s.v. *scandalizator*, 'vir perniciosi exempli'.

[49] 'quod infra annum, ubi steterat nobile edificium, uidimus fabas pullulare, et ubi iacuerant dolia uini, urticas habundare' (*Chron. Joc.*, p. 31). For the ancient association of nettles (*urticae*) with lust and pruriency cf. Juvenal, *Satires*, II, 128, XI. 168, Petronius, *Satyricon*, 138; and for nettles and 'pollution' cf. *The Owl and the Nightingale*, 592–6.

[50] Romans 1:27.

The Scansion of *Havelok* and the Use of ME *-en* and *-e* in *Havelok*[1] and by Chaucer

G. V. SMITHERS

THE matters dealt with below emerged from a study of the versification of *Havelok* for a new edition. Two of them prescribed a new explanation for the linguistic problem of how final *-e* evolved at one stage of its history. This called for separate treatment, since the evidence would have taken up disproportionate space in an edition.

In order to strip down the metrical analysis to its essentials, I have for the most part avoided aprioristic assumptions and extraneous criteria, such as reference to metres in Med. Lat., OF, or AN that are (allegedly or in fact) comparable with that of *Hav.* My concern, here and elsewhere, is with scansion not for its own sake, but as the indispensable means of eliciting linguistic facts, such as the pronunciation of internal and final unstressed syllables.[2]

The material used here is all from the text of MS Laud Misc.

[1] The line-numbering used here is that of my forthcoming edition. Since my text differs from that of Skeat–Sisam in embodying the line *He þriste in his muth wel faste* from the Cambridge fragments as line 547, my line numbers after that point exceed theirs by one.

[2] The same kind of thing (as Prof. McIntosh has kindly reminded me) has been comprehensively and powerfully done for Shakespeare's English by H. Kökeritz, 'Elizabethan Prosody and Historical Phonology', in R. Lass (ed.), *Approaches to English Historical Linguistics*, New York, 1969), 208–27. Kökeritz's basic principle (like mine) is that the material of the verse in question is the contemporary spoken language. By reference to copious phonetic and other variants of types that were current already in ME, he has shown (as I have sought to do) that the belief in the 'trisyllabic foot' is a fallacy—though in Shakespeare's case, it is admissible at the caesura.

108, without emendation except in fourteen lines (see p. 219) where a final *-e* is virtually certain to have been omitted by a scribe. This policy is not meant to imply that the extant text is at all points what the author wrote; the Laud MS has its share of corruptions, not only in major cruces, but in many small details that affect the number or the flow of syllables in a line. Anyone could plausibly emend (along with many other lines) 433:

Crist warię him . with his muth

to:

Crist him warię with his muth

(the notation being as explained below). But no-one living today could possibly produce emended lines that are all totally certain to be what the author wrote. There is often more than one textually or metrically feasible version of an individual line; and in any case we simply do not know enough about ME, or ME metre, to recover the author's words unerringly in all cases.

No account has been taken here of any intermediate degrees of linguistic stress between full stress and unstressed syllables. In any case, what seems to me to matter in this type of ME verse is the rhythmic pulse, which, being a metrical phenomenon, is distinct from word-stress, which is a linguistic fact inherent in the nature of certain syllables in various classes of words.[3] The rhythmic essence of the line in *Hav.* is that an accented beat ('on-beat') regularly alternates with a single unaccented one ('off-beat'); that each falls on a single syllable; that the line may, but need not, begin with an off-beat and end with an on-beat; and that there are always four on-beats in a line. The terms 'four-beat line', and 'five-beat line' for Chaucer's so-called 'iambic pentameter', are based on the number of on-beats, for convenience. For lack of an agreed terminology in English for scansion by rhythmic pulse, the ambiguous traditional terms

[3] On the distinction between what pertains to metre and what is linguistic (in verse) see S. R. Levin, 'The Conventions of Poetry', in S. R. Chatman (ed.), *Literary Style*, (Oxford, 1971) 177–93.

'stress(es), stressed syllables', and 'unstressed syllables' (which should properly be used only when linguistic stress is in question) are sometimes used below in discussion of the views of others who really mean by them 'metrically accented syllables' and 'unaccented syllables', or when it is doubtful whether the linguistic or the metrical implication is uppermost, or simply when it is convenient.

It follows from the approach thus defined that I am not in accord with the novel attempt of M. Halle and S. J. Keyser[4] to analyse and scan Chaucer's five-beat line in terms of 'stress maxima', i.e. of linguistic stresses. Nor am I yet able to apply to ME verse a system of scansion (such as is now used for Middle High German[5]) that takes time-duration into account. This is mainly because (*a*) I cannot confidently detect absolute differences in the length of syllables in the ME four-beat line, and (*b*) I do not see how such a system would enable one to distinguish authorial from scribal practice.

There are occasional signs that in the metre of *Hav.*, as of Chaucer's five-beat line, it is the rhythmic pulse, and not linguistic stresses, that must have primacy. In *Hav.*, in the first two lines of the actual narrative:

> 27 It wás a kíng bi áre-dáwes
> þat ín his tímę werę góde láwes,

the ἅπ. λεγ. *are-dawes* is an adoption of ON *ár-dagar* (the cognate of OE *gear-dagas*). The internal *-e-* is etymologically unjustified, and has clearly been introduced to prevent two successive on-beats here. Likewise, in *The Knight's Tale*, the Ellesmere and Hengwrt MSS agree in a reading that illustrates the

[4] M. Halle and S. J. Keyser, 'Chaucer and the Study of Prosody', *College English*, xxviii (1966), 187–219; S. J. Keyser, 'The Linguistic Basis of English Prosody', in D. A. Reibel and S. A. Schone (edd.), *Modern English Studies* (Englewood Cliffs, N.J., 1969) 79–94. See the acute comments by W. K. Wimsatt, 'The Rule and the Norm: Halle and Keyser on Chaucer's Meter', in Chatman, *op. cit.*, pp. 197–215.

[5] As Dr E. J. Morrall has kindly pointed out to me. See S. Beyschlag, *Altdeutsche Verskunst in Grundzügen*[6], (Nürnberg 1969), especially pp. 9–11, 46–7, 50–60.

same point in reverse by wrecking the metre with two successive on-beats:

1312 And ofte tymes / giltlees pardee.

Giltlees is palpably a corruption of *giltelees*, which provides the indispensable off-beat between the two on-beats. The OE antecedent was *gyltleas*, and the main ME form is the historically regular disyllabic *giltles*. But the trisyllabic form required in Chaucer's line is amply recorded as a variant; and the etymologically irregular *-e-* is syllabic (by the test of scansion) in the *Ormulum*, 8038, 12685, and the *Confessio Amantis*, II. 1702 and III. 870.

In both *are-dawes* and *giltelees* as variants (the latter of which was actually current in ordinary speech, and the former would have been acceptable, since it conformed to a well-established mode of forming the first element of a compound), the *-e-* might be explained as an example of the ME adjectival genitive in *-e* and *-ene*. But it also illustrates the tendency to avoid successive full stresses, and hence the strength of the rhythmic pattern / × / (see p. 214) in *Hav.* and comparable ME verse, and in spoken ME: the adjectival genitive (which for historical reasons does occur as the first element of compounds, e.g. *huse-lauerd*) was a linguistic form available to express this pattern. The author of *Hav.* could perfectly well have fitted a rhythmic sequence *bi ar-dawes* into the line at some point, but chose not to. In *The Knight's Tale*, 1314, in which the Ellesmere and Hengwrt MSS again agree in having *giltlees*, the line might be scanned thus:

That giltlees / tormenteth innocence.

But l. 1312 (like *Hav.* 27) suggests that Chaucer wrote (and therefore preferred):

That giltelees / tormenteth innocence.

And in this version of the line the on-beats are matched with the linguistic stresses better; Skeat and Robinson were right in adopting it in their text.

The scansion of *Havelok* can do much more for us than reveal the facts of the author's metrical practice. The prosody of a ME verse text that is sufficiently early and on the whole metrically regular is the best source (along with the rhymes) of information about the author's pronunciation and accidence and the main features of ME at large. An accurate system of scansion, in this instance and many others, determines *inter alia* the number of unaccented syllables in the line, as a norm deduced from a majority of lines. This number in turn depends on, and therefore establishes, certain phonetic reductions (by syncope, elision, and apocope) that operated in the 'spoken chain' of the verse (as declaimed to an audience), and hence necessarily in that of ordinary utterance in prose. Those reductions are only fitfully expressed in ME spelling, but are amply exposed by the metre. And *Hav.* meets both the chronological and the metrical conditions stated above.

By a lucky chance, there is very plain internal evidence in *Hav.* for the number of syllables in the line. The versicle *Benedicamus Domino* from the Mass functions as a whole line in *Hav.* 20, and also in the AN *Le Bestiaire*[6] of Philippe de Thaün, l. 3168, this part of which is in rhymed couplets of octosyllabic lines. It gives us, in a wholly unambiguous spelling, a norm of eight syllables for the ME lines in *Hav.*, and hence nine for those with feminine rhymes (e.g. *castel*:*wastel* 878–9). It confirms what we can deduce from the ME lines, as in the specially clear case of those made up of monosyllabic words:

1808 And at a dint he slow hem þre.

These two patterns may be treated as constituting a single main type, the touchstone for which is that it begins with an off-beat, and which is the commonest type of line in *Hav.*:

2221 He̽ lét hi̽s óth a̽l óue̽r-gó
1914 So̽ dós þe̽ chíld þa̽t móde̽r þárne̽s.

Note. In the notation used here:

[6] Ed. E. Walberg (Lund and Paris, 1900); composed between 1121 and 1135.

1. A dot (*a*) under a letter means that it was not sounded; and (*b*) between on-beats means that an off-beat is missing.
2. The sign ‿ between a final vowel and a following initial vowel means that they coalesce, by elision of the first or absorption of the second into it.
3. The sign ⁀ under a letter means that a vowel is to be pronounced as the corresponding semi-vowel.[7]
4. On-beats and off-beats are marked / and × respectively. Unaccented syllables in final *-e* at the end of the line are sometimes marked (×), since final *-e* within the line is open to elision and apocope, and there is no means of being certain that it was always pronounced in all types of rhymes,[8] and hence of knowing when it was not.

The system of scansion used here is of a well-tried and traditional type. It is shown to be valid and accurate by the fact that it has revealed in *Hav.* (see pp. 210–12) the systematic and historically regular distinction between what had been the 'weak' and 'strong' inflection of the adjective in OE, by the use of syllabic final *-e* to mark all grammatical cases of the singular (except the genitive) when preceded by the definite article, a demonstrative, or a possessive. This distinction has, moreover, been elicited, by the same system of scansion, in Chaucer's English. And since it accurately reflects an OE one, it cannot possibly have been invented by scribes and superimposed on the language of *Hav.*, Chaucer, and other ME writers.[9]

The incidence of on-beats in the ME line used in *Hav.* must have been based on the natural (i.e. linguistic) stresses. Besides lines that would require four stresses in prose utterance, and

[7] On the semi-vowels of English see D. Abercrombie, *Elements of General Phonetics* (Edinburgh, 1967), 50, 67.

[8] E. T. Donaldson has argued that it was always sounded at the end of Chaucer's lines: 'Chaucer's Final "*-e*"', *PMLA* lxiii (1948), 1101–24, on pp. 1121–4.

[9] As has already been pointed out by Prof. M. L. Samuels ('Chaucerian Final "-E"', *NQ* ccxvii (1972), 445–8), in demolishing certain latter-day fallacies regarding Chaucer's verse and the way it should be scanned.

others that might have been uttered (in prose) with three, there are some that might have had either according to context:

> 649 þer God wilẹ helpen nouth ne dereth
> 720 And drou him to þe heye se
> 883 And bi him mani fishes ligge.

But the rhythmic pattern of this ME verse would have been a good deal more even than that of post-medieval poetry. This is because a great many nouns, adjectives, and verbs that were monosyllabic after *c*.1400 (by the complete elimination of final *-e*) were disyllables ending in unstressed syllabic *-e* in ME. The result, when these were followed by a word beginning with a stressed syllable, was the rhythmic sequence / × /; and this, as one can see by glancing at a few pages of *Ancrene Wisse*, must even in prose have been more prominent and frequent than in post-medieval poetry. In fact, it is striking in this connection that the word-order in *Hav*. hardly differs from that of prose (see e.g. ll. 633–91).

The upshot is that expression in ME *c*.1300 would have fitted easily into verse built on the strict alternation of an on-beat and an off-beat (and vice versa). The prescribed linguistic stresses instantly fit many lines in *Hav*. into this pattern, in a form which (given seven and nine syllables as the lower and the upper limit, if we allow for the other main type of line, illustrated below, that begins with the first on-beat, and for feminine rhymes) is the maximally even one, with four on-beats:

> 2034 Mikel ioie haue he!
> 2195 Erles, barouns, drenges, theynes.

Thus the syllables *to* and *bi* as well as *ma-* in *mani-* in 720 and 883 above must be given an on-beat.

The well-known main variant of the basic type of line, which begins with the first on-beat, is extremely common in *Hav*.:[10]

> 380 In his hand a spere stark
> 390 On þe belles þat men ringes

[10] In a proportion of *c*.39 to 64 of the first type in ll. 250–350, and of *c*.93 to 142 in ll. 250–500.

The one other common rhythmic variation is 'inversion of stress' in the first measure of the first type of line:

2718 Yeld hirę þe lond, for þat is rith
2552 Brini on bac, and sheld and spere.

Examples in other positions are few and not altogether assured: see 266 (unless *be dels*), 782 (unless *shepes*), 1084 (unless *ani*), 2578 (unless *gadred*).

The main points in the scansion of *Hav.* that remain in doubt, apart from the two phenomena discussed below (*Abnormal Lines*), are whether final *-e* in rhyme was always syllabic, and how far an on-beat might in individual instances not coincide with the linguistic stress. On the whole, the author was remarkably successful in harmonizing the metrical accents and the linguistic stresses, and notably abstemious in placing on-beats on unstressed syllables[11] (as distinct from secondarily stressed elements like *-yng*), and especially on grammatical endings.[12]

One cannot accurately recognize how regular the verse in *Hav.* is unless one is aware how lavishly the well-known phenomena of elision (along with the opposite process of hiatus) and apocope are at work in it. Other but not negligible ones are synizesis (by which the vowels /i/, /u/, and /y/ in final position before an initial vowel may be converted into the corresponding semi-vowels /j/, /w/, and /j/ respectively so as to make a diphthong, and hence one syllable out of two) and the intermittent use of syllabic *r*, and of non-syllabic *w* and *n* after certain consonants. The author thus had a rich choice of words which he could at need reduce (or occasionally enlarge) by one unaccented syllable, apart from odd pairs of phonetic variants such as *heued/hed*, *louerd/lord*.[13]

One delusive example is the first of the two main problems to be discussed here. It is an important but (hitherto) imperfectly

[11] e.g. *þe* 205, 599, 832, 904, 1813, 2886.

[12] *-eth* 464, *-ed* 364 (or trisyllabic *hos*[*e*]*led* with unetymological medial *-e-*), *-en* 163, 914 (or trisyllabic *kind* [*e*] *len* likewise).

[13] Monosyllabic *heued* 1760, 1813, *louerd* 608, 628, 1229, etc.; disyllabic *heued* 1907, 2677, *louerd* 484, 1222. For *mad* (*e*)/*maked* see p. 217, 2.

understood phenomenon in the scansion of *Hav*., as of Chaucer's verse, which, if taken at face value, would wreck the rhythm of *c*.200 individual lines in *Hav*. and gravely misrepresent the author's metre in a fundamental point. It concerns lines with two successive unaccented syllables between two stressed ones (other than in examples of 'inversion'—illustrated on p. 202 above—which merely re-orders, and does not augment the number of, unstressed syllables). In a great many of these lines, the first of the two successive unaccented syllables (and occasionally the second) is the EME inflection *-en*, in one or other of five functions, as the sign of the infin., the pres. pl., the pt. pl., the past part., and the plural of a few nouns. This element rhymes only on *-e* (whether syllabic or silent): at the end of the line the spoken form of the ending in the author's idiolect had thus shed the final *-n*. The possibility of variant spoken forms of inflectional *-en* within the line remains to be examined.

In the Laud MS of *Hav*., this element is, within the line, very commonly spelt *-en* as well as *-e*. It is abbreviated as *-ē* in *c*.145 instances, and written out as *-en* in *c*.76.[14]

But the abbreviated ones are equally acceptable, since the lavish use of the titulus in other words such as *hem*, *him*, *in*, *man*, *womman*, etc. shows that in this MS it still has its original function.

The use of the phonetic variants *a* (in the two spoken forms /ei/ and /ə/) and *an* in ME and pres. E., and of *mi* and *min* in ME, before a consonant and a vowel respectively (and in the latter case within each pair to prevent hiatus), shows that a mere count of the *-en* forms in *Hav*. would be almost meaningless. The following types of phonetic and rhythmical context must be distinguished:

1. when *-en* is followed by an unaccented syllable with initial vowel or diphthong:

[14] These figures, like others given here, are necessarily approximate because a sprinkling of lines in the poem can be scanned in more than one way. There is no discernible pattern in the distribution of the two spellings except in the first 56 lines, where *-e* is used once (10) and *-en* in all the other seven examples (12, 18, 21, 26, 29, 43, 56).

1002 A̽nd hé ga̽rt kóme̽n i̽ntó þe̽ tún

and 68, 88, 102, 116, 164 (2 exx.), 176 (*seyden*), 195, 203, and the other 77 instances assembled in Appendix A below;

2. when followed by an unaccented syllable with initial *h*- + vowel:

1347 Wíth þe̽(×) wénde̽ shúle̽n he̽ yérne̽

and 56, 69, 116, 164 (*gouen hem*), 190, 242, 244, 255, 325, 348, 376, 439, 441, 519, 562, 582, 602, 722, 902, 942, 1187, 1198, 1211, 1234 (*sholen hire*), 1247, 1867, 1911, 1916, 1917, 1978, 2017, 2140, 2167, 2270, 2307, 2380, 2413, 2427, 2468, 2548, 2557, 2583, 2775, 2813, 2854, 2974

3. when followed by an unaccented syllable with initial consonant (other than *h*-) + vowel or diphthong:

449 Þér he̽ gréte̽n fo̽r húngẹr a̽nd cóld

and 145, 220, 257 (*deyen til þat*), 260, 369, 417, 464, 470, 518, 530, 732, 763, 798, 846, 861, 951, 953, 1013, 1032, 1033, 1123, 1124, 1168, 1203, 1348, 1641, 1684, 1737, 1738, 1783, 1825, 1845, 1863, 1890, 2027, 2085, 2099, 2148, 2305, 2659, 2776, 2807, 2952, 2988;

4. when *-en* is the second of two unaccented syllables, and is followed by an accented syllable

(*a*) with initial vowel:

181 A̽nd mén ha̽uẹde̽n óf hi̽m míke̽l dréde(×)

and 295, 1083,

(*b*) with initial *h*-:

1058 Wo̽lde̽n hé no̽mórẹ to̽ pútti̽ng gánge(×)

and 2414,

(*c*) with initial consonant (other than *h*-) + vowel:

161 Þa̽t yé a̽re̽n cóme̽n tó me̽ nów

and 448, 461, 1204, 1231, 1322, 1695, 1709, 1897, 1967, 2134, in nearly all of which the *-en* is the ending of modal verbs, or of the verb 'to be' used mostly as an auxiliary;

5. when followed by an accented syllable with any initial consonant:

   1024 Ånd púttĕn wíth ă míkĕl stón

   and 584, 600, 690, 1018, 1040, 1059, 1069, 1161, 1196, etc.;
6. when followed by an accented syllable
   (*a*) with initial vowel or diphthong:

   238 Ånd míkĕl sórwĕ háuędĕn állĕ(×)

   and 15, 70, 106, 128, 156, 162, 176 (*ansuereden*), 204, (*sworn* for *swóren*), 226, 238, 283, 302, 306, 317, 385, 415, 554, 604, 610, 613, 658, 747, 956, 980, 1006, 1099, 1153, 1200, 1202, 1343, 1420, 1754, 1755, 1805, 1959, 1961, 2128, 2150, 2161, 2268, 2373, 2537, 2541, 2773, 2782, 2818, 2842, 2900, 2941,
   (*b*) with initial *h*- + vowel or diphthong:

   152 Hĕ wrúngĕn hóndęs ănd wépĕn sórĕ(×)

   and 154, 172, 272, 304, 480, 533, 584, 1201, 1325, 1834, 1864, 1865, 1866, 2012, 2040, 2047, 2233, 2258, 2290, 2398, 2545, 2768, 2792, 2821, 2979, 2992, 2996.

In type 1, if -*e* was the author's form, it could (and would) have been fused with the following initial vowel by elision. In type 2, when initial *h*- was 'dropped' (as it can be, and intermittently is, today), the result would have been as in type 1. It is important to note that in types 3 and 4 (*c*) elision of the -*e*- in the -*en* is phonetically not possible (because of the following consonant), in not less than 42 examples. If the author's form was -*e*, this was subject to apocope before a consonant, even though a variant form with syllabic -*e* might coexist with it in one and the same word or grammatical form.[15] He is less likely to have used -*en* in this type of sequence, since the final -*n* would have tended in speech to be assimilated to certain consonants and thus have been shed. There is no difference in principle, where scansion is concerned, between 3 and 4 (*c*).

[15] As is demonstrable from the *Ormulum*. See Bennett and Smithers, *Early Middle English Verse and Prose*, pp. xxvi–xxx, for examples.

In type 5, since the metrically obligatory unaccented syllable is equally well supplied by *-e*, the *-n* may well be due to a scribe with an idiolect that differs from the author's. This type thus does not unequivocally require *-n*. Types 6 (*a*) and (*b*) are the only ones in which we could warrantably regard *-en* as the author's form, on the grounds that (*a*) the final *-n* prevents hiatus, and (*b*) it does not produce two successive unaccented syllables. It must be said that (*a*) is hardly conclusive, since incontestable cases of hiatus are very common in *Hav.*;[16] and here again *-e* could provide the required unaccented syllable (with hiatus) just as well as *-en*. For what they are worth, examples of *-en* (as written) that prevent hiatus in lines 1–500 are about half the number of instances of hiatus cited in n. 16.[17]

What is extremely significant is that in types 1, 2, 3, and 4 (*c*) *-en* makes one of two successive unstressed syllables. In ll. 1–100 there are no less than 13 assured examples,[18] and in the whole text of 2802 lines not less than 204, or *c*.9.8 % (some in Appendix A below); and continuous reading of the text brings out (better than the figures) how high a proportion this is. But the full force of the phenomenon can be appreciated only alongside the complementary and very weighty fact that it is not the only form used in these contexts: there are opportunities for the use of *-en* in types 1, 2, 3, and 4 (*c*) (i.e. in contexts where it would have been one of two successive unstressed syllables) that have not been taken. In not less than 82 lines *-e* is written in the same types of context (apart from the invariable use of *-e*—syllabic or not—in rhyme, where some *-en* spellings of course wreck the rhyme and must be due to a scribe).[19] The *-e* is open to elision or apocope, and if it is so treated these lines scan in a consistently even rhythm, i.e. with a single off-beat between on-beats.

[16] Within the first 500 lines there are not less than 26: 11, 122, 132, 159, 167, 169, 171, 207, 208, 248, 265, 289, 293, 296, 299, 300, 304, 311, 366, 410, 419, 454, 457, 461, 473, 491.

[17] 15, 70, 106, 128, 162, 163, 176, 238, 283, 302, 306, 317, 385, 415 (14 in all).

[18] 10, 12, 18, 21, 26, 29, 43, 56, 57, 68, 69 (twice), 88.

[19] e.g. *holden* : *holde* 29–30, *gongen* : *fonge* 856–7, *mouthen* : *douhte* 1184–5.

There is proof of what has happened in the use of *-en*. In

2525 Fór þĕ gód hĕ háuęden hĭm dón

the scribe has given himself away. Since the pronominal subject *he* is a singular (referring to *Grim*, 2522), the author could not have used the plural form of the pluperfect, but must have written *háuęde hĭm* and a metrically impeccable line. Other cases are *haueden* 2857 (subject *he* singular), *didē* 79 (subject *wo*), and *dwelle* (subject *þou*) 1352. Moreover, a scribe has shown that this kind of thing is an error by subpuncting the *-n* in the infin. *beden* 2085 (:*rede* 3 pr. sg. subjunctive). And the foregoing explanation of the hypermetrical scribal *-en* for *-e* neatly accounts for *uten* (843) as an adoption of ON *úti*: the *-n*, which is etymologically 'incorrect', has been prompted by the superficial equivalence of *-en* and *-e* in pairs like *abouten/aboute*, *wiþouten/wiþoute*, where the *-n* is historically regular.

It is important to note that in types 3 and 4 (*c*) elision of the *-e* in *-en* is commonly not phonetically feasible (because of the following consonant). It therefore cannot warrantably be invoked to eliminate one of the two successive unaccented syllables in types 1 and 2, where it would (if applicable) have the effect of preserving the *-n* and hence of endorsing *-en* as the author's form in these contexts. What is clamantly probable is that in types 1, 2, 3, and 4 (*c*) the *-en* is spurious, and that a scribe has mechanically corrupted an *-e* which in the lines as written by the author was elided or reduced to zero.

An apparent but delusive exception is the *-n* that survived, alongside an endingless form, in verbs and nouns with monosyllabic roots ending in a vowel or a diphthong.[20] This last is a general, and not essentially a regional, phenomenon in ME: it is shown e.g. by Chaucer's rhymes to have belonged to his variety of ME. The survival of both forms in conjunction is hardly by chance: it shows that the *-n* form was needed as a means of avoiding hiatus.

[20] e.g. *don*: *on* 117, *gon*: *on* 1929; but *do*: *to* 17, 252, etc., *go*: *wo* 125, 509, *be*: *me* 170, 516, *yse*: *tre* 334.

The *-en* spellings in type 5 are accordingly suspect: the author is unlikely to have used a third grammatical ending in contexts where *-e* would have sufficed, and where there was no point in doing so, when it had been reduced to *-e* or zero in the other contexts in types 1, 2, 3, and 4 (*c*) in his idiolect. In 6 (*a*) and (*b*), however, the final *-n* may well be an authentic authorial form, since it does not merely prevent hiatus in the verse, but would have been used in that function in the form of ME spoken by the author (as in others).

In other words, the *-en* of 6 (*a*) and (*b*) is not on the same footing as the variants ('allomorphs') *-e* and zero of the other phonetic contexts. If it survived, this was only because it met an extra and quite distinct need of a linguistic kind (in the speech-chain of ME, as a final *-n* does today, before an initial vowel, diphthong, or *h-* in the following word) that had nothing to do with its original role as a grammatical ending (which belongs to the 'system' of the 'language').

-En of other origins than in the five inflections dealt with above is of course treated in the same way in *Hav.*, and therefore corroborates our conclusions. In *morwen* 812, 1132 a monosyllable is required. *Abouten* is written in 1041, 2430 (where a trisyllable is needed, but the final *-n* is not), alongside *aboute* 2093 (where a disyllable with apocope of *-e* is needed). But *Abouten* 2832, where syllabic *-en* makes one of two successive unaccented syllables, is a corruption of *Aboute* with elision of *-e*.

In *boþe* 416, 600, 1013 and *boþen* 471 a monosyllable is required, and in *boþe* 1219, 1220, *boþen* 698, 2224 a syllabic *-e*. Disyllabic *siþen* 1811, 2252 and *siþe* 1815 are in order, but *siþen* (*he*) 1989 is not. In *withuten* 191 a third unaccented syllable (though not necessarily *-n*) is called for, but makes two successive unaccented syllables in 2118.

Apocope, which is generally interpreted as the suppression of a final unaccented vowel before any consonant, is vital in this inquiry, since it concerns final *-e*, which is a pivotal element in EME systems of accidence.

The system of scansion used here shows that final *-e* may (though it often does not) undergo apocope in almost any linguistic element, viz. (*a*) nouns, (*b*) adverbs, (*c*) prepositions and conjunctions, (*d*) infinitives, (*e*) the pres, pl. indicative and the pres. sg. and pl. subjunctive, (*f*) the pt. pl., (*g*) the imper. sg., (*h*) the past participle, (*i*) but in adjectives, with such far-reaching limits, and for such a reason, as set them apart. For instance:

(*a*) 2847 And seyde 'Nu is timẹ to take (x)',
2868 So mikel louẹ was hem bitwene (x)

and *timẹ* 1715, *knauẹ* 481, 568, prep. sg. *londẹ* 697, 764, and by elision *metẹ* 843, *shuldrẹ* 605, *stedẹ* 745; but *time* 1740, 2889 (OE *tima*), *loue* 2975 (OE *lufu*), *knaue* 501, 591 (OE *cnafa*), *londe* 722 (OE *lond*), *mete* 927;

(*b*) *sone* 645, 2205, 2943, *sore* 616, *yete* 495; but *sonẹ* 719, 2203, 2273, *yetẹ* 2974, and by elision *sonẹ* 813, 986;

(*c*) *abouten* 1011, 2430; but *aboutẹ* 591, and by elision 521, 671, 2832;

(*d*) *binde* 2950, *crien* 2444, *hange* 2047, *hauen* 1099, *heren* 2081, *lye* 2110, *slepen* 2109, *wayte* 2071; but *bringẹ* 2505, *criẹ* 2773, *hetẹ* 457, 457, 1719, *hauẹ* 491, 686, *herẹ* 2329, *settẹ* 2672, and by elision *cloþẹ* 1199, *comẹ* 493 (MS *comen*), *terẹ* 708, *yeuẹ* 1220;

(*e*) *biginnen* 1780, *brenne* 2584, *goule* and *grete* 454, *hauen* 1222, 2996, *strangleth* 2585 (scribal, for *strangle(n)*), *wilen* 2818; but *demẹ* 2477, *demẹṇ* 2813, *hauẹ* 2800, *louẹṇ* 1348, *sittẹṇ* 2099, and by elision *wonẹ* 105 (see n.);

(*f*) (strong): *bigunnen* 1303, *chosen* 372, *komen* 1014, 2791, *spoken* 372, *wisten* 1184, 1209, *yeuen* 1846; but *bigunnẹṇ* 2796, 2952, *komẹṇ* 1013, 1203, *nomẹṇ* 2791, *setẹṇ* 1767; and by elision *fellẹṇ* 1304, *wistẹṇ* 1188; (weak): *dide* 1685, *hauẹde(n)* 1205, 1428, *herde* 465, *sende* 1750, *seyde(n)* 1150, 1214; but *hauẹdẹ* 1431, *leddẹ(ṇ)* 1247, *liuẹdẹ* 2045, *sentẹ* 1134, *settẹ* 2572, and by elision *answerẹdẹ* 1112, *herdẹ* 1265, *stirtẹ* 567;

(*g*) *haue* 1665, *loke* 1352, *make* 677; but *hauẹ* 1332, 1363, *sit* 926.

The ending of the imper. pl. is commonly written *-es*, and occasionally *-eþ*: *bicomes* 2304, *comes* 1799, *falles* 2303, *folwes* 2602, *liþes* 2205, *lokes* 2241, and *cometh* 2248, *gripeth* 1883. The potentially monosyllabic *gripeth* 1883, *lokes* 2580, *nimes* 2595 can all be scanned /x with inversion of stress. Thus *helpe* 2422, *loke* 1681, *latẹ* 2423, *lokẹ* 1713 may be analogical adoptions of the singular.

(*h*) *comen* 1695, 1715, *eten* 658, *forfaren* 1381, *wreke* 2850; but *comẹ*

2575, *waxẹṇ* 792, *youẹṇet* 1644, and by elision *brokẹṇ* 1239, *etẹṇ* 932, *yeuẹṇ* 1251.

(*i*) There is an arresting exception and contrast to the treatment of final *-e* in the above material: apocope does not as a general rule operate in adjectives in *Hav*. This is because final *-e* has there been retained in a special function—to mark the distinction between the old 'weak' and 'strong' types of inflection (OE *se ealda mann* and *an eald mann*), and between the singular and the plural in the old 'strong' inflection. It is so used in *Hav.* with remarkable consistency, and in a form that is historically regular (even in the spelling) in a high degree.

Thus, in words with a monosyllabic OE antecedent, and with a preceding definite article, or demonstrative, or possessive:

A I. *Nominative*

(*a*) Perhaps *þe rithe eyr* 289, 2236 (MS *rith*); but *þe rith eyr*, with elision, is metrically admissible in both, on the evidence of the objective form (A II (*a*) below). With superlatives: *þe beste knith* 87, 345 (*man* 1751, *mete* 1725), *þe moste swike* 423.

(*b*) *þat fule fend* 506, 1412 (*swike* 1159, *file* 2500), *þat ilke knaue* 1088.

(*c*) In a ME monosyllabic adj. from an antecedent disyllabic one: *þi fayre fere* 1215 (*wif* 1663).

Very occasional breaches of the rule occur: *þe bestę* 1082, *þat fulę, traytour* 2534, *þe godę charbocle-ston* 2146. In 2898 (*Hauęlok þe godę*) *ne* may be a scribe's addition, despite the parallel in 2637.

Superlatives that if inflected would be trisyllabic do not have final *-e* (*þe fayrestę* 200, *strangest* 1082), and may have syncope in the suffix: *fayręst* 281, 1082.

A II. *Objective*

(*a*) *þe firste knith* 2625, *þe ricthe gate* 847 (*dom* 2474), *þe sharpe swerd* 2846. *þe rith eye* 1813 with elision; but in 2546, 2726 *rith*[*e*], with hiatus, is also possible.

(*b*) *þis fayre genge* 1736, *þat fule swike* 2452.

(*c*) *mi blake swire* 311, *his gode swerd* 2734, *his holde blame* 2461.

An exception is *þe gretę laumprei* 772. In superlatives trisyllabic form is again avoided: *þe fairest þing* 2866, *þe fayrestę man* 1111, *þe heldestę broþer* 1397. In *his gold ring* 1638, *þe gold ring* 1643, *gold ring* was probably felt to be a compound.

A III. *Prepositional*

(*a*) *þe firste siþe* (*yer*) 1053, 1334, *þe fule necke* 1823, *þe gode borw* 774, 848, *þe heye curt* (*se*) 1686, 720, *þe mirke nith* 404.
(*b*) *þat ilke grene* (*wounde*) 2841, 2675.

The metrically ambiguous *þoru* (or *þoru*) *þe rith arum* 2409 would admit of *rithe*, with hiatus; but *hise rith shuldre* 605, 2141 is an exception.

Trisyllabic form is again avoided in a superlative in *þe fayrest wymman* 1157, but forms of four syllables are not: *þe alþerbeste but* 1041, *þe alþerleste wounde* 1979, and (with an assured emendation [*þ*]*alþerlest*[*e*] *dint* 2667. The exceptions here, like some others above, bear out Lehnert's view (see note below, p. 213) about what determined the choice between a form in -*e* and one without it in various types of word.

A IV. *Plural*

These are less significant in both types of inflection, since both have -*e* throughout in all grammatical cases. Thus, for the weak-type inflection: nom, *þe beste men* 2895, *þe helde men* 2473, *þe starke laddes* 1025, *þe stronge castles* 1302, *þo foule þeues* 2045; objective *mine gode knihtes* 2707; prepositional *alþerbeste men* 2416.

In the strong-type inflection in *Hav.*, as in the other, the nom. sg. and pl. were used for all grammatical cases of the singular and the plural respectively. The sg. is endingless, and the pl. ends in -*e*, in accord with OE usage in the nom. sg. and the nom. and accus. pl. respectively. Thus in the singular:

B I. *Nominative*

A ful fayr bed 659, predicative *fayr* 1064; *an god clerk* 1178; *an iuel strong* 114, *a strong dere* 825, predicative *strong* 1067; *a ful yung knaue* 2178; *fayr man* 962; *gret dine* 1861; *rith eir* 2540; *strong man* 1072; *wis man* 180; *old sinne* 2462.

OE disyllabic adjectives in -*e* retain it here: *a riche king* (*man*) 341, 373; *trewe man* 179, but predicative *trewe* 1757; *unride* 1796 with elision. Other disyllabic adjectives of OE are endingless: *a selkuth drem* 1285.

B II. *Objective*

A birþene gret 808; *a god tre* 1883, *a ful god mast* (*ore*) 710, 1887; *a ful sor dint* 1818; *ful fair bred* 924, *ful god lith* (*stede*) 1890, 2358, *so god brede* (*shrede*) 98, 99; *god child* 2984, g(*h*)*od fey*(*th*) 255, 2270, 2854, *god man* 1694, *god þank* 2561.

OE disyllabic adjectives in *-e* retain it (*newe shame* 2462); but trisyllabic ones do not (*stalworþẹ man* 905, 1028). Other OE disyllabic adjectives are endingless in *Hav.* and thus historically regular, and are indeclinable throughout the singular: *a litel cote* (*hus*) 738, 741.

B III. *Prepositional*

The rule is again observed: *an eld cloth* 546; *a fayr staf* 2518; *a god spere* 2653, *a ful god gleiue* (*stede*) 1771, 2387; *an old seyl* 2508, *an hold with couel* 1145; *god lif* 2934; *gret ioying* 2950; *red gold* 47; predicative *gode* 283.

Exceptions are *gode wille* 2997, and *longe spere* 2300 (where *sharp* may be treated as a disyllable with syllabic *r*).

Plural

The historically regular *-e* overwhelmingly predominates in all grammatical cases, e.g. vocative *fule þeues* 1781:

B IV. *Nominative*

Faire two 2134, *gode metes* 2341, *heye men* 959, *starke laddes* 1016, (*laddẹs*) 2028; *mikle* 2015; and many examples of substantival *alle* (150, 236, 401, etc.).

Exceptions are *allẹ* 2161, 2773; *heyẹ* 1326 by elision.

B V. *Objective*

Arwe men 2116, *grete dintes* 1438 (*oþes* 2232, 2853), *alle* 169, 254, 1222, 2296, etc.

Exceptions are *allẹ* 165, 2271, and probably *al* 104, 268. *Longẹ* 1846 and *gretẹ* 2014 are due to elision. *Wilde* was disyllabic in OE (*wilde*).

B VI. *Prepositional*

Abundant examples include *alle þinge* 71 (*men* 435, *þewes* 282) *gode bowes* 1749 (*burwes* 55, 1631, *metẹs* 303, *stedes* 2573); *harde bondes* 143; *longe gleyues* 267; *wide sleues* 1958.

Exceptions are *allẹ* (substantival) 427; *godẹ drinkes* 1739; *eyne grim* 681. (*Chapmen*) ... *yung ne old* 1640, being a common formula and thus a unit, would have tended to become fixed in the endingless form of the singular.

Note. Further material regarding the treatment of final *-e* in

Hav. may be found in the monograph of F. Schmidt,[21] which is based on Holthausen's edition.

This representative sample shows that a great many words were current in two different forms, with and without final -*e*, both in verse and in speech (since the same types of phonetic environment occurred in both). It instantly points to an essentially simple solution for one of the major problems in the evolution of English, since it accounts for a decisive stage in the loss of final -*e* in ME. From the foregoing evidence (in conjunction with the massive scale on which elision is at work in *Hav*. and other ME verse), we may warrantably deduce that forms without final -*e*, in words to which it was historically proper, were first evolved in phonetic contexts where elision occurred, and that they were then naturally available for, and were carried over into, contexts in which the word was followed by an initial consonant (which is where apocope is held to have operated).

It follows that there is no such thing as 'apocope', in the sense of an independent process or sound-change. What is thus called is simply an analogical use of an elided form (as a fact of spoken usage). This explanation accounts for what is otherwise inexplicable—that one and the same word may, in one and the same grammatical function, undergo 'apocope' or not, and hence may or may not shed final -*e*.[22]

The inevitable operation of elision in the 'spoken chain', and hence in verse, is not necessarily the only factor that led to the first stage in the loss of final -*e*. Paradigmatic processes (i.e. in sub-systems of the 'language') may have worked along with it in some varieties of ME—notably the syncretism of the subject and the object case, and of the object case and the dative/prepositional case in some classes of nouns. But in *Hav*., at least, there is no palpable tendency to use metrically demonstrable forms with analogical final -*e* (though there is in the *Ormulum*).[23]

[21] *Zur Heimatbestimmung des Havelok* (Diss. Göttingen, 1900), 89–98.

[22] For examples from a very extensive text see M. Lehnert, *Sprachform und Sprachfunktion im 'Orrmulum' um 1200* (Berlin, 1953) 116–17, 119 ff., especially 134–8, and *passim*.

[23] See Lehnert, op. cit., e.g. pp. 22, 24, 116–17, 133–8.

Once the two forms of a word had emerged, the choice of one or the other before a consonant was evidently, in verse at least, a matter of rhythm,[24] i.e. of a desire to avoid two successive on-beats. Even within the short compass of *Hav.*, some of the few exceptions to the retention of final *-e*, in the weak inflection of adjectives in the singular and in the plural both strong and weak, are associated with the avoidance of two successive unaccented syllables between stresses, as in *þe fairest þing* 2866, *þe fayrestę man* 1111, beside *þę alþerbeste but* 1041, i.e. with the desire for the regular alternation of an on-beat with an off-beat.

The hypothesis offered above to account for how and why forms without final *-e* came into being concerns only one stage (but a vital one) in the process by which final *-e* came to be eliminated altogether. That stage becomes accessible to us only because there are by that time metrical means of amply establishing the facts of elision and 'apocope'. But elision (in non-metrical speech) must go well back before *Hav.* was composed (before 1310); though there are no assured means known to me of ascertaining just how far. Earlier stages of the shift from synthetic to analytic structure in accidence have been summarily formulated by M. L. Samuels.[25] He has rejected Lehnert's view[26] that the loss of form (i.e. in inflections) was due to the loss of function, itself in turn due to the increased use of prepositions (already in OE). But it should be noted that Lehnert did also take cognizance of the ME stage at which the two forms of a word (with and without final *-e*) had come to coexist, and that he sought to explain what determined the choice of one or the other in individual contexts.

Abnormal Lines

Two main issues about which some doubt remains are whether the author of *Hav.* (as distinct from scribes) (i) used two

[24] As argued by Lehnert from abundant examples, op. cit., pp. 33–4, 39, 41, 117, 119, 135, etc.

[25] *Linguistic Evolution*, Cambridge Studies in Linguistics, 5 (1972), 82–3.

[26] Op. cit., pp. 1–17 and *passim*.

successive off-beats at all within the line, and (ii) was willing to dispense with the single off-beat that normally separates two on-beats.

The answers to these two questions crucially depend on how reliable and accurate the text of the Laud MS is. That of the Cambridge fragments is too short, too late, and too debased to tell us much about the metrical accuracy of the Laud MS. But there are other instances to show that even in favourable conditions, as when there are two or three extant MSS or more, the text of a ME romance in verse is likely to run to many minor corruptions that affect the number of syllables in the line, and to be much less settled and faithful to the author than e.g. the extant relatively fixed text of *The Canterbury Tales*, with its multiple if late copies. The Laud, Auchinleck, and Lincoln's Inn MSS of *Kyng Alisaunder* are an educative example, like the six extant MSS of the *Assumptio Mariae*.[27] The Laud MS of *Hav*. is more regular in the syllabic structure, and smoother in the rhythm, of individual lines than are those parts of *Kyng Alisaunder* that are preserved in three copies. But a margin for scribal errors in *Hav*. must duly be allowed: what we can recover of the author's metrical practice cannot possibly be expected to give a totally self-consistent picture, where these two phenomena are concerned, when even the best MSS of *The Canterbury Tales* do not in regard to the first of them.

There are no secure examples in *Hav*. of lines with either more or less than four on-beats. The number of those (i) with two successive unaccented syllables within the line is greatly reduced by the elimination (above) of many with *-en* as one of the two. There are enough lines (ii) with an off-beat missing between two on-beats to require separate notice.

Many of the remaining examples of (i), especially, and some of (ii), are open to doubt in the light of certain standard types of scribal corruption, which must now be summarily illustrated. The kinds that produce overweighted, defective, or unrhythmical lines, and that can be detected in the one extant MS of *Hav*.,

[27] Ed. E. Hackauf (Berlin, 1902).

are fairly superficial. They consist mostly in the addition or the omission of superfluous words, commonly by the use of syntactic or grammatical or phonetic equivalents:

1. One form of expression may replace another as a syntactic equivalent of it. Since double and multiple negatives were idiomatically normal, a scribe might add an unnecessary one:

1123 Ne shalt þou non oþer louerd haue,

where either *Ne* or *non* is likely to be spurious, so that the line may be scanned × / × / × / × / (×).

The definite article is not idiomatically obligatory in the following lines, which are metrically normal without it:

1078 Þe king Aþelwold me dide swere
1852 So water þat fro þe welle glides
2192 And gon was þisternesse of þe nith.

But it has probably dropped out of 1133:

And day-belle at kirke rungen,

where *atte* (< *at þe*) gives a line with normal rhythm.
Similarly, the second *for* was probably added by a scribe in:

357 For gold ne siluer ne for no gyue.

Conversely, in the light of the preceding 1. 2458:

With poure mete and feble drink,

2459 is to be read as:

And [wiþ] swiþe wikke cloþes.

The preceding ll. 488–9:

þat neueremore ne shal I bere
Ayen þe, louerd, sheld ne spere

suggest that in the overloaded l. 490:

Ne oþer wepne bere þat may you dere

bere has been repeated by a scribe from 488.

The superfluous *þat was* 2535 echoes *þat was* 2533, and sounds spurious; the line is metrically normal without it.

Other syntactically unnecessary words that disrupt a line are *you*

3, *þat* 148, *and* 33, *and* or *þe* 755, *him* 859, the second *of* 897, *to* 938 and 1168, *þer* or *þou* 1163, *or* 2105, perhaps *ne* 1683 (which would then match 1867, where a single negative occurs after the infinitive dependent on *dursten*).

2. Phonetic or grammatical variants may be introduced. In 1015, *þanne weren þore* shows that the halting line 1005 should perhaps read:

In Eng[e]lond þannẹ were þere.

Bigan has probably displaced the aphetic *gan* in 724:

þat it ne bigan a wind to rise

and in 1358. *Swor*[*e*]*n* past part. 204 (MS *sworn*) would make the line normal.

Made is for metrical purposes correctly so spelt in 38, 39, 86, 95 etc., *mad* 2187, in all of which it is a monosyllable (in some with elision). A monosyllable is required in 58 (MS *maked and*), and a disyllable in 555 (MS *makeden*); in 542 a disyllable is needed if *to* is the spurious element, but otherwise a monosyllable *mad*. Disyllabic *maked* is right in 563, and is prescribed by rhymes on *naked* 5 and 2134 and on *quaked* 134.

3. A pronominal subject may be re-defined, or a personal name be expanded descriptively. In 983:

þan was Hauelok bi þe shuldren more

Hauelok may have displaced *he*, in a normal line × / × / × / × / (×). Likewise, *þe king* 2298 looks like an expansion of *Birkabeynes* 2297, and the line would be normal without it. *Grim* 598 may be a scribe's unconscious attempt to make the context more explicit.

Given 2115:

'Deus!' quoth he [sc. *Ubbe* 2094] 'hwat may þis mene?'

it may be that *Ubbe* has displaced *he* in 1931 and 2097, which are identical with that line except in the rhyme-word *be* for *mene*. But in *hwat Ubbe* 1651 the personal name is contextually necessary; and this line (and admittedly 1931 and 2097) might be scanned with inversion of stress in the second half:

'Deus!' hwat Ubbe, 'Qui ne werẹ he knith?'

Some lines are left over that are not open to doubts of this kind:

127 And a thousandẹ men bi hire syde
933 He kam to þe welle, watẹr up-drow

and 936, 1042, 1182, 1189, 1365, 1390, 1401, 1683, 1950, 2006, 2107, 2140, 2516, 2578. Lines 785, 1391, and 2688 are best not included, since they may be scanned with inversion of stress. And 886, as a near-equivalent of 869, suggests that *forth* in the latter is spurious.

Lines with two successive on-beats are more numerous. In the commonest type, the pause falls midway in the line ((×)/ × /./ × /(×)):

1119	þat she swor . swilk an oth
2185–6	And of dreng . and of thayn
	And of knith . and of sweyn
2849	þat Ich se . ride and go
472	And siþen hem . al to grotes (repeated in 1415)
1246	And made hem . glad and bliþe
2808	God leue him . sone to honge

Some lines of this type can be credibly repaired or explained: *Knict* [*and*] 32, *Eng*[*e*]*lond* 61, [*wel*] *ney* 635, *bad* [*he*] 1416, [*his*] *spures* 1677, *he* [*nouth*] 2229 (as in the virtually identical 505), [*ful*] *fele siþe* 2844; and 433 (see p. 196).

But the following resist repair:

627 Gódárd, þát . fúlé swíké(×)

and 539, 652, 702, 825, 880, 892, 1004, 1036, 1056, 1067, 1073, 1254, 1318, 1377, 1431, 1856, 2314, 2323, 2392, 2428, 2433, 2435, 2476, 2497, 2794, 2803, 2945. This is a ratio of one such line to eighty-three, or 1.2 %—though the lack of any in 458 lines (1856–2314) and the clusters of four in 69 lines (1004–1073) and eight in 185 lines (2314–2497) are curiously inconsistent.

In a few examples, the pause falls between the last two on-beats in the line:

682 Ănd séydĕ 'Wíltŭ bén . érl?'

and 635, 892, 2996. In 966 and 1163 *fir* is to be read as disyllabic, as is *fayr* 973, 2079; in 2921 *fayr* may be the adv. *fayre*.

The break is extremely rare between the first two stresses in the line:

1434 Só . þát ŭntó þĭs dáy
2748 Blód . ánd sŏ sóre hĭm sláwĕn(×).

And 1679, with a double pause, is virtually certain to be corrupt:

Ór . hé . fró hĭm férdĕ(×)

These last two varieties, at least, are too infrequent to qualify as assured elements of the author's practice. And fifteen examples of one or another type can be set aside because in them the pause depends on a missing final -*e* which the author is almost bound to have written:

274 Wislikẹ for soth[e] was him wel
578 For to don on his[e] cloþes
982 And þẹ erles men woren al[le] þore (cf. *alle* 980)
182 He may hirẹ alþerbest[e] yeme
721 þerẹ he mith alþerbest[e] fle
1138 Hwat sholdẹ Ich with wi[ue] do? (MS *wif*)
2145 It sparkedẹ and ful brith[e] shon
2172 þat Y þe with eyn[e] se (cf. *eyne grim* 681)
2218 On bok[e] and on messe-gere (as written, and metrically obligatory in 2312)
2308 O bok[e] ful grundlikẹ he swore
2547 But yif he of mi lond[e] fle (cf. *of londe* 2600)
2599 Ne hosẹled ben nẹ of prest[e] shriuen
2715 Engelond[e] euẹril del (as written in the identical line 208)
2967 And Goldẹboru quen[e], þat I wene.

Since English is a stress-timed language, i.e. with equal intervals of time between successive stresses,[28] the use of two successive off-beats within the ME four-beat line, and the omission of one between successive on-beats, would in theory have been entirely feasible and natural. One reason for doubting in practice that the author used these two rhythmic patterns is the fact that there are relatively so few secure examples of them. Another is that his English differed in one important regard (mentioned above) from present English. The survival, and the use on a large scale, of unstressed final -*e* meant that (*a*) many words that have been monosyllabic since *c.*1400 were still disyllabic (as well as monosyllabic when subject to elision and 'apocope') *c.*1300, and hence (*b*) many sequences of the rhythmic form /x/ were still of the form /x/ in ME. There would thus have been fewer oportunities and less occasion to use either of the two relatively rare phenomena considered here.

[28] See D. Abercrombie, *Elements of General Phonetics* (Edinburgh, 1967), 96–8, and 'A Phonetician's View of Verse Structure', in *Studies in Phonetics and Linguistics* (Oxford, 1965), 16–25, on pp. 16–18.

To scan *Hav.*, by the kind of system used here, is to learn that, even in details, the author's prosody is very like the practice of Chaucer in *The Canterbury Tales* and (as an example of the four-beat line) *The Hous of Fame*. In fact, it is simply not true that 'one thing may be said with security, that modern English versification starts with Chaucer. With him it was almost a *de novo* creation'.[29] Syncope, elision and hiatus, 'apocope', and synizesis all appear, and take the same forms, as in *Hav*. And of course it could hardly be otherwise, since all these things (and others) are facts of speech first and foremost, and of metrically ordered speech second. One main difference between the two writers is that e.g. hiatus, like the *-en* that produces two successive unaccented syllables, is more thinly spread in Chaucer's verse. This means *inter alia* that the scansion of *Hav*. makes certain phenomena in Chaucer's work much clearer and more definite, and their interpretation more assured. But this potential aid does not seem to have been explored (explicitly, at least) by editors of Chaucer or in recent studies of his prosody by metrists, all of whom might have profited by it.

The spelling *-en* for the infinitive, pt. pl., past part. of verbs, and the plural of a few nouns, in the most accessible MSS of Chaucer's poetry, is distributed among various types of phonetic environment in accordance with the same patterns as it has been shown above to be distributed in *Hav*. The main question to be considered here is whether the examples of *-en* that produce two successive unaccented syllables within the Chaucerian line, even in the best MSS, are the work of Chaucer or of scribes. The answer to this is in turn likely to determine whether Chaucer used two successive unaccented syllables in other sequences not involving *-en*.

It is a happy accident that the Ellesmere and the Hengwrt MSS of *The Canterbury Tales* were copies made by one and the same scribe.[30] A useful way of exploring both questions posed above

[29] Paull F. Baum, *Chaucer's Verse* (Durham, N. C., 1961), 11.

[30] See A. I. Doyle and M. B. Parkes, 'The Production of Copies of *The Canterbury Tales* and The *Confessio Amantis* in the early fifteenth century', in

is to compare the treatment of *-en* in these two MSS.[31] The relation between them in *The Knight's Tale* is as follows:

A. Before an initial vowel or *h* + vowel, where *-e* instead of *-en* would be elided and thus eliminate the extra unaccented syllable:

(*a*) both have *-en*:

> 1065 Was risen and romed in a chambre anheigh.

Also 1086, 1089, 1499, 1503, 1628, 1794, 1826, 2934.

(*b*) one has *-en* and the other *-e*:

> 1168 Is broke alday for loue in ech degree (E *broken*)

Also 1177 (E *stryuen*), 1261 (E *faren*), 1280 (E *weren*), 2425 (E *brenden*), 2516 (E *seyde*), 2622 (E *to fresshen*), 2707 (E *weren*), 2730 (E *clepen*), 2869 (E *ryden*), 2890 (H *weren*), 2917 (E *weren*). In 2866 *leyen* (E *leye*) may be monosyllabic.

B. Before a consonant, where elision is not possible:

(*a*) both have *-en*:

> 1940 Nat was foryeten the porter Ydelnesse.

Also 2021 *forgeten by*, 2074 *drawen to*, 2840 *chaungen bothe*.

(*b*) one has *-en* and the other *-e*:

> 2917 This is to seyn the bowes were so brode (E *weren*)

Just as in *Hav.*, there are a great many lines (far more than in all categories above) in which, in both MSS, an opportunity to use an *-en* that would have produced two successive unaccented syllables has not been taken. Instead, final *-e* is written; this is non-syllabic, being in most instances open to elision, or occasionally to 'apocope' (in contexts not admitting of elision):

M. B. Parkes and A. G. Watson, *Medieval Scribes, Manuscripts and Libraries: Essays Presented to N. R. Ker* (London, 1978) 163–210, on pp. 185–6.

[31] They are now conveniently available in P. G. Ruggiers, *The Canterbury Tales* (*A Variorum Edition of the Works of Geoffrey Chaucer*, i (University of Oklahoma, 1979), who prints the Hengwrt text in full with the variants of Ellesmere.

1128 This Palamon gan knytte his browes tweye
1203 And hadde hym knowe at Thebes yeer by yere
1351 That oother where hym list may ride or go.[32]

The great preponderance, in both H and E, of this usage over *-en* that produced two successive unaccented syllables is a very strong argument for concluding that the former was that of Chaucer, and hence that the latter is due to scribal lapses. This is of course said without prejudice to the status of syllabic *-en* where it prevents hiatus: many examples of this may well be 'right' (both as complying with general usage, and as representing Chaucer's practice). On the other hand, the use of *-en* before a consonant when a single unaccented syllable is needed is of uncertain status: a syllabic *-e* would have done the same work, and *-en* is on the whole less likely to be right than *-e*. What surely clinches the matter is that Chaucer (like the author of *Hav.*) never uses the *-en* type in rhyme (other than in words with monosyllabic root-syllables ending in a vowel or a diphthong).

The upshot is that:

(*a*) *-en* that produces two successive unaccented syllables is hypermetrical in Chaucer's verse, just as in *Hav.*, and hence
(*b*) that Chaucer did not countenance or use two successive unaccented syllables within the line (other than in 'inversion of stress');
(*c*) the *-en* that produces them should probably be removed from a text of Chaucer edited for ordinary purposes,[33] even at the price of potential inconsistency in relation to the *-en* of uncertain status as defined above: the former is an assured error, but the latter not.

Another important point, sufficiently illustrated by *The Knight's Tale*, is that different MSS of the same work (and even two MSS copied by the same scribe) may differ in their use of *-en* and *-e*, even within one and the same class of phonetic environ-

[32] Among many examples in *The Knight's Tale*, see 1143, 1186, 1195, 1215, 1225, 1248, 1249, 1334, 1335, 1350, 1368, 1369, 1416, 1450, 1459, 1470, 1481, 1482, 1484, 1485.

[33] The only edition, within my knowledge, in which this has been understood and consistently carried out is that of *The Pardoner's Tale* by Nevill Coghill and C. Tolkien (London, 1958).

ment. The practice even of an individual MS is not wholly consistent. It follows that an individual MS cannot be assumed to reproduce, from beginning to end, Chaucer's own use of *-en* and *-e* for the inflections in question.

That it is still necessary to state all this is vividly illustrated in practical form by F. N. Robinson's specimen scansion of ll. 285–308 of the *General Prologue*, in his account of Chaucer's versification (pp. xxxv–xxxvi of his second edition). It is no derogation of Robinson's great contribution to the study of Chaucer to point out that, in the light of the second conclusion stated above, no less than eight out of the twenty-four lines in his analysis are wrongly scanned, and should be read thus:

But looked holwe and therto sobrely	(R. *holwë and*, i.e. / × ×)
Ful thredbarę was his overestę courtepy	(R. *overestę*, i.e. / × ×)
For he haddę geten hym yet no benefice	(R. *geten hym*, i.e. / × ×)
For hym was levęre have at his beddes heed	(R. *levere have at his*, i.e. / × / × ×)
Than robes riche, or fithele, or gay sautrie	(R. *fithelę or*, i.e. / × ×)
But al that he myghte of his freendes hente	(R. *myghte of his*, i.e. / × ×)
And bisily gan for the soules preye	(R. *gan for the*, i.e. / × ×)
Of studię took he moost curę and moost heede	(R. *curę and moost*, i.e. × × /)

Robinson's belief that Chaucer 'not infrequently has an extra light syllable in a line (a trisyllabic foot in place of the regular iambus)', and that 'the extra syllable seems to have been most frequent in the caesural pause',[34] derives from Skeat,[35] and was also avowed by Manly[36] in the second of the three standard editions used in this country that aim at providing a critical text.

[34] pp. xxxv and xxxvi.

[35] *The Works of Geoffrey Chaucer*, vi, pp. xc–xci, xcvi–xcvii.

[36] *Canterbury Tales by Geoffrey Chaucer* (London, n.d.), 127–9.

Prof. N. F. Blake's edition is in a somewhat different category, as a 'plain' text (i.e. of a single MS, his choice being Hengwrt), edited 'with the minimum of emendation':[37] he has naturally reproduced the treatment in that MS of *-en* as the sign of the five grammatical endings.

Since the editions of Skeat and Robinson are the readily available ones in Britain, their handling of the *-en* and its variants is potentially important. As the scope of Robinson's edition unfortunately did not allow of his recording the MS readings in full, and as in *The Hous of Fame* 'in several instances *-n* has been silently added to infinitives to break a hiatus or mend the rhythm' (p. 899), the reader cannot learn from him exactly how the MSS treat *-en*. In practice, Robinson's emendations in *The Knight's Tale* and *The Hous of Fame* correspond extensively with those of Skeat, who does record MS readings and variants in full.

Skeat himself, however, has not been wholly consistent in his emendations. Thus, in *The Knight's Tale*, he:

1. prints hypermetrical *-en*:
   (*a*) when both E and H have it: 1065, 1086, 1089, 1499, 1503, 1628, 1794, 2825, 2934, in each case to avoid hiatus; but also before a consonant (where elision is not possible) in 1940, 2021, 2074;
   (*b*) from E, when H has metrically correct *-e*: 1261, 1280, 2730.
2. prints metrically correct *-e*:
   (*a*) from H (E with 'hypermetrical *-en*): 1168, 1177, 2425, 2622, 2707, 2869; and (before a consonant) 2917;
   (*b*) from E (H with hypermetrical *-en*): 2516;
   (*c*) when both H and E have hypermetrical *-en*: 1826.

The main inconsistency is between 1 (*a*) and 2 (*a*). There are a few individual ones such as between 1177, where he prints H *stryue* 3 pr. pl. rather than E *stryuen* with hypermetrical *-en*, and 1261, where he prints the E hypermetrical *faren* 3 pr. pl. instead of H *fare*. In both he is followed by Manly and Rickert.[38] As the *-e* of both the shorter forms is elided, the two cases are indistinguishable, and the reason for the discrepancy is inscrutable.

[37] *The Canterbury Tales* (London, 1980) 12.
[38] *The Text of the Canterbury Tales*, iii (Chicago, 1940), 53, 57.

Much the same picture emerges in Skeat's text of *The Hous of Fame*, the MS authorities for which are different ones. The Fairfax (which Skeat chose as his base) and the Bodleian MSS agree sufficiently against the Pepys MS and the Caxton and Thynne prints to imply that F and B derive from a common antecedent at some stage. Where *-en* is concerned, Skeat emends to *-en*:

(*a*) to avoid hiatus, in 85, 193, 204, 270, 353, 473, 650, 886, 1088, 1456, 2112, but does not do so in *be al* 410, *do eftsones* 359, *go as* 1106, *go into* 430;
(*b*) before *h-* + vowel or diphthong, in 50, 387, 1891, but not in *grave how* 433, *hyde hir* 1707;
(*c*) before a consonant when an unstressed syllable is needed (and *-e* would have done equally well): 227, 242, 673, 711, 1259 (*pleyen* for Th. *pleyeng*, the rest *pley*). But *grave was* 256.

Skeat's policy is evidently based both on MS authority and on the metre, with the latter as a control on the former. In the *Tales*, he generally prints hypermetrical *-en* if both E and H have it, but *-e* (with elision) if one (no matter which) has it and not the other. In *The Hous of Fame*, when F and B have *-e*, and the other three texts,[39] or only two,[40] or one,[41] have *-en*, Skeat emends to *-en*—and even when none have it.[42] His instinct, especially for the metre, was so good that the results, if inconsistent and therefore occasionally open to question, are not catastrophic. But his practice of regularly emending *-e* to *-en* to prevent hiatus is hazardous and would best be eschewed by future editors, since Chaucer demonstrably did tolerate and use hiatus.[43]

The main point is that Skeat's policy of printing *-en* when (according to the view presented here) it is hypermetrical is at best open to doubt and at worst mistaken. It is in fact clear that our established editions do not provide a fully consistent treatment of *-en*, and that editors cannot hope to recover Chaucer's

[39] 193, 473; 387 (before *h-* + vowel); 227 (before a consonant).
[40] 650, (F) 673, 886.
[41] 353; (before a consonant) 711.
[42] 85, 1456; (before *h*) 1891.
[43] See e.g. *Hous of Fame*, 12, 134, 274, 430, 507, 799, 816, 932, 1433, etc.

own usage in full (because of the uncertainty regarding the type of phonetic context classed above as 5, and in some degree 6 (*b*), in both of which either *-en* or *-e* is metrically admissible). But one thing, at least, could and should be done in an edited text: the hypermetrical *-en* should be emended to *-e*.

One of Skeat's main reasons for printing hypermetrical *-en* was his belief that in Chaucer's five-beat line the caesura involved a pause and therefore prevented elision and apocope, and thus often produced a sequence of two unaccented syllables at that point.[44] In modified form this belief is repeated by Manly.[45] Robinson is more cautious, in saying merely that 'the extra syllable [sc. of a trisyllabic foot] seems to have been most frequent in the caesural pause' (p. xxxvi).[46] But Skeat's belief has gone on reverberating in one or another degree. Baum, discussing the question of two successive unaccented syllables, would eliminate such sequences as *riden in* A57, *pynchen at* A326 by 'elision through *n* (or perhaps better called syncope)', without mentioning other phonetic contexts in which this is not possible. He recognizes that 'in some of these the *-n* may be scribal'; but he continues to believe in 'the trisyllabic foot'.

Since Skeat's view, at least, hinges on the notion of a Chaucerian caesura, the use of the term in this context needs to be clearly defined. The Chaucerian caesura seems to be commonly regarded as an essentially metrical device associated with a natural sense pause and hence a syntactic break within the five-beat line. There are moreover signs (as when Manly speaks of 'the caesural stroke'[47] in the Ellesmere MS) that the caesura is believed to be intentionally marked by the sloping stroke used in the Ellesmere and Hengwrt MSS within the line.

For the palaeographer, at any rate, this stroke is a punctuation mark—the *virgula*.[48] In Chaucer's five-beat line it is used in

[44] Ed. cit. vi, pp. xcvi, lxiv, lxxxiv–xcii.

[45] Ed. cit., pp. 128–9.

[46] Op. cit., p. 20.

[47] J. M. Manly and E. Rickert, *The Text of the Canterbury Tales*, i (Chicago, 1940), 152.

[48] See Doyle and Parkes, op. cit., p. 174.

varying positions (as Skeat and Robinson of course acknowledge). On opening the Ruggiers text of Hengwrt at random, I have found that the *virgula* occurs in e.g. lines 4393–4420 of the *Prologue* to *The Wife of Bath's Tale* after the syllables that are numbered as follows according to my scansion: 3, 3, 5, 4 and 7, 4, 6, 5, 4, 5, 3, 4, 4, 4, 7, 5, 3, 6, 3, 2, 4 and 6, 7, 5, 6, 4, 6, 2 and 6, 5, 4 and 7. Moreover, elision is to be posited in the last syllable before the *virgula* in 4396, 4403, 4410, 4411, 4414, hiatus in 4407, and 'apocope' in 4402.

The *virgula* is intermittently used twice or even three times in one line, and Hengwrt and Ellesmere occasionally disagree in their placing of it, as in the following small cluster of lines (*c.*5 % of the passage in question):

A 3815	Help water/ water/ help for Goddes herte	(E *Help/ water/ water/*)
3847	For euery clerk/ anon right heeld with oother	(E *anonright/*)
3904	Or of a soutere/ a shipman/ or a leche	(E *soutere/ shipman*)
3917	Right/ in his cherles termes/ wol I speke	(E has neither)
3919	He kan wel/in myn eye/ seen a stalke	(E no *virgula* after *eye*).

Such variations are more likely to arise in the use of a punctuation mark than of a specifically metrical sign. This suspicion is corroborated by A 3912, where, instead of a second *virgula* used in H, E has a variety of the punctuation mark called the *punctus elevatus*:

For leueful is/ with force/ force of-schowue	(E *is/ with force* ᶴ *force*).

Its use here is intended to mark a stronger pause than the *virgula* normally did,[49] and was evidently elicited by the use of

[49] As Mr M. B. Parkes has kindly suggested to me.

force twice in succession, since a rhetorical emphasis on this pointed repetition is manifestly called for.[50]

In the Laud MS of *Hav.*, in four different lines the first word, which is the last of a clause in the previous line, is followed by one or another form of punctuation mark, thus:

(1) Wan þe godemen þat sawe
(Hauelok and he þat bi þe wowe
Leye), he stirten up sone onon. (1963–5)

There are two heavy dots, one diagonally above the other, opposite the loop of the final *-e* of *Leye*.

(2) For oþer sholde he make hem lye
Ded, or þei him hauede slawen. (2000–1)

A slightly curving vertical line reaches from the top of the loop of the final *-d* in *Ded* to well below the line.

(3) Quoth erl Godrich, 'for Ich shal slo
þe, and hire forhenge heye!' (2724–5)

There is one heavy dot opposite and touching the loop of the final *-e* in *þe*.

(4) þat he hauede of him drawen
Blod, and so sore him slawen. (2747–8)

There is one heavy dot opposite and touching the loop of the *d* in *Blod*.

In these lines (as examples of enjambement, which is not uncommon in *Hav.*), the syntactic break is especially prominent: this is evidently why they are singled out for punctuation at that point, in case a reader should miss the enjambement and misinterpret the syntax.

All these things combine to suggest that the function of the *virgula* in Chaucer's five-beat line was not primarily metrical. In fact, if 'caesura' means a mandatory metrical pause used once in each line at a fixed and invariable point, there is no such

[50] For a helpful explanation of the use of the *virgula* and the *punctus elevatus*, see A. I. Doyle and M. B. Parkes in Ruggiers, op. cit., pp. xxxvii–xxxix; M. B. Parkes and R. Beadle, *Poetical Works of Geoffrey Chaucer*: a facsimile of MS C.U.L. Gg.4.27, Cambridge, 1980), iii. 56–7.

thing as a caesura in Chaucer's five-beat line.[51] There are necessarily, of course, syntactic breaks within the line. These would appropriately be marked by a *virgula*; and since syntactic pauses must inevitably be pauses in the flow of the line, the *virgula* often necessarily implies a light metrical break.

The remarkable thing is that Skeat's views had been demolished before the turn of the century, in a study by O. Bischoff[52] that was founded on notably systematic and strongly organized argument and on comprehensive material. His work has been somewhat neglected up to the present time, and his findings on the central questions at issue have even latterly been gravely misreported; they must accordingly be noticed here.

The term 'epic caesura' of Bischoff's title merely echoes the fact that in the decasyllabic line of OF epics an extra syllable (unstressed) was admissible at the caesura, i.e. after the fourth syllable, just as it was after the tenth (both of which were stressed).[53] What Bischoff means by it is a caesura with this unstressed syllable followed by another in the next part of the line (II. 385). His work is thus a study of the two related questions: did Chaucer use (*a*) two successive unaccented syllables outside the caesura, and (*b*) one unaccented syllable before the caesura and another after it?

Bischoff's treatment of Chaucer's prosody is in essentials much like that applied above to *Hav.* (and worked out without knowledge of Bischoff's monograph), though without explicit emphasis on the 'spoken chain' as the material for Chaucer's metrically patterned English. He insists on the regular alternation of an on-beat with a single off-beat as the basic rhythmic pattern of Chaucer's five-beat line. In over 30,000 lines he finds only 12

[51] A very similar statement has been made regarding the octosyllabic line of *The Anglo-Norman Voyage of St. Brendan* by E. G. R. Waters in his edition (Oxford, 1928), p. xliii. He remarks that in this poem the 'caesura' is merely a habitual break that 'does not allow of a supernumerary unstressed syllable'.

[52] 'Ueber zweisilbige Senkung und epische Caesur bei Chaucer', I, *Englische Studien*, (1897), 353–92, and II, *Englische Studien*, (1898), 339–98.

[53] See T. A. Jenkins, *La Chanson de Roland* (London, 1929), pp. cxxxviii–cxxxix.

apparent examples of two successive unaccented syllables outside the caesura; and he disposes satisfactorily (for me) of 8 of these (I. 359 ff.). He has collected all the lines that might be used as a basis (even if mistakenly) for positing an 'epic caesura'; he has classified the sequences of two unaccented syllables according to their phonetic character and environment; and he has shown that, at the caesura, the first of the successive unaccented syllables ends in *-e* that is open to elision, in all but 120 lines (out of 4,933), most of which he has been able to eliminate (II. 360).

What emerges is that, with few exceptions (for which see II. 389 ff.), Chaucer uses at the caesura only those types of final syllable which Bischoff had already shown in his part I to be open to elision or to *Verschleifung* (which he defines as reduction to non-syllabic status,[54] II. 368) by various means, especially syncope (II. 362). Moreover, one of Chaucer's practices at the caesura shows that he actually avoided having two successive unaccented syllables there. This is his use of phonetic variants (in names, which make the point especially noticeable) that differ in length by one syllable:

of Saluces/ in *The Clerk's Tale*, 414 (Ellesmere; Hengwrt metrically defective *Saluce*), *toward Saluces shapyng* 783; but *Saluce/ upon* 420, *Toward Saluce/ and* 775.

This is clearly done in order to meet the metrical requirement that an on-beat should alternate with a single off-beat (at the caesura as elsewhere).

Bischoff's answers to the two main questions of his inquiry are so massively documented and so systematically argued as to seem conclusive. In fact, so far as most works written in English are concerned, the scholarly study of these two issues (which are fundamental for the scansion of Chaucer's verse) has actually regressed during the last eighty-odd years, and the truths that he established[55] have been lost and must be rediscovered. Yet this is not due to entire neglect of his work. What is astonishing is

[54] For the importance of this definition see below, p. 232.
[55] Following the summary formulation of them by ten Brink: see below.

that it has not long since been radically misrepresented as being 'directed to proving that Chaucer admitted no trisyllabic feet *except at the so-called caesura*'[56] (my italics). And this statement has since been repeated by at least one other scholar.

The explanation seems to be that Bischoff, in summarizing his conclusions, presented them progressively, i.e. one by one, as they had emerged each in turn from the main sections of his study (II. 397–8). He did say, by way of the first, that Chaucer does not allow two successive unaccented syllables outside (*ausserhalb*, II. 397) the caesura. But he added (as his sixth and seventh conclusions) that (*a*) final syllables are treated at the caesura exactly as they are in apparent examples of a disyllabic off-beat (which are open to reduction by syncope) outside the caesura, so that (*b*) two successive unaccented syllables are reduced to one at the caesura as well as elsewhere within the line. It is difficult to understand how anyone who has actually read Bischoff's study with any care (or indeed at all) could be unaware that this is the whole drift of it. In all this, it does not matter that Bischoff (as editors have done) takes Chaucer's caesura as being marked by the *virgula*, since he duly identifies the essential features of Chaucer's caesura, and characterizes it as a light one. He analyses the practice of Chaucer's main French models (Machaut, Deschamps, Froissart, and Granson) to show that it cannot account for Chaucer's (II. 365–75).

A more recent work than Bischoff's seems likewise to have been overlooked by the editors and some of the metrists in question. To F. Wild,[57] the matter of -*en* in an apparent sequence of two successive unaccented syllables seems to have been so self-evidently clear that he hit off the essential points in half a page, without even mentioning the views exploded by Bischoff, or for that matter Bischoff's own work. Of the -*en* spellings Wild says simply (*a*) that Chaucer's own ending in the infin., pres. and

[56] Baum, op. cit., p. 20, n. 4.

[57] See his standard and authoritative monograph, *Die sprachlichen Eigentümlichkeiten der wichtigeren Chaucer-Handschriften und die Sprache Chaucers*, Wiener Beiträge zur englischen Philologie, 44 (Vienna, 1915), 296.

pt. pl., and past part. was *-e*, and that he used *-en* unsystematically (*fakultativ*) to avoid hiatus; (*b*) that the 'metrically wrong' *-en* used before initial vowel when the metre requires the final *-e* to be syllabic—which *-en* as he has noted, is common in the Ellesmere MS—is the usage not of Chaucer but of scribes. I would remark only that there is no conclusive means of deciding in individual instances whether the *-en* that prevents hiatus is the usage of Chaucer or of a scribe.

Verschleifung ('Slurring')

Bischoff's definition is important, since it differs in the vital point from the sense in which the metrists Schipper and ten Brink use the term (and hence Skeat, Manly, and others the English equivalent 'slurring'), and which in the case of Schipper and those who have followed him was closely associated with the notion of a disyllabic off-beat (and hence later a 'trisyllabic foot') in Chaucer's five-beat line. For present purposes, a good starting-point for establishing what they mean is the paragraph in which ten Brink defined and illustrated *Verschleifung*[58] as 'a kind of limited syncope or apocope. The slurred (*verschleifte*) vowel is not fully suppressed, but reduced in such a degree that in combination with a preceding syllable it does not exceed the duration of a single member of a measure [Smith: "metrical beat"]'. His examples include *werede*; *fader of*; *water he*; *ever on* (which he regards as a better analysis than *evr on*); *riden in*; *ne* after a word ending in a vowel.

Master though ten Brink was, both his scansion and his theory here are inconsistent, and hence difficult for others to apply securely. The examples given here could be straightforwardly scanned as cases of syncope, all but *riden in* as a corruption of *ride in*, and *ne*. Moreover, he adds that where unstressed (i.e. final) *-n* is open to apocope, as in the past part. of many verbs and in the infin., pres. pl., and pt. pl. throughout (i.e. four of the five endings treated above in *Hav.*), it is better to apply apocope and then elision (of the now final *-e*) than *Verschleifung*. Yet *riden in*, which is precisely of this type, is among his examples of *Verschleifung*.

[58] In his authoritative *Chaucers Sprache und Verskunst*[2] (Leipzig, 1899; the first edition had appeared in 1885), §272. See the faithful translation of the second edition by M. B. Smith, *The Language and Metre of Chaucer* (London, 1901).

Next, *Verschleifung* as a reduction that falls short of eliminating syllabic status altogether, seems unsatisfactory, for practical purposes, in the scanning of an evenly-patterned sequence of an on-beat and an off-beat: it is neither fish, flesh, nor good red herring. It is the concept of *Verschleifung* that has let in the notion that Chaucer's five-beat line allows of more than one unaccented syllable between on-beats. Yet ten Brink has elsewhere

(*a*) rejected Schipper's view that there could be an extra unaccented syllable at the caesura (§307. 3 and n.), and

(*b*) expressly affirmed that in Chaucer's four-beat line the off-beat is always monosyllabic, and that 'anapaests' or 'trochees' are not used; and he has shown how some apparent examples can be eliminated as scribal corruptions (§ 300 and n.).

It is Schipper, however, whose views are shared by Skeat, Manly, and others who believe not only that there was 'slurring', and hence a disyllabic off-beat in Chaucer's five-beat line, but that these were especially associated with the caesura. If the concept of *Verschleifung* is unsatisfactory, in its purely prosodic aspect, in ten Brink's doctrine and practice, it is still more so in Schipper's. In his own English translation of his abridged handbook,[59] Schipper usually renders *Verschleifung*, *verschleift* as 'slurring, slurred'.[60] He distinguishes *Verschleifung* from, and contrasts it with, (*a*) a process in which a vowel may 'lose syllabic value altogether'[61] or 'become quite silent',[62] (*b*) elision,[63] (*c*) syncope.[64] He explicitly assigns syllabic quality to the vowel in question: 'so that the [sc. grammatical] ending forms part of a disyllabic thesis' (p. 159).

Schipper does, however, use *Verschleifung* occasionally in other senses that seem inconsistent with all this. It is translated 'elision', p. 166, and *wirkliche Verschleifungen* as 'complete contraction', p. 156. A silent final -*e*, on the other hand, is said to be 'slurred', p. 160. It also appears that 'slurring' is a somewhat indeterminate process, since Schipper—speaking of it in much the same terms as ten Brink in the definition quoted above—regards it as varying in degree according as the vowel is uttered more or less distinctly (e.g. § 100).

[59] Respectively *A History of English Versification* (Oxford, 1910) and *Grundriss der englischen Metrik* (Vienna, 1895), abridged from *Englische Metrik* (Bonn, 1881).

[60] pp. 151, 153, 155, 156 (2 exx.), 157 (2), 158, 159, 160 (3), 161, 164, 168 (6), 169.

[61] pp. 151, 157.

[62] p. 156.

[63] p. 153.

[64] pp. 155, 156, 157, 158, 159, 160, 161, 168.

The concept of *Verschleifung* or 'slurring' in ME four- or five-beat lines thus seems to be of doubtful standing in itself, and the two concomitant notions linked with it by Schipper and his adherents look like being chimaeras.

Appendix A[65]

See lines 227, 270, 335, 346, 362, 370, 379, 463, 531, 536, 564, 623, 659, 696, 699, 741, 748 (*callen*), 783, 792, 801, 890, 915, 932, 982, 1021, 1029, 1031, 1038, 1058, 1094, 1122, 1171, 1186, 1188, 1193, 1195, 1239, 1251, 1257, 1271, 1304, 1421, 1630, 1632, 1641, 1718, 1767, 1770, 1838, 1839, 1877, 1908, 1954, 1965, 2002, 2006, 2021, 2046, 2085, 2099, 2119, 2162, 2163, 2175, 2197, 2260, 2271, 2291, 2475, 2523, 2590, 2592, 2617, 2711, 2791, 2858, 2896.

[65] See p. 203, 1.

Addendum (n. 28, p. 219): see also P. Roach, 'On the distinction between "stress-timed" and "syllable-timed" languages' in *Linguistic Controversies*, Essays in honour of F. R. Palmer, ed. D. Crystal (London, 1982), pp. 73–9.

Present Indicative Plural Forms in the Later Middle English of the North Midlands

ANGUS McINTOSH

I

IN a late Middle English text, the regular or frequent occurrence of a present indicative plural ending *-eth* can usually be taken as strong evidence of linguistic origin in the southern part of the country, or in the south or central west Midlands. The northern limit of this area is, roughly, a line running from Shrewsbury to the Thames estuary (line A–A on the map, p. 243). To the north and east of this line, but south of the domain of northern Middle English proper, the *-eth* suffix has for the most part been replaced by *-en*.[1] It is the purpose of this paper to call attention to the

[1] The forms which I write as *-eth*, *-en*, and *-es* occur of course in numerous alternative spellings, with *i*, *y*, *u*, instead of *e*, *þ*, *t* instead of *th*, *z* instead of *s* and so forth, and the various ways in which each of the three is written are by no means devoid of dialectal significance. When attached to a verb of which the stem ends in a vowel, the suffix commonly loses its own vowel: *-eth*, *-en*, and *-es* also imply *-th*, *-n*, and *-s* respectively. Note also that *-en* is often reduced to *-e* or even *-ø*, especially in texts of the later fifteenth century; see p. 238. On the history of the *-en* plural, see W. F. Bryan, 'The Midland present plural indicative in -(*e*)*n*', *MP* xviii (1921), 457–73 and references. Cf. M. L. Samuels, *Linguistic Evolution with special reference to English*, Cambridge Studies in Linguistics, 5 (1972), 85–6; K. Brunner, *Die Englische Sprache* (Tübingen, 1962), ii. 189–90. For discussion of the earlier history, with references, see Sievers–Brunner, *Altenglische Grammatik* (Tübingen, 1965), §§ 357–60.

The main distributions of the forms in question are roughly as shown by S. Moore, S. B. Meech, and H. Whitehall, 'Middle English dialect characteristics and dialect boundaries', *University of Michigan Publications, Language and Literature, xiii (1935),* 44–6 and lines G and H on the accompanying map; by

presence of *-eth* present indicative plural endings in a number of late Middle English texts whose scribes probably belonged to places well to the north and east of the main *-eth* area. I shall seek to show that the *-eth* endings here do not, in contrast to those south of line A–A, descend directly from OE -(*i*)*aþ*; they are to be explained as innovations resulting from the influence of a quite different present tense paradigm current immediately to the north of them.

Over the whole of England south of a line which runs, again roughly speaking, from Chester to the Wash, the regular ending in the third person singular of the present indicative is *-eth*. North of this line (line B–B on the map) *-eth* gives way to *-es*; the precise interpretation of B–B will be further discussed below. For the most part this line also marks more or less accurately the southern limit for *-es* as a *plural* indicative ending. In the east, however, this *-es* plural is also found beside *-eth* (with varying degrees of frequency) in a belt lying somewhat to the south of the line B–B.

It is scarcely a coincidence that most of the scribes who attest the innovatory *-eth* plural belonged—or so the available evidence would suggest—to, or just south of, that same belt, to a region, that is, which includes NE Leicestershire, Rutland, N. Northamptonshire, the extreme north of Huntingdonshire, and parts of N. Ely and NW Norfolk (the stippled areas on the map).

H. Kurath and S. Kuhn, *Middle English Dictionary, Plan and Bibliography*, (1954), 8. See also J. P. Oakden, *Alliterative Poetry in Middle English* (Manchester, 1930), i. 35–6 and the map opposite p. 38. The present indicative plural *-en* form is already in evidence, though still not in exclusive use, in the *Peterborough Chronicle*; see Cecily Clark, *The Peterborough Chronicle 1070–1154* (Oxford, 1958), pp. xliii–xliv. It is clear from the *Ormulum* that *-en* was fully established in the far NE Midlands by the end of the twelfth century. This is probably true of the NW Midlands also: the Cotton Titus D 18 text of *Ancrene Wisse*, which has a number of features characteristic of Cheshire, uses *-en* instead of the -(*i*)*eð* found in versions written in 'AB language'. The *Wohunge*, which may have indeed an anterior north Midlands history, likewise has *-en*. The rest of the texts in Titus use both *-eð* and *-en*: it is perhaps significant that their language as a whole is less internally consistent than that of the other two.

Among the texts which most clearly display this comparatively recent *-eth* ending is the ME translation of the *Rosarium Theologie* in Gonville and Caius Coll. Cambridge, MS 354/581. Since part of it is now readily available in print, the phenomena discussed in this paper will in due course be exemplified from that text.[2]

II

The fully northern paradigm of the present indicative plural differs from the normal types current further south in that it operates with alternative suffixes, the selection of which is syntactically conditioned. Expressed in somewhat simplified fashion, the rule operating north of the Chester–Wash line is that a plural form *-es* is required unless the verb has a personal pronoun subject immediately preceding or following it. When the verb has such a subject, the ending required is the reduced *-e* or zero (-ϕ) form. I shall refer to this rule as 'the personal pronoun rule'. Accordingly, the northern paradigm (N)[3] may be presented thus:

[2] *The Middle English Translation of the Rosarium Theologie*, ed. Christina von Nolcken, Middle English Texts, 10 (Heidelberg, 1979); my references are to page and line. For a tentative indication of the provenance of the text see her map on p. 48. The problem under discussion is touched on on p. 50 and (as noted there) had previously been considered by Margaret Laing in her as yet unpublished Edinburgh Ph.D. thesis, 'Studies in the Dialect Material of mediaeval Lincolnshire' (1978), i. 242–6. I first noticed the usage some twenty-five years ago but was not able till recently to localize it with any precision. I wish to express here my indebtedness to Dr Laing and to thank Mr Michael Benskin for much information bearing on this subject.

[3] This paradigm is discussed by Joseph Wright, *The English Dialect Grammar*, (Oxford, 1905), §435. See also James A. H. Murray, *The Dialect of the Southern Counties of Scotland* (Oxford, 1873), 211 ff.; Henry Sweet, *New English Grammar* (Oxford, 1892), i. §1235; pp. 93–4 of Michael Benskin and Margaret Laing, 'Translations and *Mischsprachen* in Middle English manuscripts', in Michael Benskin and M. L. Samuels (edd.), *So meny people longages and tonges* (Edinburgh, 1981); and pp. 10–12 of Michael Benskin, 'A linguistic atlas for late mediaeval English', *Mediaeval English Studies Newsletter* [Tokyo], iv (1981).

	(i) subject not a personal pronoun in contact with verb	(ii) personal pronoun subject in contact with verb
3 sg.	*-es*	*-es*
1, 2, 3 pl.	*-es*	*-e*, *-ϕ*; in the south of the N area, often *-en*

From south of the Chester–Wash line all the way to where the *-eth* plural begins to be encountered we have for the most part the simpler Midland paradigm (M) with only one form of plural suffix:

3 sg.	*-eth*
1, 2, 3 pl.	*-en* or the reduced forms *-e* and (though more rarely) *-ϕ*

Although we shall not be directly concerned with it here, it may be noted that to the south and west of the M area we have the even simpler southern paradigm (S):

3 sg.	*-eth*
1, 2, 3 pl.	*-eth*

In the area, specified earlier, where the innovatory *-eth* plural is found, the usual Midland paradigm M is replaced by another paradigm (P), the pattern of which cannot easily be explained except as being modelled on the N paradigm that characterizes the dialects immediately to the north of that area. According to the same syntactic conditions as govern the selection of plurals (i) and (ii) in N, paradigm P has the form:

	(i) subject not a personal pronoun in contact with verb	(ii) personal pronoun subject in contact with verb
3 sg.	*-eth*	*-eth*
1, 2, 3 pl.	*-eth*	*-en* (*-e*, *-ϕ*)

From the contiguous N area, this part of the M area lying immediately to the south of it adopted the same principle of selection for its two plural suffixes, namely the personal pronoun rule. The ending *-en* (together with its later derivatives *-e* and *-ϕ*) was simply the plural form already used in all syntactic conditions in the M area; the restriction of its use in paradigm P to syntactic condition (ii) was natural, because it was the very form required by this condition in the adjacent N areas. The type (i) plural ending *-eth* is, functionally speaking, a new creation which reflects the pattern of the northern paradigm N, where the plural has, in condition (i), the same form as the third singular (*-es*:*-es*). It reflects it, however, not by introducing the alien verb-morpheme *-es*, but simply by employing (in condition (i)) the morpheme *-eth*, familiar already as a third person singular form, for use in the plural as well.

For the third person singular, Dr Laing has noted that the Chester–Wash line should be considered rather as the northern limit of regular *-eth* than as the southern limit of regular *-es*. The distinction is of some importance. Like most boundaries in linguistic geography, that between *-eth* and *-es* is not sharply defined. Between the domain of *-eth* and the domain of *-es* there is a border zone of varying width in which the two forms co-occur; this zone lies just to the south, rather than just to the north, of the Chester–Wash line. Here it is by no means unusual to find texts in which third person singular *-eth* and *-es* coexist and for these also to manifest, in differing degrees, examples of plural endings conforming to the N paradigm side by side with examples conforming to the P; the *Rosarium Theologie* has such N forms, though only quite rarely.[4]

[4] It is not possible in this paper to discuss in detail the further problem of the forms of the pres. ind. 2 sg. in the *Rosarium* and in dialectally similar texts. According to Dr von Nolcken (p. 50) the forms for this in the *Rosarium* are '*-eþ*, *-es*, *-ez* in roughly equal numbers without phonetic [*sic*] pattern'. If so, the *-es*, *-ez* forms are much more prevalent in the 2 sg. than in the 3 sg., as they are in some other texts from the same area; note also the preference for 3 sg. *haþ*/*hath* beside 2 sg. *has*. As for the ('unhistorical') *-eþ* forms in the *Rosarium* where *-est* might have been expected (75/9, 78/22, 79/11), I would suggest that their use rests on the same basis as the adoption of *-eþ* forms in the plural: they simulate the more northerly paradigm in which a morphemic distinction between 2 and 3 sg. is wanting, both having *-es* (*þou spekes*, *he spekes*); this is confirmed by the rarity of *-st* forms as against either *-es* or *-eþ*.

III

In the great majority of cases the *Rosarium* faithfully follows Paradigm P and the normal pattern is as follows:[5]

(i) subject not a personal pronoun in contact with verb		(ii) personal pronoun subject in contact with verb
3 sg.	*-eþ*	*-eþ*
1, 2, 3 pl.	*-eþ*	*-e*

It should be noted that in texts which manifest paradigm M the formal distinction of present indicative and subjunctive that is preserved in the second and third persons singular has been lost in the plural. It is a consequence of the adoption of paradigm P in parts of the original M area that in condition (i) (though not in condition (ii)), this formal distinction is restored. Thus in *Forsoþ if þei kepe noȝt oþer riȝtwisnez of God, if pouer men ioy not of þar godez* ..., 69/8, *kepe*, being subjunctive (though formally ambiguous), is not an example of the correct observance of the personal pronoun rule. Conversely *ioy* is not an example of the violation of the rule, which—if the mood were indicative—would require *pouer men ioyeþ*. This partially re-

But the frequent occurrence in the *Rosarium* of *-es*, *-ez* beside *-eþ* for the 2 sg. would suggest that there was another conflicting tendency in which weight was attached to the preservation of the formal distinction characteristic of paradigm M (and of course S), signalled by the forms *-est*, *-eþ* (*þou spekest*, *he speketh*). The opposition *-es*, *-eþ* (*þou spekes*, *he spekeþ*) maintains this. It is just possible that the rather greater readiness to adopt *-es* in the 2 sg. than in the 3 sg. is connected with the phonetic conditions obtaining when (as very frequently) the 2 sg. form is followed (in questions) by *þu*. However this may be, the introduction of 2 sg. *-es* is clearly connected with the regular use of this form immediately to the north. In a fuller study, the second singular forms manifested in paradigms N and P should obviously receive careful attention.

[5] There are a few cases of *-iþ* instead of *-eþ*. Where the verb stem ends in a vowel, a final *e* is usually absent and it is sometimes wanting after certain consonants (*-ch* 86/3, *-sch* 86/5, *-st* 86/7). On the occasional appearance of *-(e)s* and *-ez* in both plural and 3 sg. see Dr von Nolcken, p. 50. I have noticed only two indicative plurals preserving the full *-en* form (59/11, 86/23); *beholden*, 66/9, is subjunctive.

stored plural indicative-subjunctive distinction mirrors, of course, that made in the N area where, in condition (i), the indicative *pouer men ioyes* differs from the subjunctive *if pouer men ioy* but where, in condition (ii), the verb forms are the same: *þay ioy* and *if þay ioy*.

There are one or two passages in the *Rosarium* where to presume that the personal pronoun rule has been observed avoids a misinterpretation. An example is *Al yuel wordez procede noȝt of ȝour mouþe*, 89/20; if this were indicative the form would have to be *procedeþ*. In this instance, the allusion to Ephesians 4:29 ('Let no corrupt communication proceed out of your mouth') makes clear that the construction is iussive. There is another passage which presents a somewhat greater difficulty. Pages 85/31–86/8 contain some twenty present plural forms which might well be assumed to be indicative but which, if so taken, would be violations of the personal pronoun rule. Since this single cluster of instances would in that case far outnumber the violations in the whole of the rest of the text, one may safely conclude that they are subjunctive in form and that they must so be interpreted.[6]

The operation of paradigm P in the *Rosarium* may now be briefly illustrated. A personal pronoun *we*, *ȝe*, or *þei* (*þai*) adjacent to (and, in the great majority of cases, before) the verb of which it is the subject requires the *-e* form: *we go*, 80/31; *we renne*, 81/9; *ȝe haue taken*, 85/19, *ȝe seme*, 102/4; *þei teche*, 63/13; *þei make*, 69/23; *werto tempte ȝe God*, 76/11.

A construction in which two verbs linked by a conjunction share a personal pronoun subject immediately preceding the first one (of the type 'they sit and gossip') normally conforms to the morphological pattern: 'pron. + vb. *-e* + conj. + vb. *-eþ*' and thus obeys the personal pronoun rule scrupulously: *þei discerne or demeþ*, 56/2; *þei pretende þam or feyneþ*, 59/20; *wiles þat þei deme and scheweþ*, 59/4; *þai aske or getteþ al* 102/36. Sometimes, however, the second verb in such circumstances also has the *-e*

[6] Respect for the rules likewise renders inadvisable the editorial insertion of *þai* before *semeþ*, 70/31. Cf. 81/18.

ending; such cases are not numerous: *þei forgiffe or wiþholde synnes*, 59/4; *þei suppose or trowe*, 55/36.

A construction of the pattern: 'they that sit' may also have either form of the verb: *þei þat edifieþ memorez of martirez*, 69/4; *þei þat chalenge þe place of a boschoprice*, 56/37. But constructions of the pattern 'them that ask' would seem, on the small amount of evidence available, to tolerate only *-eþ*: *fro þam þat makeþ*, 73/15; (*it*) *fulfilleþ ... þam þat studieþ it*, 74/18.

In all other conditions the *-eþ* form is obligatory: *þe discipules louseþ hym*, 56/18; *alonely siche* (pl.) *hath pouer*, 57/23; *some forsoþ ... neiȝeþ more nere to God*, 65/27; *þise precheþ*, 85/28; *for many goþ in þe name of Criste*, 93/31; *ȝourself* (pl.) *haþe noȝt entred*, 91/4.

IV

The attribution of paradigm P to the region already mentioned rests on the assignment to places within it of a number of texts whose characteristics point to a scribal origin in various parts of that area.[7] The *Rosarium* itself has a considerable number of features, all dialectally consistent, which would suggest that the scribe came from north Rutland. Following Dr Laing, Dr von Nolcken has indicated some of the numerous north-east Midland forms in it which point to the approximate localization indicated on her map; it is now possible to delimit the eligible area somewhat more precisely. A provenance as far west as north Rutland is suggested by the very close dialectal similarity of the text to Takamiya 59 (Chauliac). This has some features (notably the use of *hit* 'it' beside *it* and of *her* 'their' rather than of *þ-* forms) which suggest for it a provenance yet a little further west, prob-

[7] To what extent paradigm P operated further west is at present not established. In the relevant belt of the west Midlands, plural *-en* and *-eth* certainly coexist in some texts but probably for the most part simply as rival manifestations of the M and S paradigms in border areas where both were acceptable: the S paradigm extended much further north in the west Midlands than elsewhere; see the maps referred to in n. 1.

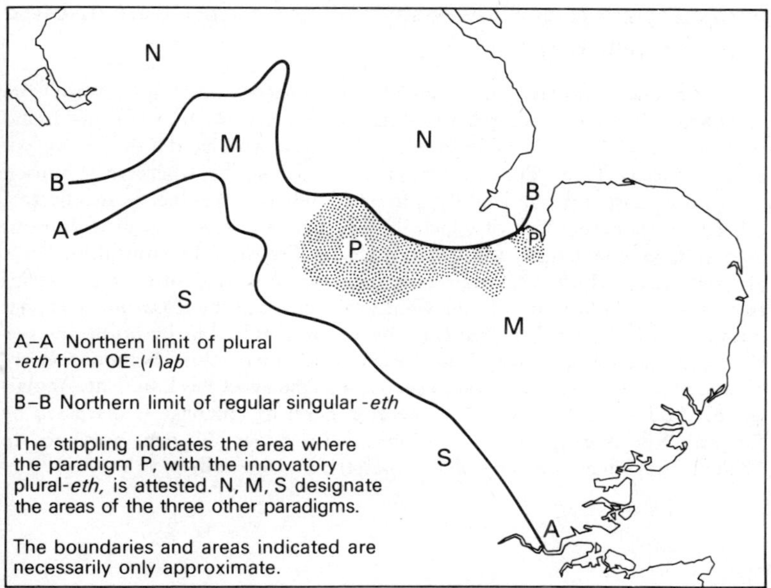

ably in north-east Leicestershire. The characteristics of the *Rosarium* are in general so similar that its scribe cannot have originated more that a quite short distance to the east.

It is of some interest that a number of other Chauliac, and also of Arderne, texts share many of the linguistic characteristics of one or both of these two manuscripts. BL Sloane 6 and Sloane 277 are quite similar in language to the *Rosarium* and Sloane 1 is very like Takamiya 59. Sloane 563 (hand C, Arderne), Sloane 3666, and New York Academy of Medicine 12 have affinities with both. Indeed, wherever in the area the various scribes of these texts originated, they share so large a number of characteristics as to suggest that their work emanated from a single scriptorium. If so, the output of that scriptorium would seem, on the evidence at present available, to have been mainly of copies of surgical works though, as the *Rosarium* indicates, not entirely so. The whole complex of texts, of which those mentioned are but a few, requires detailed investigation; it is not even clear at present how many different scribes were involved in their production.[8]

[8] It is of course possible that some of the scribes of this complex were from elsewhere and were merely perpetuating more or less exactly what they found in their exemplars. This would seem to be the case with hand B (ff. 30ʳ–33ᵛ) of Sloane 7 (see Dr Laing, op. cit., i. 371, ii. 218). This scribe, wherever he himself came from, displays two slightly different kinds of language, as if reflecting different exemplars, both of which, however, would seem to fall within our area. (Of the other hands, A is probably Derbyshire and C Lincolnshire). There are other texts which seem dialectally mixed. Sloane 610, for example, seems to be basically south Lincs., somewhat to the north of the *Rosarium* area, but with a central Leicester ingredient which is probably, but by no means certainly, an overlay. Further medical MSS which merit close examination are Sloane 374, 505, 965, 1721, 2187, 2464, 3466, 3486 and Paris Bibl. Nat. Anglais 25. BL Add. 60577 also deserves mention here; its language is discussed by Edward Wilson in the present volume in his paper 'A poem presented to William Waynflete as Bishop of Winchester'; see especially p. 128.

Early Middle English *Drihtin*

CELIA SISAM

THE Old English word *dryhten* (< Gmc. **druhtinoz*, related to *drēogan* 'perform') appears with unrounded *i* in the stem in most Old English texts from the beginning of the tenth century.[1] The original *y* was unrounded to *i* before the palatal group *ht* with great regularity in this word; the unrounding took place earlier than the south-eastern change of [y] to [e], which never affects *drihten*.[2]

OE *drihten* is the source of all Middle English forms. In the West Midland dialect of MS Bodley 34 (*c.* 1225), where other words containing OE *y* before *ht* appear with *u*,[3] OE *drihten* invariably shows *i* in the stem. It is unlikely that this *i* owes anything to the influence of the adjective *almihti*, as Miss d'Ardenne (pp. 148 f.) and A. F. Colborn (p. 71) supposed: for *drihten* is found in Old English dialects which had *-mæhtig* (not *-mihtig*), such as the late tenth-century Northumbrian gloss to the *Lindisfarne Gospels* and to the *Durham Ritual*. Consistent *i* in *drihten* may have become standardized by church usage,[4]

[1] The evidence has been collected by M. Ångström, *Studies in Old English MSS, with special reference to the delabialisation of y̆ (< ŭ + ĭ) to ı* (Uppsala, 1937).

[2] See K. Luick, *Historische Grammatik der englischen Sprache* (reprinted Stuttgart and Oxford, 1964), § 183 n. 3.

[3] e.g. *Seinte Iuliene*, 573 *wruhte* (ed. S. R. T. O. d'Ardenne, (Liége, 1936; repr. EETS 248, 1961)); *Hali Meiaðhad*, 234 *fluht* (ed. A. F. Colborn (Copenhagen, 1940)); *Seinte Margarete*, 18/26 *duhtie*, 22/5 *offruht*, 46/23 *icluhte* (ed. F. M. Mack, EETS 193 (1934)) *Sawles Warde*, noun and verb *tuht*(*e*), in *Early Middle English Verse and Prose*[2] (Oxford, 1968), edd. J. A. W. Bennett and G. V. Smithers, glossary by N. Davis, XIX. 52, 25.

[4] See Luick, § 281 nn. 1 and 2.

written and spoken. For it is in its religious,[5] not its secular, sense that the word survived in Middle English, where it continued in use till the fifteenth century in some dialects, while in others it was replaced by 'lord', 'God', etc.

Three distinct forms are found in early Middle English: *Drihten*, *Driht(e)*, and *Drihtin*. This third form is puzzling. It is regular in two carefully spelt manuscripts: Bodleian MS Junius 1, *c.* 1200 (the *Ormulum*)[6], and MS Bodley 34 (B), *c.* 1225; it is also normal in BL MSS Royal 17 A. xxvii (R), *c.* 1225, and Cotton Titus D. xviii (T), *c.* 1225–50, which, with B, preserve the texts of the 'Katherine Group'. The word is common in *Ste Katerine*[7] (B, R, T), *Ste Margarete* (B, R) and *Ste Iuliene* (B, R); it occurs once in *Hali Meiðhad* (B, T), but is absent from *Sawles Warde* (B, R, T). It is rare in *Ancrene Wisse*: *Drihtines* (g. sg.) appears in two passages where alliteration probably governed the author's choice, Corpus Christi Coll. Cambridge, MS 402 (A),[8] *c.* 1225, ff. 57ʳ9 and 117ʳ9; here A, T,[9] and BL MS Cotton Cleopatra C. vi (C),[10] *c.* 1225, all have *i* in the second syllable.[11]

Orm consistently writes *Drihhtin*, indicating that, in his dialect, the second *i* was long.[12] The length of the second syllable (and, incidentally, the fact that it was often stressed, a point to which I shall return) is confirmed by rhymes: e.g. 'Haly Thomas'[13] (Jesus Coll. Oxford, MS 29, *c.* 1275–1300) rhymes

[5] It is occasionally applied to pagan gods (see *MED*, s.v. *Drihten*, 2.

[6] Edd. R. M. White and R. Holt (Oxford, 1878).

[7] Edd. S. R. T. O. d'Ardenne and E. J. Dobson, EETS, ss 7 (1981).

[8] Ed. J. R. R. Tolkien, EETS 249 (1962).

[9] Ed. F. M. Mack, EETS 252 (1963), 68/26, 160/4.

[10] Ed. E. J. Dobson, EETS 267 (1972), 157/9, 316/19.

[11] MS Cott. Nero A. xiv, *c.* 1225–50 (ed. M. Day, EETS 225 (1952), 94/1, 195/34) has *Drihtenes*. In MS Cleopatra, hand D has written 'godis' above *Drichtines* in the second passage, suggesting that in his late thirteenth-century East Midland dialect the word had become obsolete. (On hand D, see E. J. Dobson's edition, pp. cxl ff., where he suggests (p. clx) S. Lincs. as the provenance of hand D's dialect; A. McIntosh, 'The language of the extant versions of *Havelok the Dane*', *MÆ* xlv (1976), 36–49, argues rather for W. Norfolk.)

[12] This makes influence of ON *dróttinn* unlikely.

[13] Ed. C. Brown, *English Lyrics of the XIIIth Century* (Oxford, 1932), p. 67.

Dryhtin at l. 5 with *win* 'wine'. *Cursor Mundi*[14] shows *Drightin* in rhyme with *min(e)* at, for example, l. 18702 (MSS Cotton, Fairfax, Göttingen); with *wyne* (F, *vyn* C) at l. 179. Similar rhymes appear later, for instance in *Roland and Ottwell*[15] (BL MS Add. 31042) at ll. 1283, 1356, 1570; and in *Sir Amadace*[16] (Ireland MS) at l. 759.

Such rhymes, coupled with Orm's spelling, suggest that the early Middle English *-in* spellings often represent *-īn*. Why should *Drihten* have developed *ī* in the second syllable, when other OE nouns in *-en* did not? Orm, for instance, has the nouns *efenn*, *fakenn*, *(forr)tákenn*, *gaȝhenn*, *hæþenn*, *lenntenn*, *maȝȝdenn*, *uhhtenn*, *wikenn* 'office'. The usual explanation, suggested by Luick (§ 441 n. 2) and Jordan[17] (§ 136 n. 2), is that *Drihtin* was influenced by *almihtin*, deriving from OE *ælmihtigne* (str. m. acc. sg.). This attractive theory has been generally adopted, e.g. by A. F. Colborn[18] and S. R. T. O. d'Ardenne,[19] who notes that *almihtin* might also derive from OE dative and weak oblique forms *-igum* and *-igan*, > *-iȝen* > *īn*. Miss d'Ardenne drew attention to the form *almichtin* in MS Cleopatra C. vi of *Ancrene Wisse*. Professor Dobson, in his edition of that manuscript, observes that the form *almichtin* (gen. sg. *-ines*, f. 151) is characteristic of scribe A,[20] and that forms with *-in* are 'found in a variety of texts from the late twelfth century onwards'. Examples are: *Lambeth Homilies*[21] (MS Lambeth 487, *c.* 1200) *Godalmihtin* (nom.) 15/28, *Godalmihten* 137/36, *-ines* (gen. sg.) 23/8, *-ine* (after preposition) 33/4; *Trinity Homilies*[22] (Trinity Coll.

[14] Ed. R. Morris, EETS 57, 59, 62, 66, 68, 99, 101 (1874–93).

[15] Ed. S. J. Herrtage, EETS, ES 35 (1880).

[16] Ed. C. Brookhouse, *Anglistica*, 15 (Copenhagen, 1968).

[17] R. Jordan, *Handbuch der mittelenglischen Grammatik*,[2] revd. H. C. Matthes (Heidelberg, 1934).

[18] *Hali Meiðhad*, p. 71.

[19] *Ste Iuliene*, p. 148.

[20] EETS 267, p. lxxxix; *almichtin* occurs at 12^r17, 31^v12, 109^r2, 109^v20, 169^r4, 183^r16, 187^r15, 197^r10.

[21] Ed. R. Morris, EETS 29 and 34 (1867–8; repr. as one volume, 1973).

[22] Ed. R. Morris, EETS 53 (1873).

Cambridge, MS B 14. 52, *c.* 1200) *almihtin God* (nom.) 109/27; *Vices and Virtues*[23] (BL MS Stowe 34, *c.* 1200), *Godalmihtin* (nom.) 11/16, 13/25, etc., *-ines* 41/8.[24]

That *almihtin* and *Drihten/Drihtin* were associated in dialects where the two words rhymed seems probable. In *Cursor Mundi*, l. 179, the Göttingen manuscript reads *Godd allmightin* (nom.) for *haly Drightin* (Cotton and Fairfax MSS), to rhyme with *wīn*. In Laȝamon's *Brut*,[25] (MS Cotton Caligula A. ix), the curious phrase *Ældrihten Godd* at l. 14077 is probably modelled on *almihti God*, which appears, for example, as *almiten Godd* at l. 30, *God almihten* at l. 8376 (both after prepositions). But, whereas this association is likely to have produced the anomalous forms of *almihti*[26] (final *-n* in the nominative, inflected *-ine*(*s*), and *-en* instead of *-in*)—anomalies which seem not to occur in the adjective *mihti*—it does not satisfactorily explain the second *i* in *Drihtin*. For *Drihtin* occurs in dialects where there is no sign of *almihtin* (the 'AB language' of MS Bodley 34, for example).[27] In the *Ormulum*, where the form of 'almighty' is always *allmahhtiȝ*, some other explanation must be sought.

There was another OE word in *-en* that commonly developed *-in*. Already in Old English, the adjective and noun *cristen* 'Christian' was sometimes written *cristin-*: e.g. *Old English Bede* (Bodl. MS Tanner 10, *c.* 925), *ðæs cristinan geleafan*[28] = *fidei Christianae*; the Vercelli Book (*c.* 1000), Homily XX, *cristinum*;[29] *Old English Martyrology* (BL MS Cott. Julius A. x, *c.* 1000), *þæs cristinan kyninges*;[30] *cristin,-ines, -inum* appear in the gloss to

[23] Ed. F. Holthausen, EETS 89, 159 (1888, 1921).

[24] *OED* and *MED*, *s.v. Almightin*, give further examples.

[25] Ed. G. L. Brook and R. F. Leslie, EETS 250, 277 (1963, 1978). The Otho MS, which is damaged here, reads '. .drihtene . . .'.

[26] *OED* so explains them.

[27] Scribe A of MS Cleopatra, who uses *almichtin*, had not been trained in the orthographic tradition of the 'AB language' (see Dobson, EETS 267, pp. lxxii f.).

[28] Ed. T. Miller, EETS 96 (1891), Bk. v, ch. 9, p. 410/20.

[29] F. 110ʳ22; ed. P. E. Szarmach, *Mediaeval Studies*, xxxv (1973), 9/35.

[30] Ed. G. Herzfeld, EETS 116 (1900), August 5, p. 138/17; G. Kotzor, *Das altenglische Martyrologium* (Munich, 1981), ii. 171/5.

the *Durham Ritual*[31] (Durham Cathedral MS A. IV. 19, *c.* 970). OE *cristin-* probably had the stress on the suffix,[32] under the influence of Latin *Christiánus*; and, like ME *Drihtin*, the second *i* (which may also be due to the Latin form) was presumably long. Its length and the stressing of the second syllable are attested by rhymes in Middle English: e.g. *Pearl*, l. 1202, has *Krystyin* rhyming with *fyin*, *enclyin*, *myn*, *wyn*, *hyne*. In *Sir Beues of Hamtoun*[33] (Auchinleck MS), the giant Ascopard, at his christening, protested to the officiating bishop:

> Þe deuel ȝeue þe helle pine,
> Icham to meche to be cristine. (2595 f.)

Forms with *-ine*, presumably having *ī*, appear in some late thirteenth-century manuscripts: e.g. BL MS Cott. Caligula A. ix, *c.* 1275, of Laȝamon's *Brut*,[34]

> Cristine we beoð alle: and of Cristine cunne;

MS Digby 86 (*c.* 1275), *The Fox and the Wolf*,[35]

> Hertou Cristine oþer mi fere?

Other examples of *cristine* will be found in *MED*.

But ME *cristin(e)* was not the model for ME *Drihtin*. For in the *Ormulum* and in the 'AB language' of MSS Bodley 34 and Corpus Christi Coll. Cambridge, 402 the form is *cris(s)tene*.[36] Evidently *-īn* developed in the two words independently.

In both *Drihten* and *cristen(e)*, the *-īn-* forms must have been accompanied by a shift of stress from root to second syllable,

[31] See *The Durham Ritual*, edd. T. J. Brown, F. Wormald, A. S. C. Ross, and E. G. Stanley, Early English MSS in Facsimile, 16 (Copenhagen, 1969), 60.

[32] I argue (below 250 ff.) that stressed *-īn* developed first in inflected forms; I take OE *cristin* to be a spelling for *cristen*, derived from inflected forms with *-īn-*.

[33] Ed. E. Kölbing, EETS, ES 46, 48, 65 (1885–94; repr. as one volume, 1973).

[34] EETS 277, l. 14859.

[35] In *Early Middle English Verse and Prose*, v. 120.

[36] S. R. T. O. d'Ardenne, *Ste Iuliene*, p. 209, § 64, suggests that the adjectival ending *-ene* found regularly in the AB dialect in *cristene*, *heaðene*, *guldene*, and re-formed *irnene*, may be due to association with the g. pl. ending *-ene* (OE *-ena*) originally proper to weak nouns.

which would enable a long vowel to be introduced into the originally unstressed syllable.[37] In all dialects of Middle English, the influx of loan-words, mainly from French, with an alien stress, would have weakened the English speaker's instinct to stress the root syllable. Moreover, the commoner loan-words were often stressed in two ways, in French or in English fashion: e.g. *abbái* or anglicized ábbai, *Austín* or *Aústin*.[38] Such doublets would conduce to an unstable stress in native words, so that *drihtín-* might be developed beside *dríhten*, and *cristéne*, *cristíne* beside *crísten*.[39]

MS Bodley 343, of the second half of the twelfth century (probably from the West Midlands)[40] is one of the earliest manuscripts to show *Drihtin-*; the *-in*, which presumably had *ī*, as in the *Ormulum*, occurs mainly in the inflected forms *Drihtine*(*s*), whereas *-en* is usual when the word is uninflected.[41] This suggests that shift of stress to the second syllable and lengthening of its

[37] Luick, § 390, explains ME *drightīn* as due to sporadic shift of stress; Latin *christiánus* may have influenced the stressing of OE *cristin-*. Orm always stresses *cris*(*s*)*tene* on the second syllable, and usually spells it *crisstene*; it is probable, but cannot be proved, that the *e* in the second syllable was long.

[38] e.g. *The Land of Cokaygne* (BL MS Harley 913, *c.* 1300–25) has *abbai* stressed on the first syllable at l. 103, on the second at l. 51 (in *Early Middle English Verse and Prose*, IX). Chaucer stresses *Austin* on the first syllable in e.g. *Gen. Prol.* I. 187, 188 and the *Ship. T.* VII. 259; but on the second syllable at VII. 441 and in *LGW* 1690. Orm stresses *Awwstin* (Dedication, 10) on the first syllable, though the *-īn* suggests that he knew the form with stress on the second syllable.

[39] Orm uses *hǽþéne* commonly beside *hæðenn*, e.g. 6797 f.

[40] See N. R. Ker, *Catalogue of Manuscripts containing Anglo-Saxon* (Oxford, 1957), p. 375. He notes (p. 374) that 'the drawing of a bishop on the flyleaf, f. 173, is accompanied by the unexplained inscription "ƿn biscopen ƿan ƿolstane god" (s. xiii?: insular g and *s*)'. I believe that this inscription also shows insular *r*, ill-made, with short first leg, so that it looks like *n*, and that it reads: 'wr (*for* ur) biscopen war wolstane god'. This would probably refer to bishop Wulfstan II of Worcester (d. 1095); *war* (cf. ON *var*) for *was* and the spelling *ƿ* for *u* suggest an incompetent scribe.

[41] I have made a rough count of the forms of *Drihten* in the homilies printed from MS Bodley 343 by A. O. Belfour, EETS 137 (1909), and in the homily on the Holy Rood Tree printed by A. S. Napier, EETS 103 (1894). Out of some 88 examples of the uninflected form, 55 of which were written in full, only two had *-in*; whereas *-ine*(*s*) occurred 18 times, *-ene* once, *drihtne*(*s*) 12 times.

vowel happened first when a third syllable followed: in words like *Drihtine(s)*, *cristene*,[42] a stressed and lengthened second syllable was an alternative to medial syncope; beside *Dríhten–Dríhtnes* had arisen a new paradigm, *Dríhten–Drihtínes*, with long medial vowel.

The early Middle English extension of *-īn* from *Drihtīne(s)* to the uninflected form, found regularly in the *Ormulum* and in the AB texts, is unlikely to have occurred until words and names ending in *-īn*, such as *Latin*, *Austin*, *Martin*, had become established usage. In the late Old English period and the transition period there seems to have been no model for a form like *Drihtín*, *Drihtén*, with stressed final syllable and lengthened vowel. Latin names like *Augustīnus*, *Constantīnus*, *Martīnus* in Anglo-Saxon or early twelfth-century English texts do not show a nominative ending *-īn*: *Martin*, for instance, appears regularly in Anglo-Saxon manuscripts[43] and in MS Bodley 343[44] as *Martinus* (nom.), *Martinum* (acc.); but *Martines* (gen.), *Martine* (dat.) normally have anglicized inflexions. It looks as if, in the twelfth-century West Midland dialect of MS Bodley 343, stressed *-īn* was not yet familiar in final position. The earliest example of consistent final *-in* (from Latin *-īnus*) that I have found is in the second continuation to the *Peterborough Chronicle* (*c.* 1155), where *Martin* appears in the annals for 1132 and 1137.[45] *MED* gives no example

[42] Spellings like *Drihtene(s)*, common in manuscripts, may also reflect a stressed and lengthened second syllable.

[43] e.g. *Blickling Homilies*, XVIII (ed. R. Morris, EETS 58, 63, 73 (1874–80; repr. as one volume, 1967)); Ælfric, *Catholic Homilies*, II. xxxiv (ed. M. Godden, EETS, ss 5 (1979)). Ælfric, *Lives of Saints*, II. xxxi (ed. W. W. Skeat, EETS 94 and 114 (1890–1900; repr. as one volume, 1966)); *OE Martyrology* (EETS 116), November 11.

[44] A Life of St. Martin is found on ff. 35r–39v. *Martinus* occurs at ff. 35r13 f., 18, 22, 32, etc.; *Martinum* at f. 37r25; *Martines* at ff. 36r14 f., 31, 36v6, 37v4, etc.; *Martine* at ff. 36r17, 31, 36v33, 37r3, 11, 29, etc.; *Martino* at 35v27 is exceptional.

[45] The annal for 1137 also has *Drihtin*, *Dryhtin*, *Drihtines*, beside *Drihten*.

The forms *Custantin* (*Liber Vitae*, ed. H. Sweet (EETS 83), 154/13) and *Cosstantin*, acc. (Chronicle D, *anno* 926, BL MS Cott. Tib. B.iv, *c.* 1050) were anglicized early, and probably had short *i*; the more usual *Constantinus* (D) is found īn *Brunanburh* 38, with *ī*.

of *Latin* before Orm, and I know of no earlier example of *Austin*.[46]

Orm, in a sample of some 4,500 lines, always stresses *Drihhtiness*[47] on the second syllable (e.g. ll. 752, 1165, 1415); but uninflected *Drihhtin* is stressed sometimes on the second syllable (e.g. ll. 655, 1069, Intr. 12, 16), more often on the first (e.g. 139, 237, 397, Intr. 2, 77, etc.).[48] This supports the view that shift of stress to the second syllable occurred first and persisted in inflected forms, and that it was here that the lengthened vowel arose. A similar stress pattern is found in proper names like *Adam*, *Dauiþ(þ)*, *Iesus(s)*: the uninflected forms are stressed on either the first or the second syllable, usually the first; but the inflected genitive always has the stress on the second syllable.[49]

The examples of *Dauiþ(þ)* and *Iesus(s)* are instructive: *Dauiþ(þ)*, when not stressed on the second syllable, commonly shows a short *i*, e.g. *Dauiþþ* 3594; sometimes the spelling implies a long *i*, e.g. *Dauið* 309, *Dauiþ* 310. *Iesus*, in which Orm knew the *u* to be historically long (for he discusses the Greek spelling IESOUS at ll. 4302 ff.), seems to have *-us* when the second syllable is stressed, *-uss* when it is not. Evidently the long vowel was consistently preserved in the second syllable only when that syllable was stressed;[50] when unstressed, it was commonly shortened. Uninflected *Drihtin*, to which stressed *īn* had been extended

[46] *Latin* and *Austin* are also found in the AB texts.

[47] *Drihhtine* is not found, according to White's glossary.

[48] In my sample, from the beginning to l. 4050, about 76 % of the uninflected forms (some 120 in all) had the stress on the first syllable; whereas *Drihhtiness* (8 ×) was always stressed on the second syllable.

[49] e.g. *Adam* at 16345 is stressed on the first syllable, *Adam* and *Adamess* at 16346 on the second; *Dauiþþ* (so MS) at 14912 is stressed on the first syllable, *Dauið* (so MS) at 14943, *Dauiþes* 3560 on the second; *Iesuss* 4270 on the first syllable, *Iesus* 4267, *Iesusess* 3054 on the second. In the sample passage, most of the uninflected forms were stressed on the first syllable: I counted 11 examples of *Dauiþ(þ)*, 8 of *Adam* with stress on the first syllable, against one instance of *Adam* with stress on the second syllable (Int. 31); whereas in the genitive the stress fell on the second syllable in *Dauiðes* (4 ×), *Adamess* (once).

[50] At 14911 *Dauiþþ* (so MS), with stressed second syllable, is probably a mistake, anticipating *Dauiþþ*, stressed on the first syllable, in the next line.

from the inflected forms, may often, like *Iesus*(*s*) and *Dauiþ*(*þ*), have had the stress restored to the root, with a shortened vowel in the second syllable, both in Orm's dialect and in the 'AB language'. But Orm, whose zeal for consistent spelling is well known, never admitted (as he did in *Iesuss* and *Dauiþþ*) to a short vowel in the second syllable of *Drihhtin*.

I have argued that the prerequisite for the *-īn*, *-ēne* forms of *Drihten* and *cristen*(*e*) was a shift of stress from root to second syllable; and that in the *Ormulum* such a shift occurred and persisted where a third syllable followed.[51] *Cristen*(*e*) acquired a final *-e* in early Middle English; *Drihten* derived its long vowel from the inflected forms *Drihtīnes*, *Drihtīne*. The reason why *Drihten* was affected by its inflected forms, while other OE disyllabic nouns ending in *-en* normally were not, may be that *Drihten* was constantly used in its inflected forms in such phrases as *for Drihtenes luue*, *on Drihtenes name*, *to ure Drihtene*.

It remains to consider why shift of stress and lengthening of the second syllable should produce *-īn-* rather than *-ēn-*. I doubt that it can be explained by a sound change: even if early Middle English unstressed *e* had been raised to *i* in some dialects before the nasal (and there seems to be no good evidence for such raising before the late thirteenth century),[52] lengthening of *i*

[51] The ME *-in* forms of a few other words are probably to be explained by such a shift of stress: e.g. common ME *kichin*(*e*) (OE *cycene*); the rare feminine noun *schelchine* (OE *sc*(*i*)*elcen* 'female servant'), which acquired a final *e* in early Middle English, found twice in MS Cott. Nero A. xiv of *Ancrene Wisse* (EETS 225, 6/4, 177/27), where other versions have *þuften* (MS. T *þuftin* in the second passage); possibly the form *birthyn* (OE str. fem. *byrþen*), found in 'Love is Life' 49 in rhyme with *pyne*, *wyne*, *tyne* (the spellings of the southernized MS Longleat 29, *c.* 1400–25, ed. S. Wilson, *RES*, NS x, 1959, 337–46), since the word has acquired a final *-e* in some early ME dialects.

[52] The earliest evidence of such raising that I know is in the texts written by hand D of MS Cleopatra C. vi, in an East Midland dialect (see above, p. 246 n. 11) between 1284 and *c.* 1300 (see E. J. Dobson, EETS 267, pp. xxviii f. and clx f.). Professor Dobson has shown that the same scribe was responsible for the texts copied on ff. 24^r and 24^v of Trinity Coll. Cambridge, MS B. 1.45; he gives a facsimile, facing p. 110. OE *cristin-* probably owes its second *i* to Latin *christianus*.

would probably have resulted in *ē*. The *-īn-* forms are most easily explained by influence of the common ending *-īn*(*e*) in French and Latin loan-words like *bacin*, *Latin*, *discipline*, *virgine*. Native words, when stressed like these loan-words, might also acquire their *-īn-* endings, by suffix substitution.

Another source of *-īn*(*e*) endings, which could have affected *Drihten*, was the large group of proper names ending in *-in*(*e*), such as *Austin*, *Martin*, *Constantin*(*e*).[53] That *Drihten* often functioned as a proper name is clear from phrases like *Be God and Sayn Driȝtine*.[54] Orm used *-īn* as a living proper name suffix, styling himself as both *Orrm* and *Orrmin*, with stress on the second syllable.[55] It was perhaps because he felt *Drihhtin* to be a proper name that it alone, in the *Ormulum*, shows consistent *-īn* in all its forms.[56]

[53] I am indebted to Professor E. G. Stanley for the suggestion that proper names might have influenced *Drihtin*.

[54] *Sir Amadace*, 759; also *be Sayne Drightyne* (*Roland and Ottwell*, 1570).

[55] *Ormulum*, 'Preface', 2; 'Dedication', 324, 325. H. C. Matthes, *Die Einheitlichkeit des Orrmulum* (Heidelberg, 1933), 35 ff., showed that the 'Preface' should be printed between l. 156 and l. 157 of the 'Dedication', of which it is part.

Orm's liking for suffixes appears in the extraordinary title he gave ro his work: *Orrmulum* is, as far as I know, a formation without parallel; to his name he has added a Latin diminutive suffix, as in *parvulus*, *hortulus*. Did he think of his vast work as an *opusculum*?

[56] As far as I have tested the *Ormulum* (up to l. 4050), *Drihhtin* is always without definite article, even when it is qualified by a preceding adjective: e.g. 2814 *Allmahhtiȝ Drihhtin*, 2305 *þurrh Allmahhtiȝ Drihhtiness mahht*; whereas, for example, in the AB texts we find phrases like *þe deore Drihtin* (*S.K.* 502); the *Gawain* poet also uses the article sometimes, e.g. *þe Dryȝtyn* (*Cleanness*, 669).

Clocks, Dials, and other Terms

A.G. RIGG

In Modern English we often express distance by time: a house is 'five minutes from the shops', Toronto is 'seven hours from London'. Conversely, Middle English often expressed time by distance: describing the divisions of the astrolabe, Chaucer says: '5 of these degres maken a myle wey, and 3 mile-wei maken an houre', (*Astr.* I. xvi. 12),[1] and of John the carpenter: 'This John lith stille a furlong wey or two' (*CT Rv. T.* I. 4199). It is a commonplace of cultural history that one of the greatest revolutions in man's perception of the world around him was caused by the invention, some time in the late thirteenth century, of the mechanical weight-driven clock.[2] This paper explores some of the vocabulary used in time-reckoning and the ways in which English writers of the later Middle Ages responded to this new and complex invention.[3]

A Modern English 'clock' is a German *Uhr*, a French *horloge*, and an Italian *orologio*. Conversely, a French *cloche* and a German *Glocke* are bells. A English '(clock-)dial' is a French *cadran* (i.e. quadrant), a German *Zifferblatt*; a '(sun-)dial', however, is a French *cadran solaire* but a German *Sonnenuhr*. The

[1] Chaucer quotations are taken from the second edition by F. N. Robinson (London, 1957); other Middle English texts are usually quoted in the form given, with dates, in the *Middle English Dictionary*.

[2] Cf. Lynn White, Jr., *Medieval Technology and Social Change* (Oxford and New York, 1966), 119–29; C. M. Cipolla, *Clocks and Culture 1300–1700* (London, 1967), especially pp. 103–5.

[3] I am happy to acknowledge the timely assistance of my Toronto colleagues, Dr Roy Laird and Professors Bert Hall and Bert Hansen. It was Bert Hall who first asked me why *clock* means 'bell' in French and German but 'clock' in English.

invention of the mechanical clock required each language either to borrow Latin technical terms (*horologium*, *quadrans*, *diale*) or to adapt existing words and give them more specialized senses; in either case, the vocabulary was drawn from earlier methods of measuring or announcing the time. In late Middle English the semantic field of time-reckoners was occupied by several words, which for a time appear to have competed with each other: *clock*, *bell*, *dial*, and *orloge*. Eventually, of course, the first three words acquired specialized senses and the fourth dropped out of the language entirely.

Clock

The word *clock* entered English twice, first (perhaps from Old Irish)[4] in the Old English period, when it clearly means 'bell': in the translation of Bede, the phrase *sonitum notum campanae* is rendered *hleoðor heora clucgan* (v.l. *bellan*).[5] The *cg* graph might suggest at first sight a palatal geminate /dž/, but the absence of i-umlaut probably indicates a velar stop (cf. *docga* 'dog'). Whatever the pronunciation, this form of the word (which would have produced Middle English **cludge* or **clug*) dropped out of the language.

There is a tradition, supported by Onions[6] and Förster,[7] that the word *clock* was reintroduced into English by the Dutch clockmakers imported by Edward III (Onions inadvertently says Edward I) in 1368. This view is given apparent support by the fact that the earliest examples recorded by the *OED* and the *MED* date from 1370. In fact, the word occurs in Richard of

[4] See *OED*, s.v. *Clock*; also M. Förster, 'Altenglisch *stōr*, ein altirisches Lehnwort', *Englische Studien*, lxx (1935), 51 and n. 2. I owe this reference to Professor Angus Cameron of the Dictionary of Old English, Toronto.

[5] *The Old English Version of Bede's Ecclesiastical History*, ed. T. Miller, EETS 96 (1891), 340; 111 (1898), 402; the variants for *clucgan* are: O *cluccgan*, Ca *cluggan*, B *bellan*.

[6] C. T. Onions, *Oxford Dictionary of English Etymology* (Oxford, 1966), 183.

[7] Loc. cit.

Wallingford's *Tractatus Horologii* (written between 1327 and 1336) in the section on making a clock strike (*pro sonitu unius clok*).[8] The Flemish experts are red herrings: in 1351 three Lombards were engaged on making the clock for Windsor Castle,[9] and North discusses the probability of a long tradition of English clock-making even before Richard of Wallingford.[10] The word very probably came from ONF *cloque* (beside Central French *cloche*): this is the origin of the earlier Middle English *cloke* 'cloak' (with lengthening of /ŏ/ in an open syllable), which meant originally a 'bell-shaped garment'. A simple 'clock = bell' equation is suggested by an inventory of 1393–6 of Queenborough Castle, Kent, which includes not only *i clokke infra quandam turrim* but also *i parua clokke pendens in sancta capella*.[11] This 'small clock', however, is probably a wall-clock 'hanging' on the wall of the chapel. Otherwise, Middle English *clokke* never means simply 'bell' (such as a hand-bell): it always implies time-keeping. We may note, for example, the work done in Exeter Cathedral in 1376 *circa cameram in boreali turre pro horologio quod vocatur clokke de novo construendam*, 'on the new construction of the chamber in the Northern tower for the *horologium* called "clokke"'[12] In Durham in 1380 a *cloklyn* (clock-line) ... *de 40 fathome in longitudine* was purchased for 6 shillings: the length indicates a rope for the weight, not a bell-ringing rope.[13]

All the entries in the *MED* show that a *clokke* was used to tell

[8] Richard of Wallingford, ed. J. D. North, 3 vols. (Oxford, 1976): Text, i. 441–523; Notes and Introduction, ii. 309–360; 'The St. Albans Clock in History', ii. 361–70; figures, iii. 61–74 (escapement and striking train, pp. 64–7, Plates XVII–XXI). This reference is on i. 480; North discusses the etymology of *clok* on i. 481 n. 1.

[9] C. F. C. Beeson, *English Church Clocks 1280–1850*, Antiquarian Horological Society (London and Chichester, 1971), 19–20; see also R. Allen Brown, 'King Edward's Clocks', *Antiquarian Journal*, xxxix (1959), 283–6.

[10] North, ii. 361–70: 'We not only know that there was an English craft going back to the thirteenth century, we actually know names of some of its early practitioners' (p. 370).

[11] Beeson, p. 20.

[12] Id., p. 14.

[13] Id., p. 20; also cited by the *MED*.

the time. On the other hand, the word also seems always to imply the idea of striking or sounding or of a mechanism: there is no sign that it could be used for other devices for telling the time, such as sun-dials or sand-glasses. In the passage quoted by the *MED* from Pecock's *Repressor* (*c.* 1449) the *clok* is clearly a mechanical device:

Thouȝ in Scripture mensioun is maad of orologis, schewing the houris of the dai bi schadew maad bi the sunne in a cercle, certis neuere saue in late daies was eny clok telling the houris of the dai and nyȝt by peise and bi stroke.[14]

Middle English uses suggest that a clock was primarily something one heard rather than saw. If the sounding part was distinguished from the mechanism, however, the word for the former was *chimbe* 'chime'. In a chapter-heading similar to that cited above, Richard of Wallingford describes the *quantitas horologii pro sonitu unius cimbe*, 'the quantities for a timepiece capable of ringing a bell'.[15] The word *chimbe*, however, includes the sense 'cymbal, or hand-bell' (*MED*, s.v. 1 (a)) as well as the chime of a clock (*MED* 1 (b)).

A clock was essentially a public instrument, housed in a *clocarium* or *clokhous*. Nevertheless, despite the apparently essential auditory element involved in the word *clokke*—that it chime or sound a bell—a *clokke* was always a time-keeper, never simply a bell, for which Middle English had the word *belle*.

Bell

The word *bell* (OE *belle*), from *belgan* 'bellow', is shared with the West Germanic languages: Icelandic (*bjalla*), Faroese (*bjølla*), Norwegian (*bjølle*), Danish (*bjaelde*), Swedish (*bjällra*), Dutch (*bel*), Afrikaans (*bel*), and Frisian (*bel*).[16] It has a continuous history in English. In Middle English it has most of the senses

[14] On the meaning of *orloge*, see below, pp. 260–64.

[15] North, i. 472; for a discussion of *cimba*, see i. 473 n. 6.

[16] For advice on clock-terms in modern Germanic languages I am grateful to Mr Kelly DeVries and Professor Harry Roe of Toronto.

we now associate with bells, particularly the ringing sound: see *MED*, s.v. *Belle* (n.) (1), senses 1 a (a)–(c), 1 b (a)–(b), 4 (a)–(c). All the examples under sense 4 are of a small bell; under 1 a (a)–(b) and possibly 1 b, however, we find both hand-bells and church-bells lumped together: e.g. (of hand-bells) ?*a* 1425 Mandeville (Eg) 102/17 'He knyllez a lytill bell (OF *clokette*) of siluer þat he hase in his hand'; and (of church-bells) *c.* 1325 (*c.* 1300) *Glo. Chron. A*, 10485, 'Me rong bellen in al þe toun & vaste þe ropes drou', and (*c.* 1390) Chaucer, *CT NPT* B 3970–1, 'By seint Poules belle | Ye seye right sooth.'

The distinction is (for our present purposes) an important one, as it is in the sense 'church-bell' that the word *belle* competes with *clokke*. This competition is especially evident in the 'o'clock' phrase, illustrated by the *MED* quotations under *Clokke* 1 (b) 'at, atte, of, on the clock', and *Belle* 2 (b) 'at neyne of the belle', 'bitwene vj and vij of the belle', 'vnto the houre of vij atte the belle', 'sone apon ix atte belle', etc. Note particularly: *a.* 1422 *Norwich Gild St. Geo.* 448, 'be viij of the clok, þat is for to seye, be oure ladies belle'. The near-synonymity of the two words in this context is shown by the variants in two versions of the *Jousts of Peace*, *c.* 1475 (*a.* 1486):

> To appeer at ix of the clok [v.l. belle] bofore noon, & to juste . . . vnto vi of the clok [v.l. belle] at aftir noone.[17]

Similarly, note Chaucer, *BD* 1322–3, 'In the castell ther was a belle, | As hyt hadde smyten houres twelve.' Such phrases suggest that *belle* and *clokke* occupied the same semantic area, referring to the public signal that announced the time of day by means of a ringing sound. By the late fourteenth century this public time-keeper would almost certainly be a weight-driven clock with a striking train. Although *belle* always preserved the connotation of sound, it can also imply a horological mechanism. Conversely, although *clokke* came eventually to refer solely to the mechanically driven time-keeper, nevertheless it preserved, during the

[17] On the significance of this passage for the 12- or 24-hour dial, see below, p. 266.

Middle English period, its original connotation of 'bell'. Its specialization in the modern sense of 'clock' was no doubt made possible by the existence of *belle* (to perform the functions of the modern word 'bell').

Parallel developments are seen in the other West Germanic languages that have the word *belle*: Icelandic has *bjalla* 'bell', and thus *kirkjuklukka* 'church-clock' or 'church-bell', *klukka* 'clock', *veggklukka* 'wall-clock'; the Faroese distribution of the words is similar. In Dutch both *klok* and *bel* can mean 'bell', but *klok* can also mean 'clock' (which can also be called an *uurwerk*); the situation is similar in Norwegian, Afrikaans, and Frisian. Although Danish and Swedish have *bjaelde* (a small bell) and *bjällra* (a sleigh-bell), their word for 'clock' is *ur*, like German *Uhr*. Thus, although the existence of *belle* made possible the use of *clok* to mean 'clock', the development was not inevitable. Most of these languages use some derivative of Latin *hora* 'hour' (*ur*, German *Uhr*) or *horologium* for a wall-clock (except Dutch *wandklok*), or for a pocket- or wrist-watch. In Frisian, however, a watch is either *horloazje* or *klokje*.

In English, the word *clokke* did not have an uncontested victory in its present sense. It never seems to have faced competition from (*h*)*oure*, like most Germanic languages, but for a long time it was rivalled by *orloge* and, in certain respects, by *dial*.

Orloge

In Middle English *orloge* refers to various devices for measuring time, both mechanical and astronomical.[18] In Germanic languages it is used sometimes in compounds for a wrist- or pocket-watch, and in Afrikaans *horlosie* (as well as *klok* and *uurwerk*) is used to mean 'clock'. Even in German, where it was replaced by *Uhr*, it enjoyed a short life: in 1183 in Cologne a

[18] I am grateful to Dr Karis Crawford of the *Middle English Dictionary* for providing me with the entry on *Orloge* in advance of publication, and for assistance on other words.

guild of clock-makers (presumably of water-clocks) was formed, and the street where they worked was known as *Urlogingasse* (1220).[19] As noted above, it is the usual word for a clock in French and Italian.

In Latin the word *horologium* most commonly refers to a sun-dial, particularly in the two famous passages from the Bible in which God increased Ezechiel's life by fifteen years by turning back the shadow by ten lines:

Ecce ego reverti faciam umbram linearum per quas descenderat in horologio Achaz in sole, retrorsum decem lineis. Et reversus est sol decem lineis per gradus quos descenderat. (Isa. 38: 8)[20]

'Behold, I will make the shadow of the lines through which it passed in the sun on the horologium of Achaz turn back by ten lines. And the sun turned back ten lines through the degrees by which it had passed.'

Invocavit itaque Isaias propheta Dominum, et reduxit umbram per lineas, quibus iam descenderat in horologio Achaz, retrorsum decem gradibus. (4 Reg. 20:/11).[21]

'And so the prophet Isaiah called the Lord, and He brought the shadow back by ten degrees through the lines by which it had passed on the horologium of Achaz.'

In three manuscripts of Sacrobosco's *Sphere* there is an addition in which *orologium* can refer only to a sun-dial:

clima est spatium terre in quo oportet mutare orologium secundum quantitatem medietatis unius hore.[22]

'A climate is the extent of the earth in which it is necessary to adjust an *orologium* by half an hour.'

[19] White, op. cit., p. 120.

[20] For a medieval illustration of this passage, see below, p. 263 and n. 28.

[21] In both passages the Wycliffite Bible (in all versions) renders *horologium* by 'oriloge'.

[22] *The Sphere of Sacrobosco and its commentators*, ed. Lynn Thorndike (Chicago, 1949), 112 n. 79; the three manuscripts that have this sentence are D (s. xiv, after 1328), J (late s. xiii), and K (s. xiv, second half). From usages like this, a *clima* came to mean the grid plate of an astrolabe showing the observer's map of the heavens, changed according to latitude: *revolve clima quousque duo capita* [sc. *Arietis*] *directe contra se fuerint* ('turn the plate until the two heads of Aries are directly opposite'), Richard of Wallingford. *Tractatus Albionis*, ed. North, i. 382.

Only a sun-dial would be affected by a change in latitude. Later, a *horologium* is always a mechanical clock:[23] in Robertus Anglicus' *Commentary* (1271) on Sacrobosco's *Sphere*, for example, in a well-known passage (often interpreted as a *terminus a quo* for the invention of the weight-driven clock) we read of the recording of unequal hours:

per instrumenta astronomica et etiam horologica que sunt facta secundum formam astronomicam.[24]

'By astronomical instruments and also horological instruments made according to an astronomical scheme'.

but he goes on to say that it would not be possible for a *horologium* to follow astronomical data so closely, but that clock-makers are trying to construct a clock to follow the motion of the equinoctial circle:

Nec est hoc possibile, quod aliquod horologium sequatur omnino iudicium astronomie secundum veritatem. Conantur tamen artifices horologiorum facere circulum unum qui omnino moveatur secundum motum circuli equinoctialis, sed non possunt omnino complere opus eorum, quod, si possent facere, esset horologium verax valde...

'It is not possible for any *horologium* entirely to follow the judgment of astronomy with exactitude. Clock-makers, however, are trying to make a single circle to move entirely according to the movement of the equinoctial circle, but they cannot entirely finish their work: if they could do so, it would be a really accurate *horologium*...'

The Middle English uses of *orloge* all post-date the invention of the weight-driven clock. Uses meaning 'sun-dial' (*MED*, s.v. *Orloge* (d)) seem to be confined to passages translating or com-

[23] All the early English documents containing clock terminology are assembled by Beeson, pp. 13–24. There is an earlier survey of horology and its terms by R. P. Howgrave-Graham, 'Some clocks and jacks, with notes on the history of horology', *Archaeologia*, lxxvii (1927), 257–312; this is now almost entirely out of date on the issue of chronology, because of the work of Thorndike, Beeson, and North, but remains very interesting and has excellent plates.

[24] Thorndike, op. cit., p. 180; instead of this phrase MS E reads *per astrolabium et horologium et alia instrumenta astronomica* ('by the astrolabe and *horologium* and other astronomical instruments'). For my reasons for doubting the traditional interpretation of the passage, see below, p. 269 and n. 43.

menting on the Biblical texts cited above, as in the quotation from Pecock cited above, in which *orologis schewing the houris of the dai bi schadew* are contrasted with the mechanical *clok* which operates both by day and night.[25] Otherwise an *orloge* is a mechanical clock (*MED*, s.v. *Orloge*, sense (a), 'A clock; esp. one which strikes the hours'), such as the one with which Chaunteclеer is favourably compared:

> Wel sikerer was his crowyng in his logge
> Than is a clokke or an abbey orlogge. (*CT NPT* VII 4043–4)

Lydgate specifically mentions a weight-driven clock in the *Testament*:

> Lyk a phane, ay turnyng to and fro,
> Or like an orloge whan the peys is goo.[26]

Froissart's description of a weight-driven *orloge* is discussed below.[27]

There is one apparent example of *orloge* meaning a water-clock, in the translation of Vegetius in which *orlogis* renders *clepsydram* (cited by *MED*, s.v. *Orloge*, sense (e)); the translator, however, may have been rethinking chronometry in his own terms and may have substituted a weight-driven clock for a water-driven one (which he may never have experienced). A 'translation' in the opposite direction was made by a thirteenth-century illustrator who, faced with the problem of showing God moving a shadow (to prolong Ezechiel's life), showed Him restraining the motion of a water-clock.[28]

Both *clokkemaker* (*MED*, s.v. *Clokke*, sense 2, from 1374) and *orloger* (*MED*, s.v. *Orloger*, sense (b), from 1311) occur as occupational surnames, showing, as North has done from documentary sources, that clock-making was a well-established trade in England.[29]

[25] Quoted above, p. 258.

[26] For a possible interpretation of these lines, see below, n. 36.

[27] See below, pp. 269–71.

[28] Often reproduced: e.g. by White, op. cit., Plate 10.

[29] See note 10 above; the word *bellman*, however, probably refers to bell-casting.

The word *orloge* was evidently very popular for a time; its eventual demise probably resulted from the fact that it was competing (for the position of 'mechanical time-keeper') with *clokke*, which was no longer needed in the sense 'bell'. For a time, however, there was yet another competitor, *dial*.

Dial

In Modern English the word *dial* refers to the dial-*plate* of a clock, and, by extension, to (usually round) plates with numbers, such as telephone dials; it is used in combination in the word *sun-dial*. In Middle English its range was much wider. It is derived ultimately from Latin *dialis* 'daily': compare *Thesaurus Linguae Latinae*, s.v. *dialis*, 'cotidianus, diurnus', DuCange and Niermeyer, s.v. *dialiter*, 'daily', DuCange, s.v. *diale*, 'the amount of land that can be ploughed in a day'. Daily (i.e. 24-hour) motion is the essential element in the earliest horological uses of the word. In Richard of Wallingford's treatise the very last thing to be fixed to his astronomical clock is the *diale*:

Tunc apponitur diale, in cuius circumferencia gradus et nomina signorum ecliptice ... Et figitur diale super caligam diurnam exeuntem a rota diurna ...[30]

'Then the dial is attached; on its circumference (are inscribed) degrees and the names of the signs of the Zodiac ... And the dial is fitted onto the "day-tube" which comes out of the "day-wheel".'

The point is made even clearer in Froissart's *Li Orloge Amoureus*, in which the dial is specifically called the 'daily wheel':

[30] *Tractatus*, II. vii. 6, ed. North, i. 520. North (i. 475 n. 5, 477 n. 11) explains *caliga* as a 'sleeve' or tube which rotates on a fixed axle: the *caliga diurna*, therefore, protrudes outside the workings of the clock. As the word *diurna* is etymologically the source of *journal*, the phrase may explain the origin of the noun *journal* meaning 'the part of shaft or axle which rests on its bearings' (*OED*, s.v. *Journal* B (sb.), II. 10), first recorded in 1814, of which the *OED* says: '*journal* or *journey* in this sense appears to have arisen in the Scotch workshops. No explanation of its origin has been found'.

Apres affiert à parler dou dyal;
Et ce dyal est la roe journal
Qui, en un jour naturel seulement,
Se moet et fait un tour precisement...[31]

'Next we must speak of the dial. This dial is the day-wheel which in one natural [i.e. 24-hour] day alone moves itself and makes exactly one rotation.'

On this *dyal* are marked out the twenty-four hours of the day. The expenses for the construction of an elaborate dial are given in the Computus of 1324/25 in the Sacrist's Rolls of Norwich Cathedral.[32]

The fact that the dial itself rotates makes unnecessary the definition 'the hand of a clock', suggested by the *MED* for the passage from (d) *a.* 1475, *Rev. St Bridget*, 69/1:

Above that glasse hange an horrible swerde with iij egges, neyghyng contynually to þat glasse as a dyall in ane orelege neghith to his merke.[33]

We might in a similar way explain the curious story of the seventeenth-century Frenchman who solved the problem of telling the time at night 'by designing a clock with a dial that had different kinds of spice inserted in the place of numbers. At night he reached for the point indicated by the hour hand and tastefully determined the time.' It would presumably have been easy enough to tell the time if the hand had rotated, but a fixed pointer and a turning dial would present problems in the dark.[34]

[31] *Li Orloge Amoureus*, 347–50, in *Œuvres de Froissart: Poésies*, ed. A. Scheler, 2 vols., i (Brussels, 1870), 53–86. The poem (discussed more fully below, pp. 269–71) has not been dated but was probably written 1360–70; it consists of 1174 lines in decasyllabic couplets. Note that the *roe journal* is not the internal *rota diurna* mentioned by Richard of Wallingford; both the internal and external wheels would, of course, turn simultaneously.

[32] Beeson, pp. 104–5; see also North, ii. 362.

[33] Not all dials rotated, of course: see the picture of the clock at Hampton Court, mentioned in n. 35 below. For a picture of a rotating dial, see *The unknown Leonardo*, ed. Ladislao Reti (New York, 1974), 241, illustration 3; see also J. H. Leopold, *The Almanus Manuscript* (London, 1971), 18.

[34] Cited by Cipolla, *Clocks and Culture*, p. 69; I owe this reference, and the suggested interpretation, to Bert Hansen.

The passage cited above from the *Jousts of Peace* (and several others in the *MED*) imply an a.m./p.m. distinction: 'ix of the clok bofore noone ... vi of the clok at aftir noone'. How is this to be reconciled with the *daily* motion of a dial? The sixteenth-century astronomical dial of the clock at Hampton Court, Middlesex, shows a 24-hour dial divided into two groups of 12, I–XII and I–XII.[35] This arrangement is also implied by Froissart: although 'en ce dyal ... Sont les heures vingt et quatre descrites' ('on this dial are painted the twenty-four hours'), *Li Orloge*, 353–4, the allegorical interpretation divides them into two groups of twelve: '... ces douze si sont teles. Les aultres douze aussi, qui sont moult beles, Sont ...' ('... these twelve are like this. The other twelve, which are very beautiful, are ...'), *Li Orloge*, 435–6.

Unlike *clokke* and *belle* (which one heard) a *dial* was essentially something one looked at: hence the slang use meaning 'the human face'. This usage is first recorded by the *OED*, s.v. *Dial* 6 c for 1811, but the *MED* quotes a fragment of a Middle English translation of the *Apocalypsis Goliae* (there is no direct equivalent in the Latin) that suggests that the similarity had been noticed earlier: ?*a.* 1500 in James, *Cat. MSS Eton*, 38 'There was ye deyn and ye offycyall With ij fayces lyke a dyall.'

Either because it recorded the daily motion of the sun or, more probably, because it was the visible part of a chronometer, *dial* could also mean 'sun-dial', as in Lydgate's *Troy-Book*, I. 1517:

> By þe dyal þe hour þei gan to marke
> þat Phebus southward was reised in his arke
> So hiȝe alofte þat it drowe to noon.

Similarly, Coverdale (1535) renders *in horologio Achaz* (4 Reg. 20: 11, discussed above) by the phrase 'Achas Dyall'. Some kind of portable sun-dial, perhaps a chilinder (see below), is

[35] Beeson, Plate 77, pp. 111–12; on this clock the hours are painted on the surrounding masonry, and a pointer, carrying a picture of the sun, rotates daily.

indicated by such entries in the *MED* as: (1455) *Reg. Chanc. Oxf.* '1 bursa cum diall de ligno' ('a purse with a wooden dial'). When Jacques's chance acquaintance 'drew a diall from his poake' (*As You Like It*, II. vii. 20, 33) it was almost certainly a pocket sun-dial, rather than a pocket-watch, which, even if available, would have been extremely expensive at this time.

There are, in fact, several indications that in late Middle and early Modern English *dial* could mean any kind of time-keeping device. It means a weight-driven clock in Lydgate's *Testament*, 358: 'As the peys of a diall goth'; this cannot refer to what we would call the dial, which was not driven directly by the weight (*peys*).[36] It can also mean an hour-glass, as is shown by the passage (quoted by the *MED*, s.v. *Dial* 1 (e)) from ?*c.* 1475, *Sailing Directions*, 'Upon o belille [i.e. Belle Ile in the Bay of Biscay, south of Britanny] there is in lx fadome or lxx smale diale sonde'; that is, at sixty or seventy fathoms depth there is fine sand, suitable for use in an hour-glass. Somewhat later it was used in combination in *water-dial* (*OED*, s.v. *Dial* 3, from 1552 to 1676), meaning a water-clock or clepsydra. It is thus one of the most versatile clock-terms; in the seventeenth and eighteenth centuries *dialling* referred to several kinds of surveying and precision technology. In Modern English, of course, *dialling* usually refers to turning a circular dial-plate, especially of a telephone;[37] modern push-button telephones, however, have 'touch-dials', so that *dialling* may come to acquire another range of senses.

Under *Dial*, sense 2, the *MED* gives several examples of the

[36] Twice in the *Testament* (here and in the lines cited above, p. 263) Lydgate uses the mechanism of a clock as an image for 'gerysh' fickleness. Comparison of the passages shows that *whan the peys is goo* must mean 'when the weight is moving', not 'when the weight has gone/is lost'; in any case, the loss of the weight would simply mean that the clock would stop. As the main weight of a clock imparts a constant movement, not one that could be called 'gerysh', Lydgate (assuming that he knows how a clock works) may be referring to the small weights placed on the bar of the foliot to regulate the time of its oscillation; see also below, p. 271.

[37] See *OED* Supplement, *A-G* (Oxford, 1972) s.vv. *Dial* (sb.[1]), 6 d and *Dial* (v.) 4.

word in nautical contexts: (1338) 'Un spogeour, ii seilyngnedeles, un dyall, un sherhok'; (1417) 'In j Ketille, j diolle, j Boxe'; (?*a.* 1422) 'one dyoll and one seyling-needle'; (ibid.) 'j dioll, j compasse, j boxe'.[38] It glosses all these as 'the dial of a mariner's compass; ?also, a compass'. In light of the present discussion, however, we may doubt this definition. A *dial* was not, at this date, 'an external plate or face on which revolutions, pressure, etc. are indicated by an index finger or otherwise';[39] it was a time-keeping device. The Middle English term for a mariner's compass was *nedle and ston* (see *MED*, s.v. *Nedle* 2) or *seyling-needle* (as in the quotations just given);[40] the first recorded use of *dial* meaning a mariner's compass is from 1523 (*OED*, s.v. *Dial* 5). For navigation a ship would need a compass (*nedle*), an instrument to fix its latitude (a quadrant), and something to tell the time: I would therefore suggest that dial in these nautical contexts means either a portable sundial, a chilinder (see below), or an hour-glass.

To summarize: a *clokke* is a public instrument for signalling the hour of the day; it competes in certain contexts with the word *belle*, but is mechanically powered and controlled. An *orloge* can be either a mechanically-powered time-keeper (competing with *clokke*) or a shadow-measuring device (competing with the word *dial*). A *dial* can be the (usually rotating) visible face of a mechanically-powered clock, or the clock itself (competing with both *clokke* and *orloge*), or a shadow-measuring device (competing with, and ousting, *orloge*), or an hour-glass (competing with *glas* itself), or a generic term for any chronometer.

We can now place these horological terms in the context of late medieval time-keeping devices and their literary occur-

[38] The word is often spelled *diol*: a churchwarden's account of 1560 (Beeson, fig. 71, p. 105) has both *dyoll* and *dyowle*. Neither *OED* nor the *English Dialect Dictionary* give similar spellings, which seem to indicate a rounding before *l*.

[39] *OED* s.v. *Dial* (sb.[1]), 6.

[40] There is no unambiguous case of Middle English *compas* meaning 'mariner's compass'.

rences. Essentially, there were three kinds of 'clock': the mechanical, the astronomical, and the gravitational.

(1) The first notice of a weight-driven clock is given by Robertus Anglicus in 1271;[41] his account of it is often taken to mean that the weight-driven clock had not yet been invented,[42] but it seems more likely that such a clock was in existence but did not have the precision to measure unequal hours.[43] Another Englishman, Richard of Wallingford, Abbot of St. Albans, gave a full account in 1327–36 of how to construct an astronomical clock;[44] his account, however, assumes that one already understands the mechanism of the escapement, and indeed he seems to be part of a continuing tradition of English clock-making.[45] The earliest description known to me (and apparently unknown to horologists such as North and Beeson) of the basic operations of a mechanical clock is, surprisingly, in a literary text, Froissart's *Li Orloge Amoureus*, probably also written in England in the second part of the fourteenth century.[46] In this elaborate love-

[41] See above, p. 262 and n. 24.

[42] Lynn Thorndike, 'Invention of the Mechanical Clock about 1271 A.D.', *Speculum*, xvi (1941), 242–3; White, op. cit., p. 122. Thorndike's concern was not to provide a *terminus a quo* but a *terminus ad quem*, showing that the invention was in progress half a century earlier than previously supposed. Since Thorndike, however, the passage has been taken to mean that the clock had not yet been invented in 1271. See next note.

[43] Robert describes the use of a weight to provide the power, but his main point is that the wheel should rotate once daily 'minus as much time as about 1 degree rises according to an approximately correct estimate' (Thorndike's translation. The Latin reads: *quod quidem pondus taliter moveat rotam istam quod motus ille compleatur ab ortu solis usque ad ortum preter tantum tempus per quantum oritur unus gradus fere secundum estimationem propinquam veritati*). He goes on to describe the adjustments necessary to achieve this object. It seems to me that it is the daily adjustment (to record unequal hours) that is the problem, not the movement on a regular 24-hour basis.

[44] See above, n. 8.

[45] See above, n. 10. The problem of the escapement in Richard's account is discussed by North, ii. 330–4.

[46] See above, n. 31. Cipolla (op. cit., pp. 41, 104–5) mentions the Froissart poem, but only to point to the need for a clock-keeper and the analogy of love and horology; he does not mention the significance of the poem for its account of the escapement.

allegory each part of the clock represents part of the process of love. The clock-house, 'la maison qui porte et qui soustient | Les mouvemens qu'à l'orloge appartient' ('the house which contains and supports the movements belonging to the clock'), 53–4, is the Lover's heart. The principal wheel, which gives movement to all the rest, is Desire:

> La premerainne roe qui y loge
> Celle est la mere et li commencemens
> Qui fait mouvoir les aultres mouvemens. (100–2)

'The first wheel which is fitted there is the "mother" and the source, which causes the other movements to move.'

This wheel is driven by a weight ('le plonk'), which is Beauty, suspended on a rope ('la corde'), which is Plaisance. Without a control, of course, the wheel would turn 'sans mesure'; there is therefore a second wheel (what we could call the escapement) geared to the first. The movement of this second wheel is governed by a 'foliot', which releases only one gear-tooth at a time; the term 'foliot' is still in use today in the same sense. The mechanism involves an oscillating bar or wheel, which controls a vertical shaft geared to the main wheel. Froissart writes:

> Une roe seconde et adjoustée
> Qui le (i.e. le plonk) retarde, et qui le fait mouvoir
> Par ordenance et par mesure, voir
> Par la vertu dou foliot aussi,
> Qui continuelment le moet ensi,
> Une heure à destre et puis l'autre à senestre,
> Ne il ne doit ne poet à repos estre;
> Car par li est ceste roe gardée
> Et par vraie mesure retardée (212–20)[47]

'(There is) a second, regulated, wheel, which holds back the weight and causes it to move regularly and methodically, namely by the power of the foliot, which moves it [*see note*] continually, one hour to the right, one hour to the left; it [the foliot] should not, and can not, ever be still, since by it that wheel [the first] is checked and held back according to proper measure.'

[47] In 216 it would be preferable to read *se* for *le*: the foliot does not move anything apart from itself.

This second wheel is Attemprance, the foliot is Fear ('Paours'). Apart from the impression that the *foliot* oscillates at hourly intervals (rather than seconds), this is a very accurate account of the escapement control.[48] Just as 'le foliot branle' ('oscillates'), so does the loyal heart. We have already mentioned Froissart's account of the dial:[49] it is moved by the force of the main wheel ('par la vertu de celle mere roe') by means of a small *fuiselet* ('peg'), which goes between the two wheels *sans moyen* (i.e. without an intervening gear-wheel); this peg is Purveance, and the dial is Hope. The dial is fitted with twenty-four *brochetes* ('pins, pegs'), which release the sounding train of the clock:

> Pour ce porte il vint et quatre brochetes
> Qui font sonner les petites clochetes,
> Car elles font la destente destendre
> Qui le roe chantore fait estendre
> Et li mouvoir très ordonnéement
> Pour les heures moustrer plus clerement (355–60)[50]

'For this it carries twenty-four pins which cause the little bells to ring, since they cause the release (*la destente*) to disconnect (*destendre*); this makes the wheel of the sounding train (*la roe chantore*) turn and move regularly, in order to announce the hours more clearly.'

Froissart goes on to describe the sounding train (599–604) and the regulation of the clock by the clock-keeper ('un orlogier'), who is Memory.

Chaucer never mentions the mechanism of a weight-driven

[48] It would be tempting to use the *foliot* of a clock, with its oscillating motion and monotonous tick-tock, to explain the puzzling usage in the *Owl and Nightingale*, 868, 'ne singe ih hom no foliot' (see E. G. Stanley, *English and Germanic Studies*, vi (1957), 44–6). Unfortunately this would mean dating the invention of the foliot escapement another 80 years earlier. On the other hand, a device called a *foliot* may have been used for some mechanical purpose, perhaps as a 'governor' in some other mechanism. Some have claimed that Villard de Honnecourt's sketchbook (*c.* 1235) shows the drawing of a primitive escapement, though the interpretation is generally disputed: see White, op. cit., p. 173 (note 1 to p. 122).

[49] See above, p. 266.

[50] For an account of the striking mechanism (and a mention of the *detent*), see North, ii. 334–8, and a reconstructed diagram, iii. 67.

clock, but Lydgate, as we have seen, uses it as an image in a somewhat confusing way.

(2) Next, there are the astronomical devices, those that depend on the observation of the celestial bodies or on the shadow cast by the sun. These are called, as we have seen, *orloge* or *dial*, and are generally plane surfaces mounted either horizontally or vertically, with a gnomon to make the shadow. The quadrant (first recorded by *OED a.* 1400, but a much older instrument) was hung vertically, and was marked out for 90°: from Latin *quadrantem* comes French *cadran* 'dial' and *cadran solaire* 'sun-dial'. Another useful sun-dial for travellers was the portable *chilindre*:[51] this was a cylinder, hung vertically from the finger by a ring, with a gnomon protruding horizontally; the hours were marked on the surface, and the gnomon could be placed differently according to the time of the year. This was the device carried by the monk, Daun John, by which he saw that it was 'pryme of day' (*CT Ship. T.* VII. 1396): I have suggested above that this could also be called a dial.

The most widely used astronomical time-keeper was the astrolabe, whose operation is described in detail by Chaucer. This consisted of a circular plate, representing two-dimensionally the heavens as seen by an observer at a specific latitude; above this rotated another plate, representing the daily motion of the sun and other celestial bodies. By co-ordinating the two plates, so that the sun's present position in the sky intersected with the appropriate day of the year, one could discover the time of day, according to local time. This is exactly the procedure performed so neatly by the Host (*CT ML Prol.* II. 1–14): knowing that it was 18 April and that the elevation of the sun was 45° he could

[51] The fullest account is by Claudia Kren, 'The Traveler's Dial in the Late Middle Ages: the Chilinder', *Technology and Culture*, xviii (1977), 419–35; see also Lynn Thorndike, 'Of the cylinder called the horologe of travelers', *Isis*, xiii (1929–30), 51–2. The instrument was also of interest to another Englishman, the thirteenth-century John of Hoveden, who wrote a *Practica Chilindri*: he may or may not be identical with the Latin poet of the same name. There are several chilinders (to say nothing of astrolabes, hour-glasses, and weight-driven clocks, etc.) in the History of Science Museum in Oxford.

'conclude' that it was 10 o'clock 'for that day as in that latitude'; for travellers, replacement plates were provided for different latitudes. It was not, of course, necessary to measure the height of the trees: on the back of an astrolabe was what is now known as an alidade, 'a brod reule that hath on either ende a square plate perced with certein holes, somme more and somme lasse, to resceyve the stremes of the sonne by day' (*Astr.* I. xiii). Astrolabes were used to set clocks by (*Astr.* II. iii. 63–81), but Chaucer advises against doing so in the hours before and after noon, where the lines are drawn so closely that precision is hard to attain. The astrolabe provided the model for the dial of the mechanical clock.

(3) For most people in the late Middle Ages it was perhaps interesting to know the time of day; for a mariner it was an essential factor in fixing his position. By means of his quadrant or *chilindre* he could tell when it was (say) noon; by using his astrolabe he could discover his latitude (and if he was going far south or north he might have to change the 'climate' plate on the astrolabe). He could not, however, fix his longitude: the astrolabe (and other shadow-using devices) show only local time, and the appearance of the heavens is exactly the same from any point on the same latitude. It was therefore essential to know how far one had travelled east or west; out of sight of land this could be done only by knowing the speed of the boat and the total time one had travelled. For this purpose a non-astronomically based time-keeper was essential. Clearly, a large weight-driven clock could not have been accommodated on a ship; equally, a water-driven clock would not function on a rolling vessel. Until the invention of a satisfactory marine chronometer by Harrison in the eighteenth century, the only remaining device was the hour-glass filled with sand (also called a *dial*, as we have seen).[52] In the sixteenth century the system of 'dead-reckoning' was used to calculate the speed of the ship: a log was thrown overboard, attached to a rope marked out with knots at fixed intervals; the

[52] Above, p. 267. See R. T. Balmer, 'The Operation of Sand Clocks and their medieval development', *Technology and Culture*, xix (1978), 615–32.

time of the passing of the knots was measured by the falling of the sand in the hour-glass. Thus, the rate of *knots* was entered in the *log*-book. (The system was doubtless better than nothing, but in view of (*a*) the variability of the ship's speed, (*b*) the probable movement of the log itself, by wind or current, and (*c*) the uneven 'particle-flow' of the sand in the glass, it is surprising that anyone ever knew where they were.) In fact, there is no lexical evidence for the use of this system in the Middle Ages: *log* in this sense is first recorded by *OED* for 1574, *knots* for 1633, and *log-book* for 1679. Ships' masters no doubt relied on experience to estimate their speed, and exact longitudinal position was less important before regular transatlantic crossings. Nevertheless, the total time travelled was important, and there is Middle English evidence for the use of hour-glasses on ships: we have noted the word 'dial-sand' and the possibility that the nautical 'dials' are in fact hour-glasses. We may add to these the *MED* entry (s.v. *Glas* 2 (b)): (1420–21) 'Pro ii barellis cum compac(es) et glasis'. More importantly, and an appropriate end to this paper, is the quotation from *Sailing Directions* (p. 12): 'Than must ye go south a glas or two by cause of the Rokke [i.e. in the Thames estuary]'. We have arrived at the custom of measuring distance by time. The quotation is, however, even more apposite in the context of this collection of essays, as *Sailing Directions* is preserved in British Library, MS Lansdowne 285, almost certainly the 'Grete Booke' which William Ebesham prepared for Sir John Paston in 1468.[53]

[53] *Sailing Directions for the Circumnavigation of England and for a Voyage to Gibraltar*, ed, James Gairdner, Hakluyt Soc. 79 (London, 1889). Gairdner doubted the identification of Lansdowne 285 with the 'Grete Booke', as did C. F. Bühler, 'Sir John Paston's *Grete Booke*, a Fifteenth Century "Best-seller"', *MLN* lvi (1941), 345–51, who mentions, incidentally, that there is a copy of *Sailing Directions* (together with other contents of the 'Grete Booke') in Pierpont Morgan MS 775. The identification is strongly urged, however, by A. I. Doyle, 'The works of a late Fifteenth Century English scribe, William Ebesham', *Bulletin of the John Rylands Library*, xxxix (1957), 298–325, especially pp. 299–307; on Plate IIA there is the opening of *Sailing Directions*. If the identification is accepted, we must date *Sailing Directions a.* 1468 (not ?1475, as the *MED* has it). For Ebesham's letter and accounts, see *Paston Letters and Papers of the Fifteenth Century*, ed. Norman Davis, Part II (Oxford, 1976), No. 751 (1468), pp. 386–7.

A List of the Published Writings of Norman Davis

1947

Review: L. M. Hollander, *The Skalds. RES* xxiii. 67–8

Review: E. G. Withycombe, *The Oxford Dictionary of English Christian Names*. Ibid. 84–6

Review: H. Hermannsson (ed.), *The Saga of Thorgils and Haflidi*. Ibid. 154

1949

'The Text of Margaret Paston's Letters', *MÆ* xviii. 12–28

Review: J. Hedberg, *The Syncope of the Old English Present Endings. RES* xxv. 160–1

Letter: 'Shakespeare in Bulgaria' (with P. Alexander), *TLS* 16 Dec.

1950

'Notes on the Middle English *Bestiary*', *MÆ* xix. 56–9

Review: C. L. Wrenn, *The English Language. Oxford Magazine*, lxviii. 326

1951

Review: A. Ahlgren, M. Bertschinger, B. M. Charleston, B. Danielsson, various studies in English language. *Archivum Linguisticum*, iii. 78–82

Review: Otto Funke, *Englische Sprachkunde*. Ibid. 212–13

Review: R. W. Zandvoort, *A Handbook of English Grammar*. Ibid. 213–15

Review: T. A. Kirby and H. B. Woolf (edd.), *Philologica: the Malone Anniversary Studies. MÆ* xx. 56–60

Review: T. Mustanoja, *The Good Wife taught her Daughter*, etc. Ibid. 60–3

Review: B. Sundby, *The Dialect and Provenance of the Middle English poem The Owl and the Nightingale*. Ibid. 64–70.

1952

'The Proximate Etymology of "Market"', *MLR* xlvii. 151–5

'A Paston Hand', *RES*, NS iii. 209–21

'A Scribal Problem in the Paston Letters', *English and Germanic Studies* iv. 31–64

Review: Sir Cyril Fox and Bruce Dickins (edd.), *The Early Cultures of North-West Europe (H. M. Chadwick Memorial Studies). RES*, NS iii. 63–4

Review: D. Whitelock, *The Audience of Beowulf*. Ibid. 376–7

Review: E. Schwartz, *Goten, Nordgermanen, Angelsachsen. Archivum Linguisticum*, iv. 175–7

1953

Sweet's Anglo-Saxon Primer, ninth edition revised (paperback reprint, 1980)
'The Letters of William Paston', *Neophilologus*, xxxvii. 36–41
Note: '"Hippopotamus" in Old English', *RES*, NS iv. 141–2
Review: A. Kurvinen (ed.), *Sir Gawain and the Carl of Carlisle. MÆ* xxii. 37–41

1954

Review: E. V. Gordon (ed.), *Pearl. MÆ* xxiii. 96–100
Review: A. A. Prins, *French Influence in English Phrasing. Neophilologus*, xxxviii. 154
Short Notice: A. McIntosh, *Introduction to a Survey of Scottish Dialects. MLR* xlix. 111

1955

'The Language of the Pastons' (Sir Israel Gollancz Memorial Lecture, 1954), *PBA* xl. 119–44
Review: E. V. K. Dobbie (ed.), *Beowulf and Judith. RES*, NS vi. 299–302
Short Notice: Fr. Schubel, *Englische Literaturgeschichte*, i. Ibid. 217–18

1956

Review: E. Leisi, *Das heutige Englisch. Archivum Linguisticum*, viii. 69–70
Short Notice (with P. Alexander): *PBA* xxxviii. *RES*, NS vii. 108

1958

Paston Letters selected and edited (Clarendon Medieval and Tudor Series) (paperback reprint 1971)
Review (part): D. J. Price (ed.) and R. M. Wilson, *The Equatorie of the Planetis. RES*, NS ix. 180–3
Review: H. L. Savage, *The Gawain-Poet*. Ibid. 426–8
Review: P. G. Foote and R. Quirk (edd.), *Gunnlaugs Saga Ormstungu. Durham University Journal*, i. 132–3

1959

Introductory Note to *Beowulf* reproduced in facsimile, 2nd edn. EETS 245, pp. v–xvii
'Scribal Variation in Late Fifteenth-Century English' in *Mélanges ... Fernand Mossé in Memoriam*, 95–103

Review: C. E. Wright (ed.), *Bald's Leechbook*; N. R. Ker (ed.), *The Pastoral Care* (Early English MSS in Facsimile 5, 6). *RES*, NS x. 72–5

Review: E. Partridge, *Origins*. *Library Review*, cxxix. 3

1961

'Styles in English Prose of the Late Middle and Early Modern Period', *Notes du VIIIe Congrès de la FILLM*, 165–84

Note: 'The earliest "do not"', *NQ* ccvi. 48–9

Note: 'Coal-house', ibid. 83

Review: G. Kane (ed.), *Piers Plowman: the A-Version*. Ibid. 115–16

Review: P. Clemoes (ed.), *The Anglo-Saxons. Studies ... presented to Bruce Dickins*. *RES*, NS xii. 283–5

1962

'Man and Monsters at Sutton Hoo', in N. Davis and C. L. Wrenn (edd.), *English and Medieval Studies presented to J. R. R. Tolkien*, 321–9

(with G. S. Ivy) 'MS Walter Rye 38 and its French Grammar', *MÆ* xxxi. 110–24

Review: B. Carstensen, *Studien zur Syntax des Nomens ... in den Paston Letters*. Ibid. 229–32

Review: *Malory's Le Morte Darthur*, reprint (University Books, New York). *Library Review*, cxliii. 489

Short Notice: J. Söderlind, *Verb Syntax in John Dryden's Prose*. *RES*, NS xiii. 101–2

Short Notice: *A Dictionary of American English*, reprint 1959, Ibid. 221–2

1963

The Paston Letters, A Selection in Modern Spelling (World's Classics, 591) (reissued 1978)

Review: J. A. Lauritis *et al.* (edd.), *A Critical Edition of John Lydgate's Life of Our Lady*. *RES*, NS xiv. 182–6

Review: A. C. Cawley (ed.), *Pearl and Sir Gawain and the Green Knight*. *AUMLA* xix. 132–4

1964

Review: R. Willard (ed.), *The Blickling Homilies*; P. Sawyer (ed.), *Textus Roffensis* (Early English MSS in Facsimile, 10, 11). *RES*, NS xv. 57–9

Review: M. Borroff, *Sir Gawain and the Green Knight. A Stylistic and Metrical Study*. Ibid. 194–6

Short Notice: J. Wright (ed.), *The English Dialect Dictionary*, reprint 1961. Ibid. 116–17

1965

'The *Litera Troili* and English Letters', *RES*, NS xvi. 233–4 (reprinted in S. A. Barney (ed.), *Chaucer's Troilus. Essays in Criticism* (Hamden, Conn., 1980))

Note: 'Agnostic', *NQ* ccx. 67

Review: M. W. Bloomfield and L. Newmark, *A Linguistic Introduction to the History of English*. *MÆ* xxxiv. 171–3

Review: K. Malone (ed.), *The Nowell Codex* (Early English MSS in Facsimile, 12). *RES*, NS xvi. 409–11

1966

Glossary to J. A. W. Bennett and G. V. Smithers (edd.), *Early Middle English Verse and Prose* (2nd edn. 1968; repr. with corrections, 1974)

Note: '*Sir Gawain and the Green Knight* 611–12' [pernyng], *NQ* ccxi. 448–51

Note: 'A Note on *Pearl*', *RES*, NS xvii. 403–5; continued in a letter, ibid. xviii (1967), 294. The whole reprinted with additions in J. Conley (ed.), *The Middle English Pearl. Critical Essays* (Notre Dame, Indiana, 1970)

Review: F. Th. Visser, *An Historical Syntax of the English Language*, Part One. *RES*, NS xvii. 73–5

Review: C. T. Onions *et al.* (edd.), *The Oxford Dictionary of English Etymology*. *The Listener*, 16 June, 879

1967

Sir Gawain and the Green Knight edd. J. R. R. Tolkien and E. V. Gordon, 2nd edn. revised by Norman Davis

'Style and Stereotype in Early English Letters', *Leeds Studies in English*, NS i. 1–17

Encyclopaedia Britannica, articles on English Literature, II, from Chaucer to the Renaissance, pp. 560–3, and Barclay, Alexander; Barnes, Juliana; Boece, Hector; Bokenam, Osbern; Boorde, Andrew; Fabian, Robert; *Gesta Romanorum*; Hall, Edward; Hardyng, John; Hawes, Stephen; Heywood, John; Hoccleve, Thomas; Lydgate, John; Medwell, Henry; Minot, Lawrence.

Review: J. B. Bessinger and R. P. Creed (edd.), *Medieval and Linguistic Studies in Honor of F. P. Magoun*. *RES*, NS xviii. 180–3

Review: J. Fisiak, *Morphemic Structure of Chaucer's English*. Ibid. 303–5

Review: R. H. Robbins and J. L. Cutler, *Supplement to the Index of Middle English Verse* (with an excursus on MS Astor A.2). Ibid. 444–8

Review: W. S. Ramson, *Australian English. An Historical Study of the Vocabulary 1788–1898*. *NQ* ccxii. 279–80

1968

Sir Gawain and the Green Knight, paperback edn.

Early Middle English Verse and Prose, 2nd edn.

Note: 'God and good men', *NQ* ccxiii. 376

Review: J. Kerkhof, *Studies in the Language of Geoffrey Chaucer. RES*, NS xix. 187–90

Review: G. Kristenson, *A Survey of Middle English Dialects 1290–1350. The Six Northern Counties and Lincolnshire. NQ* ccxiii. 270–2

Review: B. Kottler and A. M. Markman, *A Concordance to Five Middle English Poems. MÆ* xxxvii. 324–8

1969

'The Epistolary Usages of William Worcester', in D. A. Pearsall and R. A. Waldron (edd.), *Medieval Literature and Civilization. Studies in Memory of G. N. Garmonsway*, 249–74

'Two Unprinted Dialogues in Late Middle English, and their language', *Revue des langues vivantes*, xxxv. 461–72

Note: 'Chaucer's *Gentilesse*: A forgotten manuscript, with some proverbs', *RES*, NS xx. 43–50

Note: 'Sheep-farming terms in medieval Norfolk', *NQ* ccxiv. 404–5

Note: 'Another fragment of *Richard Coer de Lyon*', ibid. 447–52

Review: F. Th. Visser, *An Historical Syntax of the English Language*, Part Two. *RES*, NS xx. 196–200

1969–70 Six articles: 'The Changing Language', I and II, 'The Language from Chaucer to Shakespeare', 'The Language from Shakespeare to Johnson', 'English in the Eighteenth and Nineteenth Centuries', 'English Overseas', in *History of the English Speaking Peoples*, published weekly by BPC Publishing, Ltd. (consultant editor John Roberts)

1970

Non-Cycle Plays and Fragments. EETS, SS 1

Note: '*Sir Gawain and the Green Knight*, 2073', *NQ* ccxv. 163–4

Note: 'The Brome Hall Commonplace Book', *Theatre Notebook*, xxiv, 84–6

Review: *A Manual of the Writings in Middle English 1050–1500*, i. *RES*, NS xxi. 72–4

1971

Paston Letters and Papers of the Fifteenth Century, Part I

William Tyndale's English of Controversy' (Chambers Memorial Lecture)

Note: 'Kenneth Sisam', *Neuphilologische Mitteilungen*, lxxii. 762

Review: F. Th. Visser, *An Historical Syntax of the English Language*, Part Three, I. *RES*, NS xxii. 64–6

Review: R. W. Chambers and M. Daunt, *A Book of London English 1384–1425*, reissued 1967. *MÆ* xl. 75–80

Review: R. M. Wilson, *The Lost Literature of Medieval England*, 2nd edn. *RES*, NS xxii. 522–4

1972

'Margaret Paston's Uses of *DO*', in *Studies presented to T. F. Mustanoja. Neuphilologische Mitteilungen*, lxxiii. 55–62

Review: I. Michael, *English Grammatical Categories and the Tradition to 1800*. *RES*, NS xxiii. 63–7

Review: B. J. Whiting and H. W. Whiting, *Proverbs, Sentences, and Proverbial Phrases from English Writings mainly before 1500*. *MÆ* xli. 164–8

1973

'On editing the Paston letters', in *English Studies Today*, 135–48

Note: 'Two early sixteenth-century accounts of royal occasions', *NQ* ccxviii. 122–30

1974

'The Influence of Anglo-Norman on Early English Literature', Accademia Nazionale dei Lincei, quaderno no. 199 (Rome)

Review: *A Manual of the Writings in Middle English 1050–1500*, iii. *RES*, NS xxv. 67–9

Review: H. R. Loyn (ed.), *A Wulfstan Manuscript containing Institutes, Laws and Homilies* (Early English MSS in Facsimile 17. Ibid. 450–2

1975

Note: 'Well and truly', *NQ* ccxx. 450–1

Review: D. Bevington (ed.), *The Macro Plays ... A Facsimile edition*. Ibid. 78–9

Review: *A Manual of the Writings in Middle English 1050–1500*, iv. *RES*, NS xxvi. 325–7

Review: F. Th. Visser, *An Historical Syntax of the English Language*, Part Three, II. Ibid. 454–8

1976

Paston Letters and Papers of the Fifteenth Century, Part II

'J. R. R. Tolkien', *Postmaster*, 9–12

Review: J. A. W. Bennett, *Chaucer at Oxford and at Cambridge*. *RES*, NS xxvii. 336–7

Review: L. D. Benson (ed.), *King Arthur's Death. The Middle English Stanzaic Morte Arthur and Alliterative Morte Arthure*. Ibid. 453–5

Letter: 'très snob', *The Times*, 12 January

1977

'Chaucer and The English Language', Accademia Nazionale dei Lincei, quaderno no. 234 (Rome)

Note: 'Falstaff's Name', *Shakespeare Quarterly*, xxviii. 513–15

Letter: 'Middle English', *The Times*, 9 December

1978

Review: A. C. Cawley and M. Stevens, *The Towneley Cycle. A Facsimile of Huntington MS. HM 1* (Leeds Medieval Drama Facsimiles, 2). *RES*, NS xxix. 83–4

Review: R. Beadle and A. E. B. Owen (edd.), *The Findern Manuscript*, facsimile edn., and D. Pearsall and I. C. Cunningham (edd.), *The Auchinleck Manuscript*, facsimile edn. Ibid. 464–6

1979

Non-Cycle Plays and the Winchester Dialogues (Leeds Medieval Drama Facsimiles, 5)

(with D. Gray, P. Ingham, A. Wallace-Hadrill), *A Chaucer Glossary* (repr. with corrections, 1981)

Review: M. Cohen, *Sensible Words. Linguistic Practice in England 1640–1785*. *EHR* xciv. 928–9

Review: M. Parkes and A. G. Watson (edd.), *Medieval Scribes, Manuscripts and Libraries. Essays presented to N. R. Ker*. *NQ* ccxxiv. 564–6

1980

Letter: 'The Provenance of the N-Town Cycle', *The Library*, 6th Series, ii. 333–4

1981

'Language in Letters from Sir John Falstolf's Household', in P. Heyworth (ed.), *Medieval Studies for J. A. W. Bennett*, 329–46

Note: 'J. A. W. Bennett', *MÆ* i. 1–2

Review: *Aspects of English Intonation*, i and other Gothenburg Studies in English. *RES*, NS xxxii. 198–9

Review: E. Kolb *et al.*, *Atlas of English Sounds*. Ibid. 309–10

Review: P. Neuss (ed.), J. Skelton, *Magnificence*. *NQ* ccxxvi. 437–8

1982

Review: R. M. Lumiansky and D. Mills (edd.), *The Chester Mystery Cycle. A reduced facsimile of Huntington Library MS 2* (Leeds Medieval Drama Facsimiles, 6). *NQ* ccxxvii. 68–9

RECORDS *The Canterbury Tales*, *Prologue* (with N. Coghill and J. A. Burrow), *Nun's Priest's Tale* (with N. Coghill, J. A. Burrow, and L. Davis) (both with notes on the language); extracts from *Beowulf* and selections from *The Canterbury Tales* (with a section on Chaucer's pronunciation)

Index